I0121658

Anonymus

Rambles in the deserts of Syria and among the Turkomans and Bedaweens

Anonymus

Rambles in the deserts of Syria and among the Turkomans and Bedaweens

ISBN/EAN: 9783742822178

Manufactured in Europe, USA, Canada, Australia, Japa

Cover: Foto ©Thomas Meinert / pixelio.de

Manufactured and distributed by brebook publishing software
(www.brebook.com)

Anonymus

Rambles in the deserts of Syria and among the Turkomans and Bedaweens

RAMBLES

IN

THE DESERTS OF SYRIA

AND AMONG THE

TURKOMANS AND BEDAWEENS.

———

LONDON:

JOHN MURRAY, ALBEMARLE STREET.

1864.

PREFACE.

———◆———

THIS endeavour to add, be it ever so little, to the general stock of information on the state of Turkey was suggested by the author's father, at whose request the letters were written during a residence of several years in the Levant, and to whom this work is affectionately dedicated by

THE AUTHOR.

CONTENTS.

LETTER XX.

RAMBLES

IN

THE DESERTS OF SYRIA.

LETTER I.

Valley of Salt—Hanadi Arabs—Haji Batran—Anezi Arabs—
Sheikh Jedaan—Anezi Camp—Bedaween Life.

Belas : October 4, 1858.

I WRITE from a camp of the Bedaween, on the
right bank of the Euphrates. I shaped my course
in a south-easterly direction from Aleppo—not following any road or pathway, for there is none such in the
desert. Leaving on my right the Salt Lake of Jibool,
supposed to be the Valley of Salt of the 2nd Book of
Samuel, in which Hadadezer was routed by King David
with a loss of eighteen thousand men, I reached in the
evening an Arab camp of the Hanadi tribe, whose chief,
Haji Batran, I wished to take with me. He was
absent, however ; and, after partaking of the hospitality offered by his four wives, I proceeded next morning towards the east, accompanied by a few servants
and Arab followers of my own.

B

The country is woodless, houseless, uncultivated, and
inhabited only by the wildest of the Bedaween tribes.
Like most denizens of unbounded plains, these are fanatical votaries of freedom. They are also essentially
indolent. Poor and lazy, but brave, they find a ready
scope for their warlike impulses, and a timely resource
for their subsistence, in the levying of black mail from
passing caravans. To check their predatory propensi-
ties, Ibrahim Pasha of Egypt, when ruling also over
Syria some twenty years ago, brought a tribe of
African Bedaween, of tried fidelity and good conduct.
Some of these he had stationed between Aleppo and
the Salt Lake, to guard the villages from the inroads
of more unruly Arabs; and this measure answered
well until the Hanadi, or Hindawi (for so the Africans
were called, from a supposed Indian origin) became
connected by intermarriage with the native Bedaween,
and their services in opposition to the latter had assumed
a merely nominal existence. Still they were recognised
as the representatives of the government in the desert,
and our progress without Haji Batran was of doubtful
issue. The Hanadi have seventeen hundred fighting
men.

We had ridden on for a couple of hours in the fine
autumn morning without encounter. Suddenly shouts
from the rear announced an attack. Our party quickly
closed up. There they were, to be sure, at least fifty or
sixty horsemen galloping after us abreast, and in open
order, to give room for the play of the long lances, which
they brandished furiously as they advanced. On they

came, making the hard burnt-up earth sound again
with the rapid fall of many hoofs, and mingling its
rolling growl with the long monotonous notes of the
Arab song of onslaught.   In front, on a powerful bay
mare, thundered along a burly figure of sixteen stone
at least, and, as he neared us, I was not sorry to make
out the bronzed features and loud laugh of Haji Batran,
who was bringing us an escort of Hanadi.   This sem-
blance of hostile intentions is a compliment of the
Bedaween to their friends, but it renders friendly
meetings in the desert doubtful affairs before recognition.   I once knew a distinguished foreigner trust to
his being well mounted, and turn tail before those who
came to do him honour in this fashion: a very pretty
chase was performed ere his equanimity was restored.
Haji Batran collected his party close behind a mound
we had reached; and, after exchanging cordial greetings, we dismounted, and crept cautiously to its summit,
to survey together the eastern horizon.   No Arabs
were to be seen.   Batran then had our tents pitched,
saying that we must wait there till nightfall, as the two
great tribes, Anezi and Shammar, had been fighting
for several days not far from us, and we might come in
for a share in their warfare if we should not pass unob-
served.   It was a long halt, but there was no gainsay-
ing the arrangement.   To while away the weary hours,
stories were told, songs sung, pipes smoked, and various
feats of legerdemain displayed.   Amongst others of the
latter diversions, a snowy-bearded patriarch placed his
spear-point on his breast, and pretended to pierce him-

self by falling against it, while the butt was stuck fast
in the bank of the mound.   There was a trick in it of
course: perhaps a strong leather belt protected him;
but, however that might be, it passed for a miracle, and
the charmed life received all due honour accordingly.

When the sun had set, and the short twilight faded
away, we mounted again, and followed in single file
and in profound silence the stalwart form of Haji
Batran on his tall mare, who led the way.   Eight
hours in the saddle brought us, just before dawn, to
another tumulus, which we were told was on the bank
of the great river.   We halted behind it, and two
horsemen were sent round to see if no one else was
doing the same on the other side.   All being clear, we
lay down on the short grass, while a messenger went on
to the Anezi camp, for it is never safe to approach one
unannounced.   Mistakes may occur, or are afterwards
alleged as an excuse for plunder.   Our scout returned
with Sheikh Jedaan himself, the renowned chief of the
Fedan Anezi, to welcome our arrival; and with the
rising sun we proceeded along the broad and shingly
bed of the Euphrates.

A strange scene awaited us on the plain of Beles,
where the ancient Syrian kings had parks and forests,
as recorded by Xenophon, and which is still known as
a favourite haunt of wild boars, wolves, and jackals,
though now only clothed with clumps of tamarisks.   An
open space was crowded with black goat-hair tents in
such surprising numbers that they formed not only a
camp, but a mighty city of camps, while upwards of

three thousand Bedaween were careering over the plain
on their fleet mares as far as the eye could reach;
rushing at each other lance in rest, wheeling right and
left, charging in a mass, their scanty garments and long
hair streaming behind them, singing, screaming, dealing
around hard knocks with the butt end of their spears,
and laughing loud when blood was drawn by a stray
touch with the point. Some were mere children,
slenderly clad, and riding wildly, without saddles or
bridles, their docile fillies yielding at their best pace to
the mere tightening of a rope-halter. Such horsemanship is seen nowhere else. The din was deafening, the
confusion bewildering. When we reached the tent of
the sheikh, who had galloped on to receive us, we were
led to the seat of honour, a camel's packsaddle in the
centre of a long narrow carpet. No sooner installed,
than we were surrounded by two or three hundred
Bedaween, squatting on the ground in several ranks,
from each of whom we received a formal welcome.

Jedaan is a young man, under thirty years of age,
short in stature, light and wiry, with a handsome countenance and deep expressive black eyes. Elected
sheikh for his bravery in battle and wisdom in council, he had all the air and bearing of a desert prince
amongst his vassals. Before the tent, which contained
five large compartments, stood picketed his milk-white
mare, a noble animal, the gift of his enemy, Abd-ul-
Kerim, Sheikh of the Shammar. Jedaan's father had
taken refuge from a feud in his tribe with the father of
that great chief. The boys became sworn brothers;

and now that each is sheikh of his respective tribe,
they always avoid meeting in the many fights between
the Anezi and the Shammar. Last year the latter
were defeated on one occasion, and Abd-ul-Kerim was
with difficulty saved by the speed and lasting quality
of this mare. On the following day, he sent to tell
Jedaan that he would soon have his revenge when
reinforcements should come, and that, as he feared for
the life of his boyhood's friend, he sent him his mare,
which could distance every other in the Shammar tribe.
Jedaan rode her in the next engagement he had with
Abd-ul-Kerim, the Anezi were beaten, and she brought
him home unhurt after a long pursuit. There is little
bloodshed in this desert warfare, considering the frequency of battles and the numbers engaged, for the
conquered generally surrenders and is well treated,
while deaths are always avenged sooner or later.

Acts of high-minded generosity are greatly appreciated by the Bedaween, who delight in narrating
them. One of their favourite anecdotes is that of the
owner of a swift mare which a neighbouring sheikh
greatly coveted. A reward was in vain offered to any
one of his tribe who could take her for him. She was
too fleet to be obtained in the usual way. A proposal
of a hundred camels in exchange for her was made and
refused. A stratagem was resorted to. The sheikh
lay groaning on the lonely plain when the man passed
on his mare. Dismounting, the latter raised him gently,
and placed him on her to lead him home, supposing
him to be wounded or sick. The deceiver galloped off,

and the dupe called after him to take the mare as a gift on the sole condition of never telling the tale, which might deter others from being compassionate.

The Arab tents are made of long belts of coarse cloth, stitched together, and supported by poles of different lengths, with screens of reeds woven with red and blue worsted in rude patterns. All these materials are home-made. The reeds and poles are found on the banks of the Euphrates, which are covered with jungle in many places. Some of the tents are not less than eighty feet long, in squares partitioned by suspending carpets from the roof. The women and children occupy one end, the men the other, and stores are piled in the centre rooms. During winter the best mares and foals are in very bad weather admitted into the tent, and they go freely about every part of it.

The Bedaween never taste animal food, except when a sheep is slaughtered for a guest. The feast is shared on such occasions by as many as can find a morsel to seize. Their ordinary food is bread dipped in melted butter, but they are often reduced to camel's milk, either alone or with a few dates. I once stayed a week with a tribe which had had nothing but camel's milk for three months; they did not appear unusually emaciated, and I did not myself suffer in the least from hunger. It is no fable of the Arabs to attribute to that kind of milk somewhat of the sustaining quality evinced by the wonderful enduring power of the animal which produces it. They wean their foals when only one month old, in order to rear them on camel's rather

than on their mothers' milk, with the view of render-
ing them capable of long-continued exertion, and they
firmly believe in this effect on the constitution.

This singular people seems to be the only one on
the face of the globe which has remained in precisely
the same state for the last four thousand years. Often
conquerors, never subjugated, they have retained the
features of the times when the first great empires of
the world were founded. They gave sovereigns to
Babylonia and Egypt nineteen centuries before Christ.
They combated successfully the arms of the Pharaohs
and the Assyrian kings; eluded the grasp of Cyrus
and Alexander the Great; defied the Roman power;
and, when Mahomet united them in a common cause,
they carried their Oriental civilisation to the shores of
the Bosphorus and the banks of the Tagus, where
both the Eastern and the Western Empires had lost
the enlightenment of Greece and Rome. The khaliphs
of Bagdad, of Cairo, of Cordova, spread the thirst of
knowledge around them. Even the Mongolian hordes,
which attacked their eastern frontier, derived from
them their religion and their intellectual developement.
Europe sent her chivalry to assail them, and received
back its scattered remnants, bearing only scars and
rags from the holy war. Still Arabia, Syria, Egypt,
Tunis, Algiers, Morocco, offer the same spectacle of
a freedom-loving race, wandering at will over their
scorched plains; still the Syrian desert, whose roving
tribes have exercised so widely extended an influence on
other countries, serves only to furnish a bare subsistence

to a people possessing the same habits and ruled by
the same principles in their social and political condition as their fathers Ishmael and Esau.

It is a mistake to suppose that their state is in any
way analogous to that of the North American Indians
or New Zealanders. These Bedaween Arabs are not
savages. They have an organisation. It is the highest
possible developement of the pastoral life. They are
subject to the influence of public opinion. The lawlessness of the people, and the simple despotism of
their chiefs, are, therefore, not altogether untempered.
A man, who has disgraced himself by a breach of their
species of morality, is shunned by his whole tribe, and
is finally forced to leave it as an outcast. A chief, who
has drawn the bond of allegiance too tight, is deposed
or abandoned, and becomes a mere member of a tribe,
or remains without one. Their laws are certainly
somewhat peculiar, but they are laws, and, as such,
they preclude anarchy. Robbery from a hostile tribe,
from a village, caravan, or traveller, is honourable according to the Bedaween code; from an Arab of the
same tribe, it involves only restitution. Grave offences
of some kinds are punished with death. The execution
is effected simply by laying the criminal on the ground
and cutting his throat, the executioner being the sheikh
himself. Murder is subject to retaliation by the relatives of the victim, if not redeemed by the payment of
blood-money. Strange to say, no distinction is drawn
between assassination, killing in battle, and accidental
homicide.

There exists amongst the Bedaween a most salutary institution, which keeps them from waging wars of extermination. This is the ransom of blood. It falls on all kindred within five degrees. Death may thus be avenged on a large number of relatives. If the price of blood is paid in preference to suffering retaliation, the amount is divided amongst many contributors, whose lives are possibly saved thereby. It is generally the value of fifty camels, falling perhaps on fifty persons, which is not a heavy premium of insurance. This system tends greatly to preserve life, and to restrain those fierce passions which roving habits excite.

Another curious feature of Bedaween government is that by which the supreme authority changes hands provisionally when a sheikh is too old to lead the tribe in war, or another is considered a more fit and successful leader, to be restored to him at the conclusion of peace. I know an instance in which an elder brother is the sheikh in favour of his prudence, and a younger brother is the military chief by right of greater valour. The Arab tribes consider this practice to be a guarantee for the liberty of the subject, inasmuch as power is not concentrated, and jealousy prevents a coalition against popular freedom. Jedaan is the military leader of his tribe, and his uncle Deham the sheikh; but in this case the judgment and discretion of the former give him power even when not engaged in war. They are not on good terms, and when Jedaan sees his influence over the tribe diminished by intrigues on the part of Deham, who is a cunning old man, he always looks for

another tribe to quarrel with, and by declaring war
consolidates his authority.

A further check to the assumption of absolute power
is found in the judicial functions of a member of each
tribe, distinguished for sagacity, whose award is without appeal, even when it condemns the sheikh, or
aghid, as the military chief is called. This magis-
trate enjoys the title of cadi, and is generally no mean
lawyer. In the Fedan tribe there is really an upright
judge, an old man, by name Jemaijem, whom I have
heard decide cases with the greatest acumen and impartiality. He can neither read nor write, but he is
gifted with a prodigious memory, and quotes a host of
precedents in the point of law at issue, preparing his
audience for his verdict before pronouncing it.

The Anezi tribe is subdivided into many sections,
with distinctive appellations, such as Fedan, Sebaa,
Erfuddi, Ibn Haddal, Amarat, Weled Ali, and Beni
Sachar.   Other tribes, the Aghedat, Sochni, and
Aghel, live under their protection; the two former
occupying the country between Palmyra and the Euphrates, where they burn herbs producing soda for
sale in the towns, and the latter moving from camp to
camp to act as brokers for the merchants of Aleppo
and Bagdad, while they also form large caravans of
camels for the transport of goods between those two
marts.   The Anezi are in the habit of tracing every
year a great migratory orbit, which takes them to
Aleppo in summer, towards Urfa, Diarbakir, Moossul,
and Bagdad in winter, and leads them round by the

southern regions of the desert, passing near Damascus,
Homs, and Hama, back to Aleppo. They provide
themselves with grain and manufactured goods at the
last-named city, and with dates at Bagdad, selling
their wool, butter, lambs, young camels, and horses, to
raise money for these purchases. All their other wants
are supplied by the flocks and herds which they rear,
and which oblige them to wander for ever in that vast
circle to avoid the barren centre of the desert, and to
find fresh pasture-grounds on its skirts in succession
when they are exhausted.

As regards their honesty, I can say that I have been
a good deal amongst them, and I feel more disposed to
join those who have extolled their few virtues than the
exponents of their many vices. One cannot with any
degree of fairness throw all the responsibility of Bedaween misdeeds on their perpetrators. Treated as they
have been, it is only surprising that they should have
retained any virtues at all, and should not have pushed
their vices much farther. But of this hereafter.

LETTER II.

Camels — Waldi Arabs—Sheikh Mohammed-al-Ganim — Arab Warfare—Hierapolis—Koords.

Hierapolis : October 9, 1858.

I HAVE come upon this little oasis in the desert, and the charm of the spot entices me to remain. My tent is pitched on a soft green lawn, fringing the still waters of a deep pool, and surrounded by the ruins of the ancient city of Bambyce, afterwards called Hierapolis, and now, by a corruption of its former name, Mumbutsh.

We left the Anezi camp two days ago. At early dawn the numberless uncouth camels, squatting sphinx-fashion amongst the tents, began to turn their long necks impatiently from side to side. An old man arose from a group of sleeping Bedaween, and untied the fore-leg of a large camel which lay pinioned. It struggled to its feet, and at this signal they all got up, the fugleman alone having been fastened. As they yawned and stretched their ungainly limbs, the truth of an Arab saying came forcibly to my mind: The horse laughed at the crookedness of the camel's legs, and the camel asked the horse what there was so straight about him that his legs should appear crooked : a telling figure of rhetoric in a bad argument. The old man pro-

ceeded slowly towards the river, uttering a continuous
and not unmusical call of 'ho, ho!' The camel that
had been tied followed, and the whole herd filed after
him. I went to see them watered. An evolution was
performed with military precision: when the leading
camel reached the stream, the next one formed on his
right, and so on till all their heads were stretched down
to the water with a receding vista of several thousand
humps on the bank. After they had taken a sufficient
draught for a week's use, if required, the old man led
them off with his 'ho, ho!' to the pasture behind the
camp. I was told that he always lived with the camels,
and never tasted any other food than their milk.

The Euphrates is about two hundred yards wide at
that point, fifteen feet deep in the middle, and not
rapid. I had an agreeable swim in it, notwithstanding
the crocodiles that appeared to General Chesney in his
expedition of 1835. Returning to the tent of Sheikh
Jedaan, I found our party prepared for a start. We
mounted, took leave of our host, and crossed the plain
lying to the north of Beles. Under the guidance of
Haji Batran we passed from mound to mound, for these
are the only landmarks. The country is everywhere
susceptible of cultivation, but of course there is none.
In the afternoon we halted at a camp of the Weldi
tribe, whose sheikh, Mohammed-al-Ganim, received us
with true Arab hospitality.

This tribe does not properly belong to the Syrian
desert, but to that of Mesopotamia, where the majority
of it still remains. Mohammed-al-Ganim is a remark-

ably handsome man, between thirty and forty years of
age, with fine eyes and a flowing beard. He is the
nephew of the powerful Weldi sheikh, Selami-ed-
Dandan, and had been involved, by his near relation-
ship with him, in a blood-feud with the Shammar. The
last. victim having been on the side of the latter, and
both sides being too proud and obstinate to compound
their difference by the payment of ransom, a timely
retreat from their vicinity became expedient; and
Mohammed-al-Ganim was so popular a leader that he
was followed across the Euphrates by about three
hundred families. I had much conversation with him
on his prospects, and he pointed out to me how very
difficult his position had become, surrounded as he was
by the Fedan Anezi, the Hadideen, and the Mowali,
to some one of which tribes he must pay tribute for
protection from the two others, as his people were not
numerous enough to stand alone. When the protecting tribe should move, he must move with it, or be
attacked by those remaining. The Weldi, moreover,
obey him as the nephew of their common sheikh, but
they never would consent to be under the authority
of an Anezi, Hadidi, or Mowali sheikh. In short,
he found himself very critically situated. I remarked
that I could think of only one way to obviate every
difficulty, which would be to take up an independent
position as an agricultural tribe. All the argu
ments current in the desert against intercourse with
towns and Turkish officials were marshalled in opposition to my suggestion. I endeavoured to combat

them as I best could, dwelling especially on the influential ground he would occupy when possessed of
grain to barter for protection with the nomadic tribes,
each of which would prevent the other from destroying
his crops in the hope of obtaining a share of them,
while it would also become the duty and interest of
the government to give him every possible assistance.
This discussion was listened to with great attention by
the Weldi, who crowded around us in considerable
numbers, eagerly exchanging glances of approval when
any of the reasons adduced took their fancy; but I saw
that Haji Batran was also a watchful listener, and that
he did not seem to like the turn matters were taking.
He attempted more than once to put a stop to our conversation, and at last succeeded by saying that we
could not proceed farther on our journey by daylight,
as there were hostile tribes in front of us, and that,
unless we meant to stay the whole of the next day
with the Weldi, we had better mount at once, and ride
through the night. We could not escape the force of
such logic; so we left Mohammed-al-Ganim, who said
pointedly, when bidding us farewell, that he would
think of my advice.

The sun had set, but the moon was up, and the fine
air of the desert, fragrant with the aroma of herbs
crushed with our horses' hoofs, was most exhilarating.
Batran guided us still in a northerly direction, parallel
to the course of the Euphrates, and, as we rode along
together, he narrated many interesting scenes of Bedaween life. Passing a defile between two low rocky

hills, he pointed out the mouth of a cavern, which, he
said, extended eastward under the river, here at least a
mile off, and corresponded with another aperture in
Mesopotamia. If true, this might be the passage by
which Zenobia, after the fall of Palmyra, was trying
to escape when Aurelian's soldiers captured her. Batran
told me that, if I would dismount and enter it, I should
find thirteen headless Arabs of the Shammar tribe whom
he had thrown in there not long ago. On my expressing curiosity as to the fact, he told his story. He had
gone out with three hundred of his Hanadi to meet a
body of the Shammar which had crossed the Euphrates
from Mesopotamia, intent on plunder. At a Hadideen
camp on his way, he learnt that the Shammar had
sent a strong party of the Ghess tribe to swim the river
higher up, and draw attention from the main expedition,
as they had heard of Batran's approach. He met the
stratagem by opposing a Hadideen force to the Ghess,
while he marched against the Shammar. His tactics
were successful; both the Shammar and the Ghess were
driven back to Mesopotamia. Batran took twenty prisoners. This cave had been agreed upon as his rendez-
vous with the Hadideen, who soon came there to report
their victory. But they mourned the death of thirteen
of their number in the fight, which had been more
obstinate with the Ghess than with the Shammar, the
latter having at once taken to flight, leaving their worst
mounted to be captured. To avenge the Hadideen,
Batran with his own hand cut off the heads of thirteen
of his prisoners, gave them to his allies to satisfy the

c

tribe that their blood was paid, and threw the bodies
into the cavern. He released his other prisoners, he
said, concluding his horrible anecdote with a loud
laugh.

The Shammar tribe roams over the whole of Mesopotamia, from the mountains of Armenia to the walls of
Bagdad. Their number is estimated at thirty thousand tents. They are always at war with the Anezi.
Like them, they are addicted to plundering caravans,
and making raids on the agricultural population. The
predatory expeditions of the two tribes often meet, and
never fail to fight when they meet. The Ghess occupy
the left bank of the Euphrates from the town of Urfa,
the ancient Ur of the Chaldees, to the country of the
Barazi tribe of Koords. These two tribes are generally
on friendly terms. The former numbers fifteen hundred
tents. The Hadideen are the shepherds of Aleppo
and Hama, whose inhabitants invest a considerable
amount of capital in flocks intrusted to their care.
They supply those towns with milk and butter, and
carry on a large trade in wool for exportation. They
are a peaceful tribe, always submissive to the government, often giving timely notice of hostile intentions
on the part of marauding Bedaween, and occasionally
suffering for it when discovered. Their strength does
not exceed two thousand tents.

We rode on without apparently any definite object.
Sometimes Batran seemed to swerve to the right,
sometimes to the left. The horses were getting
tired. At last we pulled up in the middle of a barren

wilderness. Haji Batran confessed that he had not the
least notion where we were. There was nothing for
it but to picket our horses, pitch our tent, and wait for
daylight. The want of water was very distressing.
A guard of Hanadi was placed to watch for Arabs and
wild beasts. Batran lay down still further in advance.
I went to commend his zeal, and found him with a
bottle raised to his mouth. Hoping to assuage my
intolerable thirst, I took it from his hand, but, instead
of water, it had contained brandy, which he had stolen
from one of the servants. The emptiness of the bottle
fully accounted for the erratic course we had followed.
I returned to the tent, and contrived to sleep an hour
or two. When I awoke, the dawn was breaking the
gloom which had enveloped us after the moon had set.
On looking round the horizon, I descried towards the
north something like a building very near us. I roused
Batran, who gazed at it awhile, and announced, with
his usual sonorous hilarity, that we were close to
Mumbutah. The tent was soon struck, the poor hungry
horses prepared, and we rode on hither.

The town must have been large and important.
Greek remains are strewed amongst Saracenic tombs.
Sculptured sarcophagi lie half buried beneath turbaned
headstones with Cuphic inscriptions. The ruins of a
temple, possibly that of the great goddess, whose
worship at Hierapolis is explained by Lucian, have
been repaired to form a mosque, now crumbling in its
turn. When Julian was here, that temple, which was
said to have been wealthy enough to maintain three

hundred priests, seems to have been already fallen, but
the city must still have been more or less flourishing,
as he found there the philosopher and friend who could
afford to give hospitality to Constantius and Gallus,
and he made it the base of his military operations
beyond the Euphrates, which his army crossed here on
a bridge of boats. The great fertility of the surrounding country, and its favourable position for trade with
both the east and the west, are perfectly consistent
with the recorded wealth of Hierapolis; and vast sub-
terranean store chambers still exist to remind one that
its granaries supplied the populous Antioch during the
scarcity which caused the quarrel with Julian, ending
in the publication of his witty but indiscreetly satirical
Misopogon. Even down to the middle of the fifth
century of our era, when Chosroes King of Persia
besieged Hierapolis, the inhabitants could redeem their
city by the payment of a heavy ransom. Their freedom
was subsequently secured to them for a time by the
military genius of Belisarius, whose firm attitude, with
the Roman army drawn up to the east of the town so
as to appear twice as numerous as it really was, deterred
the Persians from attempting the passage of the river;
this being one of the many distinguished services
rendered by Justinian's lieutenant, the great general of
the day, which hastened his death by the jealousy of
his rivals, though neither through want nor the loss of
sight, as a fiction of later times has represented. In
the beginning of the seventh century, Hierapolis was
again attacked; money or skill could not save it then,

and it became subject to the aggressive kingdom of
Persia; the Euphrates, which Augustus made the boundary of the Roman empire, being no longer defensible,
in its decline.　This period of the history of Hierapolis
has left its stamp on many fine edifices, now fallen, but
displaying in · their ruins the profuse architectural
ornaments of the dynasty of Chosroes.　Finally, it sank
before the conquering arms of Khalid's Saracen forces,
when Syria again changed masters seven hundred years
after Pompey had overthrown the last of her Macedonian kings.　Many are the vestiges of that Arab
occupation, but their buildings, though massive and
substantial in appearance, were constructed of materials
less durable than those of their predecessors, a soft
yellow limestone and bad cement, little calculated to
resist the shocks of earthquakes, so frequent and severe
in this country; and the Saracenic remains are thus less
perfect than those of the Greek and Persian populations
of the place.

Its only inhabitants now are a few miserable Koords
of the Barazi tribe, which is often to be found encamped
in different parts of the valley of the Euphrates between
Beles and Bir, though rarely on its right bank.　They
have some sheep grazing on the grass-grown ramparts
of the ancient city; and their wretched ragged tents,
much smaller than those of the Anezi Arabs, crouch
amid the ruins of temples and mosques; the former
showing what the country was under the Greeks and
under the Saracens; the latter, what it is under the
Turks.

The Koords are supposed to be the descendants of the Carduchians of Xenophon, who so stoutly opposed the retreat of the Ten Thousand. Their present name may be the original one, which was transformed by the Greek general and author. They are a taller and better-looking race than the Arabs; as brave, but more treacherous. Their religion is that of Islam, with the exception of one of their tribes, the Yezidi, who are called devil-worshippers, but in reality believe merely that it is necessary for man to propitiate Ariman, the Spirit of Evil, by sacrifices. They differ little in other respects from the great wandering hordes of Syria, on all of whom religion sits lightly. The Koords cover the whole of the southern watershed of Mount Taurus, and extend to the frontiers of Persia in the east, migrating frequently northwards in Armenia as far as Mount Ararat. In Northern Syria their number is computed at about fifty thousand. Their occupation is pastoral, plundering, and, when located, agricultural. From these tribes are recruited for the most part the irregular troops kept by Turkish governors in Syria.

LETTER III.

Batna: October 9, 1858.

STILL under advice to travel only by night, we left
Mumbutah yesterday afternoon; having spent a
delightful morning there, in rest, in writing, in rambling
over the ruins, and swimming in the small lake. Our
course was south-westerly. The first object of interest
we saw was the ancient aqueduct which feeds that
lake with the clear cool water of a spring rising at a
distance of twelve miles. The stream is almost always
under ground, as the plain undulates, and a level con-
duit has been excavated for it by means of shafts about
fifteen yards from each other. This was probably a
work of the Persians, with whom it was a religious
duty, after the precept of Zoroaster, to multiply the
principles of life and abundance, fire and water. Aque-
ducts thus constructed are certainly less perishable
than those whose level is maintained above ground by
arches; this one must have been twelve centuries in
operation without care or repair, and it may continue
to work well for ever.

As we passed one of the shafts, an enormous hyena
suddenly sprang from its funnel-shaped mouth. A

shout from Batran, and a bound of his vigorous mare
under a severe application of sharp-pointed shovel
stirrups, gave the signal for a furious chase. The wild
beast strained his every nerve, and doubled over and
over again, to escape the screaming Batran. On we
rushed at our best pace for a couple of miles. At last
Batran got a favourable opening for a pistol-shot
which broke the hyena's hind leg. He jumped off his
mare, put the butt-end of his lance into the brute's
mouth, and, while it was biting at the iron spike, he
placed his knee on its body, and, drawing a long knife
with his other hand, cut its throat amid loud bursts of
jovial laughter. It would be difficult to determine
which seemed the wilder beast of the two.

Returning to our course we were soon benighted.
As we rode along slowly, Haji Batran, now calm after
his mad excitement, narrated some of his adventures to
keep me awake, as he said. One of these was striking,
and I have since ascertained by enquiries here that it
was strictly true. When offering to guide us by a
circuitous route, passing through a valley called Saffi,
where we should find some tents to rest at, a proposal
which we declined, he remarked that it might indeed be
better not to go that way, because his last visit there
could not have been forgotten. Three years ago, he
said, in answer to my question as to the visit he alluded
to, there was great difficulty in obtaining the pay of
the irregular troops. Having at last become desperate,
he informed the authorities that, if he received no
money up to a certain day, he would plunder the Arabs

nearest his camp, who happened to be those of Saffi.
The reply was a civil request to go to town and receive
his pay.   He went, was admitted to the governor's
presence, and was kept in conversation by him until
the room, passage, and stairs were filled with soldiers.
Batran chanced to look round, and, understanding at
once the governor's design, uttered a yell of rage, drew
his sword, and, being a man of great strength, pushed
and cut his way through the crowd, which fell back dis-
mayed as he vaulted on his mare and galloped out of the
town.   From Saffi he sent a message to the governor that
he might still save the Arabs of that valley by sending
his money thither.   The messenger brought back word
that there was no answer, but that troops were preparing to march against him.   Haji Batran then fell
upon the unfortunate people of Saffi, killed sixteen of
them, and carried off everything they had.   It soon
became known that he had joined the Anezi, and, pursuit being in vain, no further steps were taken.   When
a new governor came, some months afterwards, his
depredations were put a stop to by condoning all his
past misdeeds, and settling his accounts.   He then resumed his previous functions, as if they had never been
interrupted.   I could not refrain from expressing my
opinion of his conduct at Saffi, to which he replied in a
deprecatory manner that he had done nothing wrong,
as he had spared the women and children, and as
no Arab ever expects to die a natural death like the
cowardly townspeople.

Our horses, meanwhile, were beginning to knock up,

and we were still a long way from our halting-place.
We alighted, and pitched our tent to rest a little. We
suffered greatly from thirst. Some complained of
hunger too, but our stock of provisions was exhausted
by the seventy mouths we had to fill, and we had had
no opportunity of replenishing the supply for several
days. I was trying to sleep in the tent, while the
Arabs sat round a fire of brushwood they had kindled
outside. One of them entered, preceded by a savoury
odour, and put a plate before me. To my astonished
enquiries he replied, with the utmost indifference, that
it was a slice of roast hyena. My hunger seemed
satisfied by the mere announcement, and the plate was
soon on its way back to the circle round the fire, where
the whole carcase of the unclean animal was devoured
with great apparent relish.

At dawn the tent was struck, and we came on to this
place, now called Tadif. It is the ancient Batnæ. The
small town is pleasantly situated in a grove of cypresses,
which received Julian in so congenial a manner with
sacrifices to Apollo and Jupiter; and it has still the
appearance described. This is now a resort of pilgrims
from amongst the Jews of all Syria, on account of a
tradition that Ezra wrote his reproduction of the Mosaic
law in a cavern shown by them with great reverence.
The government has selected Tadif as a central point
for the controlling of Bedaween movements by irregular
troops. With how much success may be deduced from
the following cases in point.

A few mornings ago the plain was seen at break of day

to be covered with small parties of Arabs, endeavouring to drive off the sheep and cattle pasturing there. The people of Tadif, who muster upwards of four hundred well-armed and mounted men, soon assembled to defend their property. The assailants were repulsed, leaving three of their number killed, four wounded, and several mares taken, while the villagers had five wounded, of whom one mortally, and lost a flock of sheep which the Arabs succeeded in keeping before them as they retreated. No assistance was afforded by the irregular troops employed to defend Tadif. They were not forthcoming when their presence might have been of use, although they inflict on the peasantry the burden of supporting them, for they rarely receive a sufficient portion of their pay to meet their necessary expenses.

On a recent occasion a detachment was sent out against some Anezi who had committed depredations. The troops attacked the peaceful and submissive Hadideen, and carried off a quantity of property which they represented, and possibly believed, to belong to the great marauding tribe. A public sale took place, and the imperial treasury received the spoil of the Sultan's faithful subjects.

All endeavours of the Turkish authorities to preserve tranquillity in the desert prove abortive. A battle may be fought with a favourable result in so far as success in the field is concerned, but the permanent effect produced is still injurious. The Arabs retire exasperated, collect other tribes, and return to plunder unguarded villages. The idea of coercing them by

preventing trade is of self-evident inexpediency.   It
deprives some towns of supplies, while the produce is
carried to other markets, perhaps already overstocked.
Last year the Anezi, Shammar, and Mowali, got
into a complicated state of warfare, fighting amongst
themselves and plundering all others.   The authorities
issued a sweeping interdiction of all intercourse with
them.   To procure money for the purchase of grain,
they sell annually, besides wool and butter, young
camels and horses to dealers in live stock from Asia
Minor.   Those dealers had arrived, and were waiting
with their money for permission to trade.   Seeing that
there was no chance of obtaining it, they returned home;
and the Arab tribes, despairing of being able to purchase
what they required, took it by force when the harvests
were gathered on the threshing-floors around the villages.   The Turks pay dear for a display of authority so
little in harmony with their power of maintaining it.

This year an opposite policy is adopted.   A species of
tribute is given to keep the Bedaween quiet.   They
are allowed to draw the pay of irregular troops.   Encouraged by this acknowledgment of weakness, they
are becoming more and more daring in their attacks
on villages, caravans, and travellers.   Complaints have
been made, but, to the surprise of the complainants, the
sheikhs are frequent and honoured guests of the governor, past faults are forgiven, robes of honour are
bestowed on them, and they are sent back to the desert
to bring their produce to the towns for sale.   The fact
is that the Arab tribes of the Syrian desert are not

under the rule of the Sultan. Such troops as can be
employed against them are not reliable either for
courage or fidelity ; and the Bedaween can easily defeat
their attack, elude their pursuit, or tamper with their
integrity, according as circumstances may dictate.
Each tribe knows no authority but that of its sheikh.
This anomaly exists *jure caduco*, and it is so little likely
ever to be brought politically into notice, that it con-
tinues to exist almost entirely without the knowledge
of Europe.

The Anezi are the greatest of the tribes. They
migrated from the Nejd, or Central Arabia, about
eighty years since, on the failure of pasturage for their
increasing flocks. After repeated struggles with the
Mowali, who are a Syrian tribe, and who disputed their
advance, they finally succeeded in maintaining their
ground. They pay no taxes to the government; nor
do they furnish recruits for the army when military
conscription is enforced in the provinces they frequent.
They are always careful to encamp at a distance from
the towns on account of their rooted distrust of the
Turkish authorities, while they rarely remain more
than a week on the same spot, in order to avoid attacks,
and to procure fresh pasture for their sheep and camels.
Notwithstanding these precautions, they are often engaged in hostilities with the government troops, both
regular and irregular, when they are sent to punish
them for more than a usual measure of depredation.
War is thus a national habit with them, not only against
other tribes, but also in their own defence when attacked

by the Turks. They do not suffer much, however, at
the hands of the latter, who can no more cope with
them now than could Aurelian on his march from
Emesa to Palmyra, when they are said to have watched
the moment for surprising his legions, and eluded their
slow pursuit. An expedition was sent against Jedaan
during the summer before last which furnishes an apt
illustration of this. At the first bivouac, all the artillery horses were stolen, and a message was left with a
pinioned sentry that, if the troops ventured further into
the desert, they would not only have to drag their guns
themselves, but their cavalry should also go on foot.
To the credit of the Turks be it recorded, they took
their field-pieces with them another day's march. In
the night twenty cavalry horses disappeared. The
troops still advanced. They even succeeded in surprising a camp on the bank of the Euphrates. Tents were
struck, and loaded on the camels. Women and children
mounted. Jedaan covered the retreat with a thousand
horsemen, until the river was crossed by fording, swimming, rafting, any way in short. Then he turned, and,
seeing a large herd of camels captured and guarded by
a lieutenant with a sergeant and fifty dragoons, he galloped forward with only seven followers. He ran the
lieutenant through the body with his lance. The
Turkish commander was on a height with a field-piece,
which he pointed at Jedaan and fired. The ball killed
the sergeant then in command of the party. The report frightened the camels, which took flight and ran
over the dragoons. The Arabs got the camels together

by calling to them, and took them safely across the
river under the unavailing fire of the troops. The
latter returned to their barracks, announcing with a
flourish of trumpets the great victory they had gained.

I happened once to be in a camp which was attacked
by troops. The women and live stock were immediately concealed in a ravine, and the men mounted to
meet their enemy. When in sight, they made a feint
of retreating in a panic. The Turks pursued, and,
after a fruitless chase in the opposite direction from the
hiding-place of the women, the Arabs put their mares
to their speed, and vanished, leaving the former to go
quietly home again. All this I saw, and then, going
round another way, reached the town. I was present
when the Turkish officer reported having fought a
pitched battle, and having left thirty of the Bedaween
dead on the field. The truth underlying these facts
is that the Arab tribes are better mounted than any
regular cavalry in the world, but the pleasant fiction of
keeping them in check must be administered to the
chief authorities. Speed is naturally the first consideration with a people who fight amongst themselves
without fire-arms, and, when pitted against ordinary
troops, whether regular or irregular, they can ride
round them. If they could be induced to submit to the
restraints of discipline, and taught to stand under fire,
no such cavalry would exist anywhere. But, as it is,
I fear they have neither sympathy nor training enough
to be of any use to the Sultan, and the best thing he
can do is to let them alone, if he does not mean to

adopt a more rational mode of improving them. These
fruitless expeditions only serve to keep up their traditional hatred of the Turks, and, when they have an
opportunity, they will always retaliate with impunity.
Two or three thousand Bedaween sweep down upon
the regulars at night, cut their tent-ropes, steal their
horses, plunder, kill, and are lost in the sands of the
desert before a sentry can challenge. The Turks are
no match for them at this sort of work. A common
practice of pashas is to keep for a time on terms of
amity with some of the tribes, allowing them to trade,
and then to incite the hostility of other tribes against
them when they indulge in their habits of license.
This practice is not more successful than it is moral.

When war spreads amongst the Bedaween, the village and caravans always suffer more than they do from
the depredations of tribes at peace with one another.
Last year this occurred. The Anezi had become troublesome. The Shammar were set at them. Jedaan
marched north to seek revenge. Ten parties of Anezi
horsemen, each five hundred strong, crossed the Euphrates, and attacked the Shammar. After three days'
fighting, the latter were forced to retire with no small
loss in killed and wounded, and in mares, besides a
thousand tents, and camels and sheep captured by the
Anezi. The Shammar got the Koordish tribes and the
inhabitants of Mesopotamian villages to espouse their
cause. Another great battle was fought, in which the
Anezi were driven back, leaving all the spoil they had
taken, with two hundred and seventy mares in addition.

The total loss of life in these two engagements was
seven hundred and four on the side of the Anezi, and
two hundred and fifteen on that of the Shammar.   On
recrossing the Euphrates the Anezi found Omer Pasha
on his way to Bagdad, where he had been appointed
governor-general.   He had with him two battalions
of rifles and a regiment of cavalry, besides about two
hundred irregulars.   Jedaan fancied he wished to subjugate the Bedaween, and fell back on the walled town
of Deir, the ancient Thapsacus.   The pasha sent on a
party to prepare provisions there.   The gates were
closed, and all communication refused.   When the
great general came up, and found no provisions ready,
he took the place by storm, and gave it to his troops to
pillage, losing seven men, amongst whom was an Hungarian colonel.   The consequence of this was the sudden
appearance of Jedaan with a thousand Anezi on the
skirts of the desert, plundering villages and caravans
with the greatest ferocity.   Irregulars were sent out,
but the first party was sent back with a loss of five
men; and no others ventured to show themselves.   A
very large number of sheep and cattle was driven off
by the Anezi, crops were destroyed, and houses rifled,
without further opposition.   Such is always the result
of wars in the tribes, whether fomented by the government or undertaken with troops.   The payment of a
subsidy, or bribe to remain quiet, by recruiting a
nominal force in a tribe, is a disgraceful homage, which,
like that paid to the barbarians by the Greek emperors,
weakens rather than strengthens the state.   I have,

D

therefore, come to the conviction that the only humane
and feasible expedient is to induce the Bedaween to
settle and cultivate. It cannot be done all at once, but
the progressive extension of such a measure would be
a protection to the villages within the advancing cordon,
which might be further strengthened by the establishment of defensive military stations at intervals along its
inner margin; not to fight the nomads, but to support
the settlers who will fight in their own defence, Arab
against Arab.   These wild sons of Ishmael should be
tamed, instead of being punished for their wildness.

LETTER IV.

Castle of Aleppo—Persian Invasion—Saracen Conquest—Timour
the Tartar—Rise of the Turks—Their Decline—Population of
Aleppo—Christians—Mussulmans.

Aleppo: October 16, 1858.

THE approach to Aleppo from the east produces a
widely different impression from that which is felt
on coming to it from the coast. This is the case with
all the inland towns of Syria. After enjoying a higher
degree of Europeanism, one reaches them in a spirit of
disparagement. They appear only as places of banishment. From the desert, however, one enters Aleppo
with the feeling of a return to civilisation. Mosques
and minarets apart, blind walls and rough streets over-
looked, Aleppo is quite a little London after the fallen
cities and desert plains we have been visiting. But
Aleppo is also more or less a fallen city. A century
ago, it possessed four hundred thousand inhabitants,
while there are now only one quarter of that number;
and, forty years back, a fearful earthquake shook down
the greater part of the city, killing a thousand persons,
and leaving mounds of rubbish between houses newly
built far asunder. The Christian inhabitants of Aleppo
are twenty thousand.

The Castle of Aleppo is a tumulus on a large scale,

raised by enormous labour, like the pyramids.   If,
as Herodotus records, Cheops took twenty years with
the third of the whole population of Egypt to build the
gigantic piece of masonry bearing his name, there is
nothing surprising in so much earth being heaped up
into a small mountain.   The tumuli are expressions of
the same idea as the pyramids.   Where earth would
lie, we have tumuli; where sands were shifting, pyramids
were built of stone.   Both were probably meant for
altars, when high places were desired for worship.   It
is thus that I understand also the tower of Babel.
Sepulchres were in many of the tumuli, as in the pyramids; and even now, when a sheikh of renown dies, he
is generally buried on one of the many mounds that stud
the plains, which thus becomes again a sacred spot.
The Arabs, if asked who made the tumuli, invariably
call them the work of Ghiaoors—that is, infidels,
non-Mussulmans—in fact, Pagans; and they certainly
were raised by Pagans.   The largest of them generally
show evidence of having been made into citadels, probably long after their first construction.   These are for
the most part in ruins, but at Aleppo, the walls and
towers have been repaired by the Saracens, and are
still standing.   There are also architectural vestiges of
the Persian occupation, commencing in the middle of
the fifth century when Chosroes in his war with the
Roman Empire successfully besieged Aleppo.   In the
beginning of the seventh century, the benevolent Abu
Obaidah and the fierce Khalid, surnamed the Sword of
God, marched against it.   The Christian inhabitants of

the town paid a ransom for the preservation of their lives
and religion. Those in the castle, trusting to its steep
declivities faced with cut stone, and to its broad and
deep moat, refused to surrender, even after the loss of
three thousand men on the walls. Yukinna, its de-
fender, killed his brother, a monk, for having dared
to propose that he should capitulate. Three hundred
Christian prisoners were beheaded before the ramparts
by the besieging commanders. A slave of colossal
stature, named Dames, undertook to enter the citadel.
The Saracens feigned to raise the siege and retire.
Yukinna was celebrating their retreat with revelry in
his palace, when Dames scaled the wall by a ladder of
seven men, each standing on another's shoulders. To
stab the sentries on the battlements, attack and overpower the guard inside the gate, was the work of a few
moments, and the Mahometans rushed in victorious.
It were well for the fame of Yukinna if history told no
sequel to this tale, for he afterwards became a renegade
and a sanguinary leader of the Saracen invaders of
Syria. Towards the end of the tenth century, which
Gibbon calls the most splendid period of the Byzantine
annals, in the time of the Emperors Nicephorus, Phocas,
and his assassin John Zimisces, the imperial army, still
honoured by the name of Roman, forced the pass of
Mount Amanus, and restored Antioch to Christendom
and the Lower Empire. Aleppo, then a royal residence,
was occupied by a Saracen emir of the dynasty of
Hamadan, named Seif-ed-Dowleh, or Sword of the
State, who took to flight. His palace, now a tannery,

outside the western wall was plundered by the invaders,
but the garrison closed the city gates, and the former
encamped on the neighbouring hill of Janshan, or
Isoletti as it is called by the present Aleppines. A
quarrel having arisen between the Christian townspeople and the Saracen troops, they fought in the streets,
while the imperial army, on hearing of it, stormed the
ramparts, and put the Mussulmans to the sword. After
a brilliant campaign, which closed at Bagdad, the conquerors returned to Byzantium, leaving the Saracens to
resume their sway at Aleppo; the only city of Syria
which remained in the possession of the Greeks being
Antioch. Three centuries later, Aleppo was again attacked. To the utter dismay of its Mameluke defenders,
a line of Indian elephants, bearing turrets full of archers,
appeared on the plain, announcing the resistless advance
of Timour the Tartar. The outposts were driven in,
and the assailants entered the town with the fugitives.
The citadel surrendered. Timour called the doctors of
Islam to discuss controversial questions with him, while
the streets were filled with the shrieks of a population
given up to the ferocity of his Tartar soldiery. From
the banks of the Oxus came next, in the beginning of
the fourteenth century, the hordes of the successors of
Gengis Khan, and then the disbanded army of Gelaled-
din, who had died in Kurdistan. Thus was resumed
that inevitable invasion from the east which had been
averted for some time by treaties and alliances in favour
of the Greek Empire, and which was owing to the
pressure of China on the territory of the Scythians,

Huns, Turks, and other Tartar tribes. From the latter race, Syria suffered much. One of their chiefs,
Suleyman Shah, was drowned when attempting to cross
the Euphrates; his son Ortogrul reached the river
Sangarius, where he settled with four hundred tents;
and of him was born Othman, who founded, and gave
his name to, the Ottoman Empire. From Othman
to Suleyman II., twelve sultans reigned, all men of
transcendent ability and energy; from Suleyman II.
to the present Sultan, twenty-two have been at best
barely above mediocrity. The camp was the favourite haunt of the first series; the harem, of the second.
After two centuries and a half of aggrandisement and
consolidation, follows a period of decline. The Janissaries, who had extended the Turkish Empire when
their military organisation and discipline were superior
to those of Byzantine and European armies, undermined
its strength when their ascendency became paramount
in the state. Eight sultans, murdered or dethroned
by them, warned Mahmoud II., whose vigorous grasp
crushed them, and opened for Turkey an era of reform,
with such results as now appear.

Pritchard attributes to the Syro-Arabian race the
most perfect physical structure and the highest standard of intellectual powers of all mankind, and he
gives as an illustration of the latter superiority the
fact that the three great systems of theism which have
divided the civilised world came forth from nations of
Shemite origin. I made this remark the other day to
a very acute Turkish pasha, with whom I was con-

versing about the state of the country, and he replied
that Mahometanism, Judaism, and Christianity had
certainly all come out of Syria, and, as they had come
out of it, there is neither a good Mussulman, Jew, nor
Christian left here. Such was the judgment passed by
the Mongolian on the Semitic and Indo-European inhabitants of the present day, and it is far from being
unfounded. The union of three great races has not
formed an ethnological combination of much intrinsic
value. Whatever the Shemites might be alone, they
have been adulterated by too many infusions of foreign
blood, distracted by too frequent uprisings and down-
fallings of fantastic creeds, to retain any character,
either national or religious. The Phœnician with his
homicidal sacrifice to Moloch, the Chaldean prostrate
before his serpent, the Persian Gheber bowing down
to the sun, the Macedonian of Alexander the Great
and the Roman under Pompey with their licentious
polytheism, the Hebrew clinging through persecution
and contempt to his theocratic Deism, the Christian of
the East worshipping his saints and images, and the
Mussulman in his lordly exclusiveness of faith, have
clothed the people of Syria with a motley garb of political systems and religious creeds so commingled that
no distinct colour remains. Fortunately, it is now
thoroughly worn out, and a new suit is wanted. The
Greeks of the Lower Empire, the Arabs who subjugated them, and the Turks, at present dominant over
both, offer here a boundless field for ethnological study.
Their respective national character is still displayed.

The Greek of Syria has all the love of the beautiful and aptitude for recondite learning and analytic enquiry of the Indo-European family; the Arab possesses the pride of descent, impatience of restraint, poetic imagination, and impassioned eloquence of the Shemite; while the Turk, indolent when not excited, impetuous when roused, devoid of method and perseverance, without taste for literature, science, or arts, wields power with the ease and satisfaction of the Scythic invader of Herodotus and Mongolian conqueror in the decline of the Roman Empire. Abu el Ferraj, called by historians Abulpharagius, says that God gave heads to the Greeks, tongues to the Arabs, and hands to the Turks. Not only in their inherent nature, but even in outward form and features, these three races can at once be recognised in Syria, where alone they meet to form a nation.

The Christians of this province are not a warlike people, like those of Mount Lebanon or the Albanian and Cretan highlanders. They have neither a taste for arms nor any knowledge of their use. Being hardly ever sportsmen, there is nothing to give them manliness; they tremble at the sight of a gun or sword, and dare not approach a horse. This is what essentially they are not, and the Porte in consequence knew well that they could bear a tax in lieu of military service when abolishing the capitation assessment to please England and France at the Paris Congress. What they are supereminently is a keen money-making people, clever in trade, miserly at home, abject when

without foreign support, and insolent under protection.
They have a marked aversion to agricultural pursuits.
Of the four species of tenure of land existing in Turkey, two are open to them, *mulk* or freehold property,
and *miri* or crown lands, which they can occupy by
right of a title-deed, called *tapoo*, conferring on them
a perpetual usufruct, on condition of cultivation at least
once in three years, under the penalty of reversion to the
Sultan.   The only rent paid is a tithe of the produce
levied from all property.

The other two species of tenure can be enjoyed by
Mussulman holders only, and the nature of their origin
accounts for this distinction.   Vakoof, or pious foundations, are in the hands of the descendants of those who
bequeathed them for the maintenance of mosques, and
cannot be alienated.   Malikaneh, or fiefs, still belong to
the families of Sipahis who had received grants in payment of assistance rendered in the wars of the state.
In all of these kind of titles, the real property of the
land is vested in the Sultan alone, who, though feudalism is nominally abolished in Turkey, retains the fee-
simple of the whole of his dominions.   Unlike that
of the northern nations which subverted the Roman
Empire in the West, the feudal system of the East
secured a seigneurial right over the people to the
sovereign, without its being in any way shared by the
landed aristocracy otherwise than by delegation; and
this peculiarity of the Turkish social compact still exists.
Sultan Mahmoud II., in pursuance of the purpose
of his enlightened and well-meaning but less energetic

uncle, Selim III., decreed that feudalism should no longer be the law of the land. Imperial edicts, however, and practical results, are often at variance in Turkey. Freehold property, the best of tenures notwithstanding this modification, is thus within the reach of the Sultan's Christian subjects; but the fear of unjust treatment, and the love of liquid capital, deter them from becoming landholders. Their national tendency, also, inclines them to prefer commerce, on however small a scale, to cultivation. Here they live in a, state of chronic terror. It is difficult to explain this otherwise than as constituting a reflex of the panic caused by the incidents of 1850. Eye-witnesses of the horrors then perpetrated, and many of them actual sufferers by plunder and violence, one can hardly be surprised at their systematic concealment of wealth, and seclusion of their families in the Christian quarters of the towns. Before the Egyptian occupation of Syria, in 1832, the native Christians had grounds of alarm and complaint which cannot now be adduced. They were not allowed to ride through the streets, or to walk in the gardens. Rich merchants were fain to dress in the humblest garb to escape notice. They were often forced to carry burdens as common street-porters, or sweep the gutters, to give proofs of their submission, and they were rarely addressed by Mohammedans without expressions of contempt. But the Egyptians treated the Christians differently during their rule in Syria, and, since the return of the Turks, nothing has been outwardly renewed of the previous

relations between the two classes of the population. I
believe in little or no change in the inward feelings of
the Mussulmans towards the Christians, who themselves
believe in none, and they talk of pillage and massacre
as being imminent on every occasion when the ancient
spirit of Islam is fired by the excitement of religious
festivals. Hence their state of dread.

The Mussulmans of the interior of Turkey are a
different people from those of the capital and the great
seaports. There, a contact with European ideas exists,
which is unfelt here. The dominant race is still in the
provinces of the Ottoman Empire what it was four
centuries ago, proud, bigoted, and indolent. It is not
here, as at Constantinople, Smyrna, and Alexandria,
a mongrel transformed by the inroads of Frank trade.
Commerce flourishes more or less in the inland towns,
no doubt, but it is an element apart, which has not
exercised any great influence on the thoughts and habits
of the Mussulman. The descendant of the Arab grandee,
as of his Turkish conqueror, remains unconscious of the
gradual encroachment of foreign enterprise, and blind
to the rise of Christian ascendency. The traditions of
the two great factions which have always divided Mo-
hammedan society, the green-turbaned Shereefs claiming kindred with the prophet, and the fierce Janissaries
trusting only to the favour of sultans, though forgotten
on the coasts, are still fresh inland. In vain one talks
to a Mussulman here of the altered circumstances of
Turkey, which appear incredible to him ; and he con-
tinues to live on in his narrow circle of contemptuous

exclusiveness, animated only by personal and party
rivalries. His religion, essentially a religion of pride,
forbids his admitting the possibility of Christianity,
which he knows to be a religion of humility, ever
becoming compatible with power abroad or prosperity
at home. The condition of this northern capital of
Syria is thus a remnant of what Turkey has been,
rather than a production of any new system or influence.
The Sultan's authority is represented by a governor-
general, who puts his seal to all acts of the administration, which is practically in the hands of the Ayans
or notables of the town. These latter are always
squabbling amongst themselves for a predominance of
power. Few pashas have the energy or patriotism to
resist their usurpation. They might oppose it successfully, were they so inclined. In 1815, when Cha-
panoglu, the deposed Prince of Ynzkat, was sent to
govern Northern Syria, thirty of the Ayans were summoned to his presence, and summarily beheaded. In
1819, the different local parties united against his
successor, whom they murdered for levying a house-
tax; and the town was besieged for four months by
the Sultan's troops before order could be restored.
The vigour of the Egyptian government kept the
Ayans in subjection from 1832 to 1841, but, when
Syria again fell under Turkish rule, their rebellious
and overbearing spirit was unchecked, and in 1850 it
went so far as to produce bloodshed. That spirit is
fed by the weakness of Turkish governors, and by the
encouragement found in the non-realisation of the

various reforms which have been decreed. The Mussulman here has thus seen nothing to corroborate the
statements made of Turkey having entered a new era
of her existence as an empire. He falls back on his
old traditional sturdiness, and remains what he was in
her period of barbaric power.

LETTER V.

Effects of the Crimean War—Financial Administration—Taxation—Provincial Councils—Tithe Farming—Sipahis—Roadmaking—Police—Judicial Establishment.

Aleppo: October 22, 1858.

THE intelligence of the bombardment of Jedda, and execution of the instigators of the massacre, has created a strong sensation in Syria. The effect produced seems to be favourable to the repression of seditious movements on the part of the Mussulman population. Some few of the influential inhabitants of the towns attempted at first to talk of the disgrace inflicted on Islam, but a salutary fear of sharing the fate of the ringleaders at Jedda prevents such insinuations from finding an echo amongst the people. This city is quiet, if the absence of overt turbulence can be called tranquillity. But there are several quarters whence a storm may emerge at any moment. One of them is the great distress in which the poorer classes are plunged. This is a somewhat new feature in Turkey, where existence is so easy that little indigence has hitherto been noticed. A bread riot is a thing quite unheard of in this country, and yet the crowds daily gathered round the bakers' shops and corn stores portend nothing less. No steps are taken to

avert the evil, although the price of provisions is already
very high. The Turks generally trust to the chapter
of accidents, and it is astonishing how often their administration, both provincial and metropolitan, scrambles
through its difficulties, and sometimes even stumbles into
success. If it be true, as has been said, that, ever since
the birth of society, the chief agency by which great
changes have been effected in the world is that of war,
then should we have the right to expect a complete
metamorphosis of Turkey after the momentous incidents of the last five years. But we learn from all
history, sacred as well as profane, that war, be its
immediate object the increase of territory, the overthrow of a dynasty, the establishment of a principle,
or other national interest whatsoever, leaves consequences in no way connected with the cause of contention, whether concurrent with success or with failure,
to baffle and mystify all human foresight. The results
of the Crimean war seem to me to furnish a case
in point. A paltry squabble between the Greek and
Roman Catholic monks at Jerusalem produced a mighty
struggle, involving the chances of life or death to
empires. For a time, the question of a key of one
church and a silver star in another was but as a little
cloud no bigger than a man's hand. It soon swelled
and darkened, however, engulfing almost the whole of
Europe in its gloom and devastation. The sky once
clear again, the contending states, having gathered
what lesson they could, each after its kind, turned to
the consideration of the future arising out of their

war. The first statesmen of the world assembled at
Paris. Stipulations were signed and sealed. The
Sultan secured the civil and religious liberty of all
classes and creeds amongst his subjects. Codes of law
were to be framed, banks established, roads constructed,
and foreigners admitted as settlers by the purchase of
land in Turkey. Fiscal burdens were to be equally
balanced. The civil and military services, even in the
highest ranks, were to be open to every persuasion.
Now for the first time had the heavy hand of Western
power and enlightenment been brought down on the
tottering institutions of Turkey, and they crumbled in
the iron grasp. Terror succeeded surprise in the
Mahometan mind—surprise at foreign strength—terror
at its own weakness. Spasmodic efforts to keep pace
with Europe brought about wide concessions to the
previously unfavoured classes of the population. The
agricultural labourer would thenceforth eat the produce
of his plough in peace, the pastoral tribes would no
longer take to the hill or road to compensate the loss
of a violently appropriated flock, the artisan would have
elbow-room for his work, and the trading community
would find security to encourage a healthful spirit of
speculation. All these prospects, if ever realised at
home, would open a wider field, too, for commerce
abroad; and Turkey, whose decay and impending fall
had been so often proclaimed, yet possessing still an
undeniable fund of productive vitality, would be in-
vigorated by the powerful tonic of a ready outlet to
attach her to the wheel of traffic circling incessantly

E

around the countries of Europe. The Emperor of
Russia announced that the aggressive policy of Peter
the Great, Catherine II., and Nicholas, was at an
end. That hereditary system had collapsed after
resulting only in defeated armies, dismantled fortifica-
tions, sunk fleets, blown-up arsenals, depopulated provinces, an exhausted treasury, and a ruined trade.
Alexander II. would prefer the real prosperity flowing
from the arts of peace to the vain glory of combats
and the ambition of conquest. Projected railways,
river navigation, the construction of roads and canals,
and custom-house reforms—throwing open the ports of
Russia to the commerce of the world, and her land
frontiers to the free circulation of foreign produce—were
to take the place of the complicated mechanism of vast
armies drawn from the class now destined to provide
labour for agricultural, commercial, and industrial pur-
poses, while they would also supersede the intricate
efforts of diplomatic activity hitherto used in mediation
between the Sultan and his Christian subjects. The
thunders of war were silenced in the East, soldiers
would rest from their work of destruction, and the
navies of the trading world were to be wafted to the
shores of Russia by the four winds of heaven. On
the fulfilment of this programme depended the future
political destiny and material prosperity of Turkey.
France engaged to abstain from all single-handed interference in the internal administration of the Ottoman
Empire, and more especially to discontinue that illegal
protection of native members of the Church of Rome

in Turkey, which is generally believed to have been in a great measure instrumental in creating, from time to time, disturbances such as those occurring on Mount Lebanon and elsewhere. The other Powers represented at the Congress of Paris had no call to enter into stipulations which can be regarded as applicable to themselves, but in signing the treaty they assumed the duty of watching over, and enforcing if necessary, the strict performance of the international contract by all who were parties to it. How far these respective obligations and professions have been fulfilled, will hereafter appear.

The financial administration of the Turkish provinces may offer an apt illustration of their existing state. The Turks are notorious for a want of method in all their official arrangements, and for a singular degree of blindness to malversation, if not always of connivance at it. In no department, of course, are these defects more ruinous than in that of the public revenues. Surrounded by productive tracts of country, possessing a trade of considerable extent and activity, and amply provided by nature with the elements of abundance, the Turkish authorities have become callously accustomed to the unvarying spectacle of an empty chest. There are amongst them men of undoubted integrity; but they have sunk to so hopeless a depth of apathy that the greedy accomplices in the wholesale robbery of the people and the government ply their nefarious traffic with impunity. The chief device practised is to allow debts to accumulate by

the non-payment of taxes, tithe-farms, and other contracts. These debts are placed to the credit of the
local treasury, while the remittances sent to the capital are in cash. A deficit is thus produced in the
portion of the revenue left in the province for local
expenditure. Payments are consequently in arrear,
each sum received being disposed of before it is en-
cashed, by means of orders on the treasury. These
are discounted at twenty-five, and sometimes even
thirty-five and forty per cent., in default of ready
money in the chest. The discounters, who are generally in the public service, though represented in the
transaction by petty bankers, watch the influx of revenue, and pounce upon it as soon as it reaches the
treasurer's hands. Then, at the season when there
are few receipts, they induce the governor to contract
loans at onerous rates of interest from usurers, with
whom they are in collusion, and the money borrowed
returns to them in payment of the discounted orders.
By the loans is produced another class of clamorous
claimants to beset the treasury. Thirty and forty per
cent. per annum are generally paid, and there have
even been instances of six per cent. per month being
levied as interest on money thus invested. Besides
these exorbitant charges, and the loss of revenue by
the accumulation of outstanding debts, there is also a
more simple drainage by that under-current of direct
robbery of the public purse which is rarely wanting
in Turkey. The result of all this is that a province
enjoying a nominal income of about a quarter of a

million sterling, with an establishment costing much
less, annually exporting raw produce to the amount of
half a million, and importing manufactured goods worth
a million, has coffers perseveringly inane, civil servants
pilfering or starving, and usurers steadily fattening on
its wants.

And what is the remedial measure about to be
applied to such a state of things? Instead of adopting the obvious course of forcing those indebted to
the government to pay up, which they could and
would do under due pressure, it is said that the currency is to be reduced in nominal value. The tithes
having been sold, their purchasers will have to pay at
the reduced rate; a rise will then be allowed, and the
treasury will expend the revenue at a higher value
than it was received. Irrespective of the essential
perniciousness of this expedient in its ulterior effects,
the immediate aim will in all likelihood be frustrated
by the inability of many of the tithe-farmers to meet
their engagements on such terms. It has been, however, an immemorial remedy for Turkish impecuniosity,
and its gross unsoundness is not yet understood. Two
hundred years ago the piastre was four shillings; it is
now twopence. To trade, this measure, if adopted,
will be simply ruin. Goods are imported by merchants, and sold to retail dealers for piastres at the
current value payable in four monthly instalments,
commencing after the expiration of four months, and
the purchaser may have to pay for them more than he
has sold them for in the meantime; while the merchant

receiving a remunerative price may find the coin en-
cashed worth less than he paid to the manufacturer
abroad, in consequence of a further change of rates.
But it is a loss of time even to enumerate briefly
the reasons militating against this financial policy,
which is too shallow to require or bear serious consideration.

One might think it an easy task to check official
corruption in Turkey. I have often seen it tried,
with what success one remarkable instance of recent
date will show. A functionary was accused of peculation. Another functionary was sent to audit his
accounts. The selection was in every respect unex-
ceptionable, for the auditor was well known to be a
man of rigid integrity and perfect fidelity to his government. Besides these qualities, he was gifted with
a rare degree of perseverance and ability. He soon
discovered that the field of corruption extended over
other branches of the administration. Patiently following clue after clue, amid a general outcry against
him, he traced all their disgraceful ramifications, im-
plicating a great number of persons in the intricate
network of embezzlement and collusion. Witnesses
were bought off, bribes returned to those who had paid
them, accounts falsified or destroyed, and hush-money
circulated freely. Protectors in higher quarters were
enlisted in the cause of the self-called victims of persecution and animosity. Large sums changed hands.
The auditor, meanwhile, stood alone against this formidable array of opponents, unmoved, and seeking only to

discharge his irksome and onerous duty with uprightness,
actuated, as I feel sure, solely by the patriotic motive of
furnishing an opportunity for making an example of
many who had given way to the dominant weakness of
official life in Turkey.   At last, this mortal struggle
between administrative corruption and a praiseworthy
endeavour to stigmatise it was cut short by its summary
removal to another sphere, where it died a natural death,
representations having been made that disturbances
would take place if the enquiry were continued on the
spot.   Those who had trembled on the brink of exposure triumphed over the conscientious functionary
recalled for his zeal.   Instead of doing good, his offensive scrutiny furnished an example of impunity, and a
lesson in the mode of defence to all practising, or
tempted to practise, the inherent vice of the Turkish
bureaucracy.   A more striking illustration of the extreme difficulty attending all attempts to arrest the
downward course of internal decline in the Ottoman
Empire could not well be conceived.

The tithe of agricultural produce is the main source
of revenue.   It is collected by speculators, who purchase from the government the right of collection,
hoping to receive from cultivators a greater amount
than the price paid.   When the tithes are about to be
thus farmed, an auction is announced, dividing the villages and districts into lots.   Each member of the
provincial council selects the lot he wishes to purchase, and puts forward a retainer to bid for it under
his own guarantee for its payment.   All the members

agree not to compete with each other, and to use their
best endeavours to deter others from bidding. When
the highest price is obtained, the governor consults the
council, which declares it to be the full value, and a
profitable investment is secured to the councillor whose
turn has come. Then follows extortion in the villages.
There are instances of thirty-five per cent. being taken
instead of ten. The peasant is, moreover, forced to
convey the collector's share to the town without remu-
neration, to feed his numerous satellites, to bring him
presents of lambs, poultry, and forage for his horses,
which are not subject to the payment of tithes. There
is no possibility of redress. The voice of the all-
powerful council drowns that of every complainant,
be his complaint ever so well founded. The governor
may hear of it, but he shrugs his shoulders, while the
public revenue suffers, the people are oppressed, and
the provincial council enriched.

The land taxes are further diminished by the removal of boundaries. A village, for instance, which
has to pay a tithe of its produce is surrounded by
others, which have been devoted to the support of
mosques, or are held on feudal tenure without assessment; their holders are notables of the towns, from whose
number the councillors are drawn ; and encroachment
sometimes goes so far as to blot out the official existence of the surrounded village, the tithes of which are
clubbed with those condoned as belonging to the privi-
leged tenures. The encroachers occasionally quarrel
over the spoil. When recriminations reach the point

of establishing the right of the government to the tithes thus usurped, the litigants generally come to some arrangement, and the village suddenly vanishes, to be no more heard of until they quarrel again. These cases, however, may not recur, as the Sipahis, whose feudal rights were nominally abrogated all over Turkey in the commencement of the present reign, had succeeded in maintaining their position in return for service while protecting the great annual caravan of Mussulman pilgrims to Mecca. That service, when rendered at all, was of little efficacy, and, after a robbery committed last year in this neighbourhood, when the Soor Emini, or leader of the pilgrimage, was murdered, the Porte has very properly put an end to the corresponding privilege by incorporating the feudal taxation with the ordinary tithes. It remains to be seen, nevertheless, whether or not this enactment will be practically carried out, for it will meet with every opposition that Oriental chicane can devise to defeat it. The intention of the government is that regular troops should escort the caravans of pilgrims, which will have the effect of adding about four thousand pounds sterling per annum to the provincial revenue. The rights of pious foundations are still intact, but the day must come, and is perhaps not distant, when the government will appropriate them, and the maintenance of the religious establishment devolve on the State, to the great advantage of the revenues.

The trabieh, or house-tax, is not farmed, but annually claimed in advance from householders by the chief

of each quarter of the towns. There is some degree
of injustice also in this mode of collection, for that
dignitary does not always hesitate to assess the property
of Christians at a rate beyond its real value, making a
corresponding reduction in the estimate of that of his
own community. This hardship is, of course, not
suffered by the Christians where they occupy separate
quarters under chiefs of their own, whose distribution is
more equitable.

A new tax has been decreed, an *ad valorem* duty of
twenty per cent. on spirituous liquors, to be levied not
only on those distilled for sale, but also on such as are
intended for domestic consumption. Great distilleries
do not exist in Turkey, and small quantities of arrak
are made with the refuse of grapes after wine has been
extracted from them. Now, to enter private houses
by authority, and measure the spirituous liquors found
in them, is a very different thing from taking tithes
of agricultural produce on the open threshing floors
that surround the villages. Annoyance may be purposely given on unfounded suspicions in a country so
full of family feuds, and a system of domiciliary visits
is repugnant to the ideas and habits of an Eastern
people. Feelings of outraged privacy cannot fail to
resent the violation of the domestic sanctuary, especially when a payment has to be avoided.

The bedelieh askerieh, or tax in lieu of military
service, is drawn exclusively from the Christian population. That the principle is a just one, is readily
admitted, but fault is found with the mode of its appli-

cation. The Christians think they should not be called upon to pay the tax when the conscription is not in activity. If the Mussulmans give men, it is fair to take money from the Christians, while, by levying the tax from one class without enlisting recruits from the other, the government relieves the Mussulman population of a burden which it throws on the Christian communities; professing, at the same time, to favour the latter by abolishing the kharadj, or former capitation tax. That tax amounted to a hundred thousand piastres in this province: two hundred and forty thousand piastres are now claimed, in lieu of forty-eight soldiers at five thousand piastres each. This appears the more onerous from the change having been represented as a boon granted by the Sultan to his Christian subjects under pressure from abroad. It does not amount to much, however—only two shillings per head per annum. I believe that, in comparison with other countries, the population of Turkey is on the whole lightly taxed. But there is no people on earth more remarkable for what Lord Castlereagh called an ignorant impatience of taxation than Eastern Christians.

Besides an improved collection, and the appropriation of mosque property, the chief desideratum for increasing the revenues is road-making. The country is impoverished by the decline of exportation on account of the difficulty and expense of conveying produce from the interior to the coast, which often exceeds its first price. Money thus leaving Turkey by importa-

tion of foreign goods, does not return by any exchange
of commodities with other nations in an equal, not to
say a superior, *ratio*.   Yet, not only is nothing done
for the construction of roads, but even the existing
mule-tracks are not protected from plunderers.   The
government, too, impedes the movement of merchandise without the least scruple, on every occasion when
troops or pashas travel, by seizing all the beasts of
burden to be found, sometimes even when they are
actually laden by the merchants.   This evil is not confined to the mere number of animals required for the
public service, because it is made an opportunity for
gain by the police officers, who take possession of
whole caravans of mules and camels, releasing those
whose owners bribe them.   Thus, when a hundred
animals are wanted, a thousand may be seized, and
perhaps five thousand are concealed, their drivers not
daring to approach the towns until the demand has
ceased.

The working of the provincial councils, as I have
already explained in part, is very defective.   As a
first step in the career of reform, much was expected
from their organisation.   But it is now abundantly de-
monstrated by its mode of action that, however beneficial it may be in other countries and under different
circumstances, it was adopted prematurely here, being
incompatible with the stage of political education at
which the population had arrived, and not in the least
in harmony with their social condition.   I allude, of
course, only to the provincial population of Turkey, for

that of the capital is in a widely different state, and
seems to belong to another age.   Those who judge the
former by the latter, and write on the shores of the
Bosphorus sanguine disquisitions, inspired by the more
advanced and intelligent members of the patriotic party
amongst Ottoman statesmen, on the prosperity of the
rural class, the safety of life, honour, and property, and
on the great and favourable changes which have taken
place within the last twenty years, deceive themselves
and others in so far as the provinces of the empire
are concerned.   I used to be one of those myself,
but a deeper insight into the state of the interior
of Turkey has since then forced me to give up some
of the bright theories I indulged in.   I now see that
the great change to the agricultural population, which
was often oppressed by a pasha cruel and rapacious,
is the substitution of fifteen or twenty councillors,
always greedy of gain, full of enmities, and more skilled
by local knowledge to oppress whenever oppression is
safe and profitable.   It is idle to talk of the influence
of Christian members of provincial councils, for they
hardly presume even to sit in the presence of their
Mussulman colleagues, and never venture to express
dissent, calculated though the decision may be to fall
heavily on their own constituents.   These councils, in
point of fact, hamper a good governor without acting
as a check on a bad one.   They are, in addition to this,
a new source of evil in themselves.   Men of public
spirit and integrity are not to be found in the class of
notables in the interior.   The councils are conse-

quently composed of unscrupulous speculators. They
do not give themselves the trouble to attend their
sittings unless they have some personal interests to
further. Collusion supplies the means of serving such
interests, and pashas are powerless, when willing, to
cope with their deep collective chicanery. Possessed
of great experience, wielding a dangerous ascendency
over the people, and well versed in all the trickery of
the East, they rarely fail to reduce the best-intentioned
governor to the condition of an instrument in their
hands. He is soon made to feel the weight of their
displeasure, and the value of their support, by the unwise credit given at Constantinople to their censure or
approbation, and he then resigns himself to let them
govern the province in his stead. The same familiar
phases of such struggles, with the same results, have
come under my notice in the provinces of European
Turkey and Asia Minor, as now in Syria. Still the
agricultural population is not immersed in that hopeless
state of destitution that might be expected under these
conditions: so fertile is the soil, so frugal the labourer.
I have also too great a respect for municipal institutions
to condemn them entirely here, even when convinced
that they are far from working well. I therefore regard the formation of provincial councils as an experiment which has not been successful only because it was
made in too precipitate a manner. The tyranny of some
of the pashas of the old school called for a counterpoise:
the remedy has outweighed the evil. For each tyrant
we have many tyrants, all seeking their own advantage,

and every one of them inferior to the pasha in qualifications for government.   Were the practice of sending
memorials to the Porte, laudatory as well as censorious,
put a stop to, and were the desired control over governors exercised by inspectors of high rank instead of
by local magistrates, I am inclined to think that these
councils might still assume the place in the mechanism
of provincial government they were meant to occupy.
The feudal system of the East had degenerated when it
produced the great barons of Turkey in the commencement of the present century. Ali Tepedeleni of Janina,
Ali of Stolatz, Kara Osmanoglu of Magnesia, Chapan-
oglu of Yuzkat, Haznadaroglu of the Djanik, and others,
had reduced the mass of the people to a state of actual
servitude.   All spirit of industry was crushed out of
them by the narrow maxims of a military aristocracy.
The country was on the verge of ruin.   It was saved
by the destruction of the Janissaries, the formation of
a regular army, and the abolition of feudalism.   To
prevent a relapse under another form to the evils reme-
died, the provincial councils inaugurated the reign of
principles based on the ancient municipal system. But
the new institutions were not regulated so as to be
consonant with the social and political state of the
country.   The pendulum has to be brought back to its
centre after an equally pernicious vibration on either
side.   In saying that Turkey was saved by the first
reforms, I do not mean to say more than that the evil day
was then postponed.   Facts are too stubborn for me to
hope any longer for her regeneration as a result of her

present policy and under the present *régime.* The only
old empire in all history that has ever become new is
the Mogul empire, and to that end it had to become
British. Until some such change of masters, or modification of the dominant class, come over Turkey, there
can be no reasonable chance for her. The whole vast
assemblage of heterogeneous peoples under the Sultan's
sway have lost confidence in his rule. Promised immunities and acts of justice remain unrealised, and
Turkish and Punic faith have come to be synonymous
terms in their estimation. But a change of masters
and systems is commonly acceptable to subject nations :
the elements of prosperity and power are certainly in
existence, though dormant ; and the motley population
of this worn-out tottering empire may one day joyfully
blossom into another India under some new form of
rule.

The next in importance of the details of provincial
misgovernment in Turkey appears to me to be the mode
of conducting the police establishment. It not only
forms by its professed organisation one of the chief
items of expenditure, and accordingly one of the most
assiduously cultivated fields for peculation, but also
leaves, by its inefficient operation, life and property
lamentably insecure. In this province an irregular
force of two thousand men is allowed for the protection
of the towns and villages. This force consists of twenty
troops, each under the command of a dehlibash or
captain. The pay of the corps is regularly charged
to the government, but its full existence is confined to

the muster-rolls. The captain presents his monthly
pay-list, and receives an order on the treasury for the
amount. On application there, he is told there is no
money in the chest. A discounter, often official, makes
an offer for the order, which is accepted, and then the
balance is paid—perhaps out of the empty chest. Receiving thus only enough to pay sixty or seventy of his
hundred men, the captain can hardly be expected to keep
the whole number. He may even do a little business
on his own account, and, encouraged by the example
of the payment being sufficient for only two-thirds of
his troop, he does not see any reason for keeping more
than one-third. Then, his appointment having cost
him a large bribe to some influential member of the
provincial council, which sum he has borrowed from
a usurer on condition that the latter shall reimburse
himself with enormous interest by drawing the pay of
a fixed number of nominal troopers, the unfortunate
troop is condemned to a further reduction of its numerical strength. The day of muster and inspection
comes round. This does not matter in the least. Young
men of ragged outfit and martial bearing are always to
be found in the streets, ready for any job by the day.
Horses are easily borrowed or hired. The formality of
verifying the numbers in the ranks is perfectly understood by all who take a part in it. The majority of the
troop returns to the coffee-houses and khans whence it
was drawn, and the captain goes back with the small
remainder to his respective out-station.

Irregular pay is not confined to the irregular troops.

F

The regiments in garrison have upwards of fifteen
months' arrears to receive. The private soldiers are
fed by the government, and their extraordinary discipline and submission keep them quiet. But the
officers, many of whom have families to support out of
barracks, are exceedingly dissatisfied, being obliged to
sell their effects to procure daily bread. The other
day, two captains of infantry came to me in great distress, saying they had nothing left to sell but their
swords, and begging me to give them a small loan.

The judicial establishment is composed of three courts.
The first, called the Mejlis el Tahkik, consists of a president and four members, and confines its operations
to the investigation of minor offences, without passing
sentence, unless ordered by the Governor-General to
do so. The second is the provincial council, numbering from thirteen to twenty of the chief functionaries
and notables of the town, which passes judgment on the
evidence taken by the first court, from which it is also
the court of appeal. The Mehkemeh is the court of law,
conducted by the Cadi with the assistance of the Mufti,
who is neither a colleague nor a superior, and merely
issues oracular expositions of the law applicable to the
case on trial. The only judicial authority above the
Mehkemeh is the Sheikh ul Islam at Constantinople.
The Cadi is moved annually from town to town, while
the Mufti is a native and stationary. As a theoretical
organisation this may seem well arranged, but here
again the difficulty of finding trustworthy men to carry
it out is severely felt. The Cadi seeks only to enrich

himself during his short stay, and the last month of his
year generally sees a great number of causes settled at
a cheap rate to leave no gleanings for his successor.
The Mufti sells his fetwa, or written opinion, to the
highest bidder.   The proceedings are not recorded,
testimony is merely oral, the witnesses are often bribed,
the judges almost always, and the heaviest purse gains
every cause.   The entrance to the different courts on
days of hearing is crowded by persons making a livelihood by giving false evidence.   Witnesses are wanted,
they are found at the door, ready to swear to anything
for a couple of dollars.

The evidence of Christians is not yet received by any
court, notwithstanding all that has been said, written,
and proclaimed on the subject.

A commercial tribunal was instituted a short time
since.   Four European merchants were appointed to
judge cases brought before it, with four Mussulmans,
four native Christians, and a president selected from
amongst the all-pervading notables of the town.   But
the weight of foreign impartiality and integrity could
not long be borne by the majority of the court, who
found themselves shamed into honesty.   A pretext only
was wanting to throw it off.   The farmer of the customs
received an inconvenient summons, and refused to appear.   The president and Mussulman members resigned,
and the Chamber of Commerce, as it was pompously
styled, ceased to exist.   The previous practice was resumed, and a notoriously corrupt Turkish merchant,
with four Mussulman assessors, arbitrates by private

contract with one, and sometimes both, of the litigants.
European merchants renounce a right or claim against
a Mussulman rather than take it for trial to that judicial counting-house.

A new penal code has been promulgated for police
cases. It would seem to work well, if one may judge
by the diminution of petty punishments. But this may
also arise from the introduction of the novel penalty of
fines. The power to inflict them is certainly not always
justly exercised, and accused persons, though innocent
and prosecuted only through private enmity, prefer
paying a small sum to defending themselves. In its
ultimate result this method differs little from the more
habitual purchase of acquittal from the judge. On the
other hand, the substitution of fines for corporal punishment tells on those disposed to become real offenders,
who are sometimes more cautious to avoid the liability
of their pocket than to escape the rod.

LETTER VI.

Aintab : October 27, 1852.

RAIN pattered on my windows, and the morning was cold and comfortless; but it was the day fixed for an excursion northwards, and we mounted our horses in the hope of the weather improving. Nor were we disappointed, for the sun soon broke the heavy clouds, and followed us, as we advanced on our road to Killis, with his enlivening rays. The country was perfectly level, and the soil appeared very rich under the many rude ploughshares which were turning it over to cover the seed just sown. In the evening we pitched our tents at the small village of Bashkieni, and it was full time, for we were no sooner sheltered by our canvas roofs than the sky became again overclouded, and the rain fell in torrents. One of the tents was watertight, but the other leaked, and dismal voices were heard in the night enquiring after umbrellas.

Another fine day on the great plain stretching from the Euphrates to the long range of Mount Amanus, another rainy night encamped near a village, and a short ride on the following morning over fine cultivated

land, then through shady orchards, brought us to Killis.
Killis, the ancient Ciliza, is now a half-ruined town of
twelve thousand inhabitants. We had just taken up our
quarters in the house of a worthy Protestant Armenian,
when a visitor was announced. He was a handsome
dark-visaged youth, in a rich Koordish dress, bristling
with arms. This was Dehli Halil Aga, whose nickname of Dehli, the Mad, is not usurped, if all tales told
of him be true. He is the actual ruler of this part of
the country, though not acknowledged as such by the
government. Indeed, the government does not seem
to think it worth while disputing his authority. There
is a nominal Turkish governor, however; but he is
quite secondary in local importance. He also came to
make our acquaintance after the mad Aga had gone.
We had asked the latter about the state of the country,
and were informed in reply that it was perfectly quiet
and orderly. To the same question the Governor answered that the Koordish tribes in the neighbourhood
had taken up arms, and intercepted the roads from
Malatyah, Sivas, Kharpoot, and other towns of Asia
Minor, plundering caravans, and beating back the irregular troops sent to protect them. The Turkomans of
the plains of Antioch and Aintab, together with the
formidable mountaineers, of the same race, occupying
the impenetrable ravines and heights of Amanus, were
committing the same excesses towards the south-west.
The Bedaween on the east of Killis, after having been
so well treated this year, and after having behaved so
much better than usual, had commenced pillaging the

villages. Several of their inhabitants had been killed, and almost all their flocks and herds had been taken possession of. The town was entirely at the mercy of the Koords and their mad chief. On a recent occasion, a merchant of Aleppo had obtained from the Governor-General some policemen to enforce a claim he had against a Koord for money advanced to purchase wool which had never been delivered. The policemen went to the camp of the debtor, where they were told that if they did not immediately return to Aleppo they would be fired upon. When passing through Killis they learnt that the Koord, whom they sought, had come there before them. They met him in the bazaar, and dragged him before the Cadi. Dehli Halil Aga was soon informed of this act of violence against one of his people; he surrounded the Cadi's house with two or three hundred armed men, went in himself, and, after expressing great indignation, carried off the prisoner. This state of matters was giving rise to well-founded apprehensions amongst the townspeople, whose only safety is found in conciliating the favour of the Koords and their chief. The notorious weakness of the government, the disaffection of the nomadic population, and, above all, the hope of plunder, would, it was feared, lead to still more serious consequences.

Since my arrival here I have heard that the Koordish, Turkoman, and Arab tribes, above alluded to, on finding that no further opposition to their depredations was even attempted by the Turkish authorities, thought of coming to an understanding by which that part of

the province should be divided amongst them for the purpose of robbery and devastation. Fortunately they were
unable to agree, and began fighting with each other.
Rival chiefs appeared, too, all claiming supremacy.
Although their strength has thus been broken up, small
parties continue to ravage the country. This may, I
think, be regarded as a seditious movement suggested
by dislike and contempt of the Turkish rule in Syria,
but resulting in pillage rather than insurrection. The
particulars consist merely in a series of robberies, and
of skirmishes between different bands of the robbers.

We found some dissension amongst the Christian
inhabitants of Killis, chiefly arising from religious
differences. Many Armenians there having become
Protestants, through the instrumentality of those most
able and worthy servants of Christ, the American
missionaries, the other Churches seem to have been
moved to some activity. The Roman Catholic priests
took the field, and succeeded in bringing over to their
Church about twenty families of the Greek community.
The Greek Bishop of Aleppo sent an emissary to
Killis, who induced the perverts to return to his fold
after he had redressed their grievances, some tangible
interest of a temporal character being almost always
at the bottom of spiritual contests between the Eastern
Churches. Several Jews of Killis have likewise courted
conversion by applying for religious instruction to
the Rev. Mr. Grant Brown, a greatly and deservedly
respected missionary of the United Presbyterian Church
of Scotland at Aleppo, and they have announced their

readiness to receive his teaching. The Jews do not often brave the persecution raised by inclining towards Christianity in the East, for the Rabbis have many resources; they can banish, imprison, and excommunicate more effectually than the Pope himself, as their victim runs the risk of actual starvation unless he be a baker, no other baker daring to sell him bread, which of course has the result of making him join a Christian community out of sheer hunger. All this religious excitement has much disturbed the tranquillity of Killis, but it was most gratifying to see one sect calmly building a large and handsome place of worship, so numerous and zealous have the new Protestants become.

After four long days at Killis, where we were detained by the illness of one of our party, we proceeded on our way under the bright sunshine of that second summer which follows the first rains in this climate, not too bright to be agreeable, and cool and fresh as a May morning. We skirted, then crossed, a low range of volcanic hills, stopped to fish in a clear deep stream spanned by a fine old bridge, and late in the afternoon reached a squalid hamlet called Kehriz. The next day, still on high ground, was not far spent when we entered this pretty town of Aintab, the ancient Antiochia ad Taurum, now boasting of five-and-forty thousand inhabitants. The beauty of its situation in the centre of a partially-wooded and well-watered plain has gained for it the honourable name of Little Damascus.

This is the metropolis of Oriental Protestantism.
Here the reformation worked out by the American
missionaries has its head-quarters, and is represented
by no less than fourteen hundred persons. The Presbyterian Church of Killis numbers one hundred members; that of Birejik, fifty; Marash, a thousand; Diar-
bekir, four hundred; Urfa, forty; Aleppo, thirty;
Beitias, a hundred; Kissab, five hundred; and Yeko-
look, a hundred: in all, three thousand seven hundred
and twenty in Northern Syria alone. Education, as
well as preaching the Gospel, has been spread to a great
extent, schools having been established by the American
missionaries in every considerable place in the province.
Besides those which are merely elementary, there are
theological classes for the preparation of natives for the
ministry, upper schools affording classical and scientific
tuition, and a girls' boarding school under the enlightened
charge of American ladies. Independently of its all-
important effect in purifying the religion of the country,
these missionary labours are of obvious advantage to a
population which has been plunged into a state of
lamentable ignorance by centuries of servitude, and
they have raised the standard of morality which had
fallen to so low a degree. The Protestants as a community are very poor, and yet those illicit gains, eagerly
sought by all classes in Turkey, are conscientiously
avoided by them. Thus, in trade, to defraud the public
revenue by smuggling is regarded generally as a legitimate profit; but the Protestants, having learnt the
meaning of truth, rise above such practices.

This movement, the exclusive merit of which belongs to the United States, commenced in Syria under circumstances equally remarkable with any that occurred in the early Christian Church. The first convert was from the Maronite community, the secretary of the patriarch. Employed to refute a tract published by an American missionary, he was convinced by it. Imprisoned, starved, beaten, his constancy did not give way. He escaped, was recaptured, and died the death of a martyr, chained by the neck to the wall of a dungeon. Persecution on the part of the Eastern Churches has not yet ceased, whether directly as in this sad but glorious instance, or through influence with the Turkish authorities; but persecution never injured a good cause, and in Syria it has evidently benefited it by the frequent adoption of the injudicious measure of banishment, which disseminated the new doctrine. The opposition to the spread of Protestantism, though still existing within certain limits, is now less violent, being for the most part confined to the ejection of teachers from any new field they may enter, since it has been recognised by the government as a distinct and independent religious denomination.

A party has been formed amongst the native converts to Presbyterian Protestantism, with the view of establishing an Episcopalian Protestant Church in the East. This idea seems to have been in some degree prompted by the extreme rigour of the Presbyterian system with regard to church-membership, a sort of jury having to scrutinise the private life of every applicant for

admission to the Holy Communion, and baptism being
refused to the children of those not admitted. Besides
this motive, there may be under it a lurking hope that an
Episcopal Protestant might enjoy the especial protection of England. It is hardly to be wondered at that
mixed motives for religious professions of this nature
should be entertained in Syria, for the example of the
Roman Catholics, still openly protected by France,
and the Greeks and Armenians by Russia, in spite of
the stipulations on that subject in the Treaty of Paris,
cannot be without its effect on the minds of a people
always anxious to escape from Turkish jurisdiction.
Instances are recorded even of alleged murderers elud-
ing trial, not to mention many cases of insolvent
debtors obtaining protection from creditors, by joining
one or other of those favoured Churches. On one
occasion a man offered to become a Protestant on condition of relief from pecuniary engagements; he was
of course refused, and he joined another Church on the
same terms a few days afterwards. Such proceedings
for the purpose of extending political influence may
well inspire the belief that Great Britain would be
actuated by similar views. The Episcopal party does
not acknowledge that hope, however, and attributes
their movement to the accident of a Turkish translation
of our Prayer-book having fallen into their hands, and
to their having been so pleased with it that they have
continued to use it in preference to the Presbyterian
extempore prayers, and the Armenian Liturgy which
is in a language they do not understand. They have

consequently been cast off by the former Church, and
excommunicated by the latter. In number they say
they can reckon on three hundred actually united, and on
at least a thousand more who would join them from the
Armenian Church, were they recognised as a separate
community. The want of bishops in the Presbyterian
Church is considered by them one of the chief obstacles
to the universal reformation of the Eastern Churches;
and the consideration is not without weight in a country
where bishops are allowed to exercise a civil as well
as an ecclesiastical jurisdiction, the alternative being
Turkish jurisdiction.

The precept of the Coran, that there shall be no
violence in affairs of religion (the truth distinguishing
itself sufficiently from error), and the Sultan's decree,
that a convert shall not be executed, were carried out
in a case that occurred here last year. A young
Armenian woman became a Mahometan in order to
obtain a divorce from an uncongenial husband. After
some time it was said that she wished to return to
her Church. A zealous sheikh kidnapped her to prevent a scandal to Islam. The Armenian priests
complained to the Turkish authorities, who had her
brought before them by the sheikh. She publicly
declared herself a Moslem, and denied ever having
thought of abjuring her new faith. Her relatives
petitioned for permission to remonstrate with her. It
was granted, and she was placed for a week in a
Turkish house to which they were allowed free access.
All persuasion was in vain until the Armenian priests

bethought themselves of pronouncing a formal divorce
from her husband, which they had refused to do previously, not seeing then adequate grounds for it. When
again taken before the authorities, she said that she had
repented of her error, and wished to return to Christianity.   She was allowed to go free, and a warning
was published to all Mussulmans who might think of
molesting her, that any attempt to do so would be
severely punished.   Turkey has made some progress:
that woman would have been beheaded, had the case
happened twenty years earlier.

The state of the population of Aintab may be appreciated by the following incident.   A short time ago a
Turkoman Bey from Mount Amanus rode into the
town in broad daylight with a party of armed horsemen, entered the house of one of the principal Turkish
inhabitants, forced the door of the harem, and carried
off his daughter, who was famed for beauty.   They
were soon pursued by all who could mount in time.
The Turkomans separated to divide the superior number
of their pursuers, who were in sight, each horseman
taking a line of his own in the hope that the townspeople would follow, some in threes and fours, and others
not at all, while the Bey contrived to be the last to
leave the straight road.   The manœuvre was skilful,
but unsuccessful, for the Bey soon found himself riding
alone with his fair burden through a ravine, and eight
or ten of the avengers close up to him.   When on the
point of being overtaken, he dashed the screaming girl
to the ground, and his swift horse, relieved of the addi-

tional weight, sprang forward and saved him.   The
girl was killed by the fall.   The Bey, not long afterwards, was seen in the streets of Aintab as if nothing
had happened.   The authorities sent soldiers to capture
him, but retribution was nearer at hand.   The bereaved
father, hearing his enemy was there, outran the guards,
and shot him, with his own hand, in their presence.   No
further notice was taken of the affair.

LETTER VII.

Saam—Sacred Fish—Mussulman Prayer—Islam—Turkoman
Camp—Kilijli Tribe—Mount Taurus—Turks—Marash—Death
of Guarmani—Armenians—Governor.

Marash : November 3, 1858.

ON leaving Aintab we ascended the eastern slopes
of a broad belt of mountains, over which lay our
road to Marash.   The first halt was at a pretty village
called Saam, where we lunched under the shade of
gigantic walnut-trees spreading their ponderous boughs
over a copious spring.   The clear cool water flowed
into an ancient reservoir full of large fish, rendered
sacred by some forgotten tradition, possibly that which
is attributed by Lucian to the reverence of the Syrians
for Derceto, who, according to Diodorus Siculus, threw
herself into a lake and was transformed into a fish after
giving birth to Semiramis.   Certain it is that in many
parts of Syria, at Urfa, Tripoli, and elsewhere, there
are to this day, near the mosques, large tanks full of fish
which no one is allowed to molest, and which are very
tame from being frequently fed by visitors with crumbs
of bread.   The faithful of our party crowded round the
fountain, washing their hands, head, and feet, and comb-
ing their beards with their fingers ; then turning to the
south and spreading their cloaks on the ground like

carpets, they raised their hands behind their ears, held
them before their eyes to simulate an open book, knelt,
rose, stooped, fell prostrate, pressed their foreheads to
the earth, sat complacently awhile on their heels, looked
over each shoulder to exorcise evil spirits, and rose good
Mussulmans to enjoy the simple fare laid out before us.
To pray five times a day, to eat no pork, drink no wine,
touch nothing unclean, fast from sunrise to sunset and
feast all night for a month each year, give a tithe of
their income to a mosque, and make a pilgrimage to
Mecca, constitute the whole duty of a pious Moslem
life. It is a pity that Mahomet inconsistently appended
his own recognition as a prophet to the otherwise pure
deism of Islam, or Resignation, which he founded, for
without that imposture there would be a certain genial
dignity about the rest. In converting the Arabs from
Sabianism, he did well, but he did not know where to
stop. The morality he inculcated was excellent, and
it might have been a preparation for that foundation
other than which can no man lay. One must not take
into account the traditional legislation of Islam which
has been subsequently added to the original institution
by Mahomet; the sensual paradise, the inferiority of the
female sex, polygamy, and other degrading doctrines,
have not the warrant of coexistence with the precepts
of sobriety, hospitality, almsgiving, religious tolerance,
cleanliness, veracity, and prayer to one God, which he
introduced in a pagan state of society. Much of what
has rendered the Mussulman faith odious to us, has also
been added after his death, and it is even doubtful how

far he is responsible for all that is attributed to his life.
The Coran expressly affirms that Mahomet was but a
man charged with a divine mission, and, when a miracle
was required by his hearers, he asked them whether
they thought he was other than a man. His claim to
the honours of a prophet, as also his practical sanction
of polygamy, did not appear until his mind had been
affected by enthusiasm and epilepsy, and he had fallen
into the hands of a servile Jewish adviser, who led him
into a raving imitation of the prophets of Israel, and the
plurality of wives of the patriarchs. His conscience,
moreover, was evidently not at rest on the latter point,
for he never ceased to bewail the loss of his faithful
Cadija, with whom alone he had lived so many years,
and her memory was a subject of constant reproach to
those he married afterwards for presuming to share her
privilege of having been a prophet's wife. The chapter of the Coran generally quoted as sanctioning
polygamy is the most obscure and ambiguous of that
whole collection of mystic rhapsodies; and many learned
Mussulmans regard it as a weak attempt at a compromise with his conscience under the commission of what
he felt to be sinful. Now there is but a small minority
of the professors of Mahometanism to be found with
more than one wife. A witty Turk once said that the
chief difference he perceived between his and our creeds
was, that his allowed many wives and one God, while
ours admitted the existence of many gods, but permitted
us to have only one wife. It is a melancholy truth that
in the East the practice of the Mussulman religion is

purer than that of Christianity, which the Moslems not unjustly tax with idolatry and polytheism when they see prayers offered to images and saints. If we look on that picture and on this, the conviction that the Church of Christ does not shine beside Islam comes sadly home to us. The divisions amongst sects scandalise the Turks. The history of the world furnishes no instance of a creed or community with such an absolute and compact unity as that of Mahomet, while the religious institutions founded by Moses, Zoroaster, Confucius, and even our own true Church, have all been split asunder into pugnacious and mutually-hating communities, both doctrinal and political. Islam alone is still as it was twelve centuries ago, strong in its singleness of nature and purpose, whether as a faith or as a civil system, imperturbable as a half-truth fossilised in pre-maturity. The Coran, like the Pentateuch, is a guide for this life as well as for the next, a source of law as well as of divinity, a code of polity as well as of religion, laying down not only what is to be believed of things spiritual, but also what is to be done in things temporal, requiring strict literal obedience, and never accommodating itself to circumstances. Freed from its jurisprudence and its ritual, the stand-point of the faith is but another covenant of works, professing only to revive the religion of Abraham, revealing no truth not already known, but ignoring many essential to salvation. As a faith it is thus as strong as Judaism, and may last as long; losing, like it, however, its dominant position. In Turkey there is no artificial union of

Church and State, but the two are essentially one, and
the Church prevents progress in the State. Raised to
be a scourge to the corrupt Christian Churches of the
East, they have, ever since its rise, been forced to bear
its heavy yoke. In numbers Islam greatly exceeds the
Christian faith in Asiatic Turkey, and it is more deeply
rooted in the hearts of its votaries. Assuming to be
the final revelation of God, it subdues their reason and
engages their affection, instilling its chief maxim of
resignation to the Divine will in a manner far from
being evinced by the Christians of the East. Then it
has no mysteries to baffle and mortify their intellect, and
it gratifies their pride by making man his own saviour
in the merit ascribed to good works. They censure
what they call the inconsistencies of Christianity, such
as justification by faith alone when works are still required; and, with a seeming plausibility derived from an
epigrammatic antithesis of language covering a confusion of thought, they say that their God created man
in his own image, but that Christians have created gods
in their image as unreasonable as themselves. Mussulmans have the name of God constantly in their mouths,
not without reverence, but with a sort of familiarity
that we can hardly understand. Salutations, leave-
takings, thanks, even the most trivial requests, are all
in the name of God, accompanied by emphatic professions of faith. These latter constitute at least a third
part of every dialogue in this country. But there is
no great thought of piety in this habit, which rather
originates in an unholy pride and a defiant spirit. An

assertion of superiority is all that is meant, and a wish
to provoke religious antagonism generally inspires the
Mussulman formulas of civility towards those of other
creeds. Their curses, too, which may be said to contribute another third to conversation, are far from
conveying the import of the expressions used, but
merely revert to the former greatness of their race, by
addressing to an awkward slave, the threats of a conqueror to a vanquished foe, when they hope the fire
may be extinguished on his father's hearth, or to a lame
donkey, when they wish his mother's grave may be
defiled.

We slept at Arablar, a small colony of Bedaween,
finely situated on a height; and continued next day
our picturesque ride over hill and dale, stopping to
lunch in a deep ravine below a village called Kara-
buyukli, and halting for the night at a Turkoman
camp. We had reached the plain of Buzarjik, and,
tempted by the grassy bank of a stream covered with
the tents of Suleyman Aga, the rebel chief of the
Kilijli tribe, we pitched ours amongst them. The
chief was hospitable, though in open revolt against the
government, and he posted a guard of his men to protect our horses from the wolves which howled around
us all night. Our party took in turns the duty of
sitting up, revolver in hand, to watch our guard, which
might have been as dangerous to us as the wolves.
Nothing untoward happened, and we left the camp in
the morning, escorted by Suleyman Aga and twenty
Turkoman horsemen, who flanked our march to drive

from the brushwood any stragglers who might fancy to
attack us. A chain of mountains detaches itself from
the high plateau of Lesser Armenia, and extends
southwards to terminate abruptly on the plains of
Northern Syria. This range of rugged heights leaves
room for fertile fields in some of its narrow valleys.
Richly clothed with gigantic timber, plane, oak, and
beech trees, and affording abundant pasture, it is
tenanted principally by a scanty population of shepherds, whose rude cottages nestle in ravines lined
with myrtle, oleander, and briars of prodigious growth.
The undulating lowlands at its feet display a considerable breadth of culture around the small town of
Marash, peopled by the worst of the Turks, and a few
Christians, trading in their produce. The lower slopes
of the mountain are the orchards of the province.
Cherry, apricot, plum, and walnut trees, grow there
in thickets. Higher up, amongst various kinds of
oak and ilex, are those yielding gallnuts for dyeing,
and the *vallonea* whose acorn cup is an article of exportation for the use of tanneries. Gum Tragacanth
and Scammony are brought in abundance from the
hills, as well as the berries of the *Rhamnus infectoria*,
which supply a beautiful yellow colour. The agricultural implements seen on the plain are still very primitive, and the science of husbandry remains in a stunted
infancy; but the soil is so marvellously productive
that heavy crops are obtained by merely throwing seed
into shallow furrows scraped by the most wretched
of ploughs, without harrowing, rolling, or weeding.

The town of Marash, known under the name of
Germanicia in Roman times, has now about twenty-
seven thousand inhabitants.   Its chief characteristic is
the gushing rivulets which occupy the centre of almost
every street.   It has a declining, depopulated appearance.   The plague, once a check to the increase of
population in Turkey, has now ceased to exist and to
decimate her inhabitants as it did every tenth year in
the beginning of this century, but other causes of the
progressive diminution of their number remain, amongst
which infanticide, and the drain of the recent war, are
at present conspicuous.   The Christians are increasing
in number, and consequently in proportion to that of
the Mussulmans, all over the Ottoman Empire.   In this
part of the country, however, they do not yet exceed
an eighth part of the population.   Their distinctive
habits, costume, and even their language, have almost
totally merged into those of the dominant race.   Christian influence is thus less felt here than farther
south.   The Malikaneh tenure of the Moslem land-
owners is prevalent at Marash, and their accumulation of wealth by extortion and corruption keeps the
Christians in a state of serf-like dependence, with the
exception only of the Armenian mountaineers.   In
districts like this of Asiatic Turkey, therefore, lies
the greatest national vigour of the Turks, founded
on centuries of political consolidation, while their less
comprehensive sway in European Turkey over a more
numerous Christian population betrays greater inherent
debility.   Here are no Arabs, and we have to do with

the pure Turkish race.   Those of the villages differ
entirely from those of the towns, as the latter do in
their turn from the Turks of the capital and seaports.
This may in some measure account for the conflicting
opinions of the nation given by travellers.   Those
who have seen much of the Turkish peasantry talk of
the truthfulness, honesty, kindliness, hospitality, and
natural dignity of the race ; others, having gone by
the post road from town to town, descant on their
falsehood, avarice, and knavishness.   Both views are
correct.   At Marash the Turks have retained all
their pristine ferocity.

This was displayed two years ago in a very tragical
incident.   Signor Guarmani was a young Italian who
had been employed by a mercantile house of Beyrout to
purchase silk on Mount Lebanon.   In a Druze village he
engaged the affections of a handsome girl, who agreed
to become a Christian and marry him.   The difficulty
was to get her safe away from her relations, who would
certainly have put her to death rather than give their
consent.   Guarmani found a muleteer carrying grapes
to town, hired his mule and panniers, as also his dress,
and gave a preconcerted signal under the house of his
bride, who joined him at once.   Her father, brothers,
cousins, soon discovered her flight, and, armed to the
teeth, galloped after the fugitives, whom they overtook,
but did not recognise in the muleteer singing Arab
songs as he jogged along on his panniers, in one of which
crouched the resolute girl.   A few words of enquiry
as to any other party which might have passed him on

the road, were adroitly answered, and the danger was
over. The Druze bride was baptised and married at
Beyrout. For some time concealment was necessary, and
finally Guarmani accepted service in the British Land
Transport Corps during the Crimean war. He was at
Marash purchasing baggage animals for our army, when
a disputed contract was taken before the Cadi. In the
belief that his adversary had bribed that judge, he used
strong language to the latter. A tumult arose. He
had scarcely reached his house when it was attacked
by a yelling mob. Attempts were made to gain admit-
tance, and volleys of pistol-shots were directed against
the door and windows, but Guarmani was brave and
determined. His Druze wife assisted him to keep up
a close fire on the assailants, in the hope that succour
would not be long of coming. She loaded his arms,
and was even seen herself firing from a small window.
So stout a resistance made the Turks furious, and the
house, which was entirely of wood, was set on fire. A
faithful Turkish soldier of our Land Transport Corps,
named Ahmed Aga, who told me the particulars, got
to a back door, and called to the Guarmanis that he
would save them if they would but come out that way
to him. The woman knew his voice, opened the door,
told him hurriedly that her husband was badly wounded
and could not move, and that she would never leave
him, but she besought him to take their child, which
he carried away in safety. The last Ahmed Aga saw
of the Guarmanis was the graceful form of the devoted
wife tenderly trying to stanch the blood that flowed

from her fallen husband's side, while the roof was
crashing down upon them. Before another hour had
passed, the house was a heap of ashes, from which the
remains of the unfortunate couple were never dug out.

The Christians of Marash all belong to the old Armenian Church founded on the heresy of Eutyches.
The Armenians have hitherto been best known in Europe as a scattered nation submitting to the domination
of the Turks, and exclusively addicted to trade, in
which they are eminently successful. Light is beginning at last, however, to dawn on the fact that they
are a nation, computed at four millions in number,
possessing political aspirations, and rallying round one
or two strongholds of their nationality. The most remarkable of these is in the neighbourhood of Marash,
as yet obscure, but likely some day to bring its name,
Zeitoon, under the notice of Europe. The Armenians
look upon it as the nucleus of their possible independence. They call their country Haikaodan, from Haik,
the son of Togarmah, the son of Gomer, the son of
Japheth, whom they regard as their progenitor. They
are thus one of the most ancient nations on the face of
the globe, and we accordingly find them mentioned as
contemporary with the first empire of Nineveh, and
as tributary to Egypt with the Assyrians fifteen centuries before the Christian era. They had a dynasty
of kings from Valarsaces to Tigranes, who overthrew
the Macedonian throne of the Seleucidæ in Syria, and
finally they fell before the Persian conquerors of the
Sassanide line. They believe that they owed Chris-

tianity to the Apostle Jude, who suffered martyrdom,
they say, when converting them. They call him by
his surname Thaddeus. In the eleventh century, the
Armenians of Mount Taurus achieved their independence under a native prince of the name of Roopin;
his successors made alliances with the Crusaders, who
recognised them as kings; and the last of them were of
the French family of Lusignan. Leo, the sixth of this
dynasty, was deposed by the Mamelukes, and died at
Paris in 1393, leaving the kingdom of Armenia in the
hands of the Saracens, who lost it in their turn to the
Turks. Some of the Armenian princes and nobles retired to the rocky region of Zeitoon, where they have
never been completely subjugated; and their descendants
still enjoy there a sort of semi-independence. Zeitoon
is the Asiatic Montenegro of Turkey.

The Governor of Marash, a young man brought up
in a great pasha's harem, having been bought when a
child in Circassia, comes often to chat with us, and to
play chess, at which game he is an adept. But our intercourse, which might otherwise be agreeable enough,
for he is very clever and full of Oriental information,
is sadly marred by his unbounded propensity in favour
of arrak. We dined with him once, but heartily wished
ourselves at home again without our meal, as the host
was rolling on the sofa quite intoxicated before it was
announced.

LETTER VIII.

Passage of Mount Amanus—Ahmed Bey—Great Cilician Plain
—Turkomans—Payass—Mustuk Pasha—Battle of Issus—Scanderoon—Pass of Beylan—Templars' Castle—Antioch—Crusades.

Antioch : November 17, 1858.

A LONG narrow plain extends southwards from
Marash, bounded on the west by the huge masses
of Mount Amanus, now called the Ghiaoor Dagh.
Leaving the town in the afternoon, we followed this
plain for about two hours, and encamped for the night
near some Turkoman tents. Striking off to the right
next morning, we commenced a laborious ascent of the
great mountain amid noble pine forests. Our steep
path offered many favourable spots for the attacks so
much dreaded by the few travellers that ever attempt
to pass this way. No European had ever been on the
Ghiaoor Dagh before us. I suppose every one we met
was a potential robber, who, seeing a strong party,
passed with kindly greetings. In fact, the opportunity
makes the robber here. We had about forty horsemen,
sent to escort us by Ahmed Aga of Bulaulik, a powerful
Turkoman chief of the mountain, and we were thus
perfectly safe. When we halted at Bulaulik, and
thanked the Bey for his guard, adding that we had not
seen any of the notorious banditti who are so much

talked of as infesting these passes, he replied that we
had seen many of them, and that the most notorious
were our escort. The castle of the feudal chief ruling
over the northern portion of the Ghisoor Dagh is a
fine old building, defensible if attacked, and hospitable
to all wayfarers. We pitched our tents on the green
sward before the gate. As soon as we were comfortably installed in them, a stream of savoury dishes
borne by as many lads inundated us, but we turned it
off upon another group formed by our guard, to their
no small satisfaction, and we were content to accept
only a lamb roasted whole and stuffed with pilaw. All
who pass this way are the guests of the wealthy chief,
who thus nobly exercises the profuse old Turkish hospitality. In the morning we continued our journey,
accompanied by Ahmed Bey himself, with a great
many Turkomans on foot, who kept groping in the
thick jungle on either side to dislodge stray marauders.
This manœuvre having produced on our minds a due
impression of the dangers surrounding us, our surprise
was unbounded when the Bey suddenly pulled up,
called in his men, and took leave of us, saying that we
were about to enter the district of Chikoor Ova, where
the Turkoman tribes were hostile to his own. There
was nothing for it but to proceed alone amongst thickets
of trees and caverns in the rocks, every one of which
looked mischievous, with the best heart we could. The
country is more picturesque than productive, in romantic beauty matchless, densely wooded, diversified
with hill and dale, torn up by foaming torrents, and

towering above us the lofty summits of Amanus reared
their craggy brows.   No cultivation, not even flocks,
met our eye during our whole descent.   It must then
be true, as it is said, that the population of the Ghisoor
Dagh lives by plundering the adjacent plains.   The
very Bey's wealth can have no other source.

On reaching the Chikoor Ova, the great Cilician
plain, we directed our course towards a large camp of
white round-topped tents in the distance.   Horsemen
galloped out to meet us.   While their purpose was
still unannounced, we demanded hospitality for the
night in tones calculated to convey the impression that
we had either a right to it, or full confidence in their
readiness to afford it.   A curious pause ensued, during
which the wild Turkomans gazed at us undecided, then
interrogated each other's thoughts by astonished glances,
and we put spurs to our horses and galloped in amongst
the tents.   We were surrounded by the whole tribe,
from amongst whom advanced an old man with a snow-
white beard, who, after hearing the account of our
arrival by those we had first met, gravely bade us
welcome.   When seated in his tent, he told us he was
Hussein Aga, the great man of the greatest Turkoman
tribe, the Tajerli, and asked who we were.   Our answer fully satisfied him and those standing around,
who immediately dispersed, some to picket and tend our
horses, others to bring in our baggage, while our servants were pitching our tents.   Hussein Aga asked,
on remarking the latter operation, if his humble tents
might not be honoured, and we ordered that our own

should be rolled up again, which greatly pleased the
Tajerli, and our journey through their country became
at once secure, the bond of hospitality having been acknowledged.　This broad plain is the central haunt of
the nomadic tribes descended from the warrior hordes,
whose constant stream had poured over the Lower
Empire with unebbing tide from the commencement of
the Christian era, when the Sienpi overthrew the supremacy of the Tanjoos, which had lasted no less than
thirteen hundred years, and drove them westwards
under the guidance of Suleyman Shah, Timour the
Tartar, and Gengis Khan.　When the Scythian Empire of the sixth century had been broken up into
fragments of the great Turkish race, more or less independent, they covered that vast portion of the globe
stretching from the Wall of China to the banks of the
Danube, where one of its offsets, the Magyars, had
settled.　So astonishing a career of conquest was not
followed by consolidation of the subjugated territory,
and small states were formed here and there.　Amongst
their chiefs of renown was Seljook, who had been
banished from Eastern Tartary for an infraction of the
sanctity of his sovereign's harem.　He encamped near
Samarcand, and adopted the Mussulman faith.　His
grandson, Togrul, was elected sultan of all the Turkoman tribes in that part of Asia.　This was a bold and
ambitious invader.　Having pushed his conquests to
the frontier of the Roman Empire, he had the hardi-
hood to send ambassadors to Byzantium to summon the
emperor to pay him tribute.　His nephew, Alp Aslan,

the Brave Lion, fierce and generous as his prototype,
resolved to take it by force, invaded the empire, and
placed his foot on the wounded and captive emperor's
neck, after defeating him at Malazkerd, then raised him
from the ground to the place of honour in his tent. A
ransom was paid, a tribute promised, and a marriage
arranged between the children of the conqueror and
the conquered. All the country extending from Antioch to the Euxine then became Turkish territory.
On the death of the next sultan, Malek, the Seljookian
dynasty and empire were divided; the eldest branch
occupied the throne of Persia, the second founded a
kingdom on the Indian Ocean with Kerman for its
capital, the third succeeded the Arab Emirs of Damascus and Aleppo as kings of Syria, and the fourth
formed the subjugated provinces of Asia Minor into
the Turkoman kingdom of Room. The last of these
states, nominally including Constantinople and all the
unknown regions further west, was then ruled over
by Suleyman, the great-grandson of Seljook, and the
cousin of Alp Aslan. The capital of this Turkish
state of Rome, or Room, as they call it, was first
Nicea, and, after that city was taken by the Crusaders,
Konia, the ancient Iconium. The sober and hardy
Turkomans had found only cowardly and enervated
nations to dispute their progress, while they were more
skilled in the art of war as practised then, simple in
their manners, honest in their ferocity, just even to
their enemies, and, above all, united. The Greeks, on
the contrary, were so little of all this, that, when Con-

stantinople was on the point of falling, they declared
that they preferred Mussulmans as conquerors to
Christians of other churches as allies, and rejected the
proffered aid of the Genoese occupying Galata on the
other shore of the Golden Horn. Provinces submitted
to the Turks to escape the oppression of Christian governors and princes. But the Turks in time adopted
the manners and learnt the vices of those whom they
had conquered. Indolence succeeded to impetuosity.
The sultan no longer governed. Place and power became an object of traffic. A chain of bribery and
corruption bound the tent or hovel to the palace, its
links comprising all official grades from the lowest to
the highest. Insane luxury and extravagance required
this aliment to maintain them. Venality introduced
universal depravity. Ministers bought their seals of
office, and sold the provinces. Magistrates paid for the
judgment-seat, and traded on justice. The collection
of revenues, the command of troops, the administration
of local affairs, were put up to auction, and sublet by
the purchasers, to supply the means of bribery. Trade
was mulcted to swell the customs dues, agriculture
ground down to extract pillage, and usury became the
resource and the ruin of both. Wars, famine, and
plague, in the quick succession of cause and effect,
carried off the population. Brigandage put an end to
all security of life and property. The state crumbled
to pieces under its own weight. Europe had trembled
at the sudden rise of the Turkish power; an era of
fear lest it should as suddenly fall and disturb the

H

European system, followed. After a three years' residence in Egypt and Syria, Volney, a keen observer, announced, so far back as the year 1788, that it was on the brink of annihilation. Sobieski, Montecuculli, and Prince Eugene, dissipated the former alarm; time is disposing of the latter. Those who have lived for years with the Turks, not at Constantinople alone, where their real state is not apparent, must come to the conviction that no sudden fall is imminent, but that a steady and gradual decline is bringing the dominant race to the inevitable necessity of a change of domination in the country. The Turks neither investigate the real cause of their decline, nor seek to apply the only possible remedy. The few who admit that it exists, say they conquered in Asia, Europe, and Africa, without organisation, and decline cannot arise from the want of it, but rather from the degeneracy of Islam, of which all attempts to organise the Empire are merely symptoms.

These Turkomans are descended from those who under Seljook overran the Syrian kingdom of the Abasside Khalifs at the commencement of the twelfth century. They inhabit the whole tract of country stretching from Urfa to the Cilician gates on Mount Taurus, and northwards, and are to be found in almost all the eastern portion of Asia Minor. They retain the characteristics of their savage, intractable ancestors, whose language they have preserved as pure, and their large features as prominent, as when they issued from the Altai Mountains. They profess the Mahometan

religion. In number, those on the Taurus and Amanus
ranges with their adjacent plains may reach the aggre-
gate of a hundred and twenty thousand, while their
brethren on the level country of Cilicia and Northern
Syria may be computed at about half as many. Like
the Bedaween, they are divided into tribes under their
respective chiefs, whose authority, though far from being
absolute, has more hold on their allegiance than that
of the Arab sheikh over his people. Amongst themselves there are frequent and enduring feuds, as there
are also between them and the Koords and Bedaween.
They acknowledge the sovereignty of the Sultan, whom
they boast of as a scion of their old stock, but the
Turkish governors of provinces can rarely enforce a
measure in opposition to the wishes of the majority.
They rear immense herds of cattle, which they use as
beasts of burden. Though known to be robbers of
caravans, they are commonly employed as guards
against other plunderers. Ibrahim Pasha of Egypt
attempted in vain to subjugate them, and that resolute and skilful general was obliged to admit that
his twenty thousand regular troops could not force
their mountain fastnesses. These are a ready refuge
to the inhabitants of the plains when some act of
more than ordinary violence has rendered them obnoxious to the government, and obliges them to retire
thither till the affair has blown over sufficiently for
them to venture to show themselves again. Less
addicted to petty thieving than the Koord or Arab,
the Turkoman is more prone to shed blood, and, where

from the hands of the former a traveller would escape
with the loss of his property, the latter do not scruple
to take also his life on the slightest show of resistance.

Hussein Aga, chief of the Tajerli, gave us a guard
on the following day, when we left his camp, with
many friendly wishes for our safety and prosperity.
We travelled southwards over the rich but uncultivated tract of level country called Chikoor Ova.
About noon we came to the ruins of a fine castle
bearing the name of Yuzlab; what it was I cannot
say, but its appearance would ascribe it to the Lower
Empire, and its position would imply that its purpose
had been the defence of the great line of ancient
traffic, now destroyed, between Syria and Asia Minor
by the plain of Issus, on the confines of which it
stands.   We forded the river Pinarus, and passed
the remains of a considerable town near the head of
the Gulf of Scanderoon, which does not seem to have
been yet identified. Its area is very extensive, and
water had been brought to it from a distance by a fine
aqueduct, some of the arches of which are still almost
entire, showing traces of Roman construction, if I am
not mistaken. We slept at another Turkoman camp,
where we were most cordially received in favour of
our escort from the tribe of Hussein Aga. The tents
were full of people, but there was no cultivation in
sight, not many cattle, and no appearance to indicate
their occupation and means of support, unless the stout
little horses picketed before them, and the abundance
of arms suspended within, may be allowed to tell their

tale about their masters' livelihood. Next day we
approached Mount Amanus, following a track on its
lower slopes, with the bright sea gleaming in the sunshine at no great distance on our right. In the afternoon we reached Payass, the ancient Issus, a jumble of
ruins of all ages, the most recent being very interesting. These consist in a large fort, containing caravan-
serais, baths, mosques, and a long bazaar of shops, all
perfectly entire and capable of being used and occupied
on the shortest notice and with hardly any repairs.
The explanation of this is simply, that the want of
security on the line of road we were traversing had
completely put an end to a trade which continued until
fifty years ago to flow from Asia Minor and Northern
Syria to this point, where the harbour, without being
altogether safe, was sufficiently so in the summer
months to make it a much-frequented shipping port
for the produce of the interior. Payass is still the
seat of a local pasha, who may be considered the last
of the Dereh Beys, or semi-independent hereditary
chiefs who ruled over all the provinces of Turkey
before the reigns of the last two sultans. In this
case an attempt was made four years ago to substitute
a governor appointed by the Porte for the powerful
but rebellious Mustuk Pasha. Before any suspicion
entered the mind of the old Turkoman, he was induced
to visit Constantinople, and was detained there on
various pretexts. He contrived to send secret orders
to Payass. Robberies of travellers, wholesale plunder of caravans, assassinations, seizure even of the

government mails, rapidly succeeded each other.   At
last the new governor admitted his inability to restore
order.   Mustuk Pasha was sent back, and all disorders
immediately ceased.   He is now above eighty years of
age, but still active and influential.   We did not see
him on this occasion, as he was absent on a tour of
collection from his vassals of the only revenue he
enjoys; but I know the old fox well.

After heavy rain in the night, more or less trying to
our tents and to the temper of those in the leaky one,
we left the pomegranate orchard in which we had
encamped, and crossed the narrow field of the battle
of Issus, enclosed between inaccessible mountains and
the sea.   The morning was fine, and we lingered over
the scene of that event so great in its influence on the
East twenty-two centuries ago.   Then first was felt
in Asia the power of Europe.   The army of Darius,
six hundred thousand strong when it left Babylon,
with the sacred fire burning before him on silver altars
as he marched, the chariot of the sun surrounded by
three hundred and sixty-five youths in purple, to represent the days of the year, the immortal band of ten
thousand men with golden collars and robes glittering
with precious stones, were scattered as chaff before the
wind by Alexander the Great with his phalanx of five-
and-thirty thousand Macedonians in simple armour.
This first step in that wonderful career which diffused
the light of knowledge, and extended the benefits of
commerce, over the rich domains of the East, invests
Payas with an interest contrasting painfully with the

present degraded state of this country. Bishop Thirl-
wall, and Alexander's other biographer, Archdeacon
Williams, from whose teaching I derived the little
classic lore and school reminiscences remaining to me,
would have admitted with me the accuracy of Xenophon, and, had they seen the spot, would have given up
the theory of the battle having been fought on the great
plain to the north of Payass. I was fully convinced that
the Cilician and Syrian gates, instead of being the
passes of Taurus and Amanus, were the actual stone and
mortar gates described by Xenophon. Remains of the
two fortresses can be traced; between them runs a river
exactly corresponding with his account of the Kersus,
one hundred feet in breadth; and the length of the plain
is a short half-mile, about three stadia as he describes
it, with the sea on one side, and inaccessible rocks on the
other, the only rocks of this character along the base of
the range of mountains. Following the shore, and halting to lunch at a ruined arch of Roman construction, now
unaccountably called Jonah's Pillars, we reached in the
evening the port of Scanderoon or Alexandretta, probably the ancient Myriandrus, where Xenias the Arca-
dian general and Pasion the Megarean took ship and
abandoned Cyrus. It is not now much of a town,
some ten or twelve houses occupied by commercial
agents being the whole amount of building beyond
the huts formed of branches and raised on stakes above
the level of the swamp, which are inhabited by a population of porters and boatmen. The harbour is the
only good one on the coast of Syria, but the air is

infected by miasmata from the large marshes around, as is amply attested by the Greek burial-ground, recording many English names during the last two centuries. Three days' detention in this uninteresting place ended at last, and we mounted our horses again with great satisfaction. Crossing the Ghiaoor Dagh by the pass of Beylan, which Ibrahim Pasha of Egypt forced from the east, when it was held by the Turkish army in the hope of cutting him off from his fleet at Scanderoon, we descended to the plain of Antioch, now almost entirely covered with water. Near the foot of the mountain on our right, we visited a fine old castle standing high on a rock. It is called Bagraas. Some of the halls and the chapel, which had rung with the revelry and orisons of the Knights Templars who built it, are still almost perfect. In the evening we came to the bridge of the Orontes, and entered Antioch.

Little now remains but the site of a city, which has played as distinguished a part in the history of the world, as most others. The ruined walls may still be traced, however, ascending the craggy heights of Mount Silpius, and lines and heaps of stones indicate the long streets which Antiochus Epiphanes and Herod the Great adorned with colonnades, and the amphitheatres contributed by the early Greek emperors to the noble edifices of Antioch. The whole area between the river and the mountain is now occupied by a series of mulberry plantations, with a poor Turkish town in their centre. The flight of Seleucus Nicator's eagle from the summit of Mount Casius three centuries before

Christ, raised a city to revel in all the refined license of
polytheistic paganism, while another city not far distant
retained the pure worship of one God; their antagonism
fulfilling the struggle so minutely prophesied by Daniel.
That struggle, after ending in the full restoration of the
ancient faith of Israel under the Maccabees, was succeeded by the greater contest establishing Christianity,
and giving it a name in this city, which received the
fugitive disciples driven from Jerusalem by the martyrdom of Stephen, had St. Peter for its first bishop, and,
later, gave to the primitive Church its most eloquent
preacher, St. John Chrysostom. Few cities have had
a more eventful past than this. Its population was
half a million, one-third of the present inhabitants of
the whole of Syria. Now there are barely twenty
thousand souls at Antioch. The walls were twelve
miles long, with four hundred towers and only five
gates. This may appear an improbable arrangement
to those who have not visited it, but at sight of the
rugged precipices overhanging one of the longer sides
of the parallelogram, and of the deep broad Orontes
washing the other, it becomes comprehensible that the
city might have been twice as large, and still have had
no more than five gates. Despite the many towers, the
place was taken by the Crusaders—not by storm, however. Godfrey of Bouillon, and Robert Duke of Nor-
mandy, clove Turks in twain, their head and shoulders
falling to the ground while their remainder stuck to
the saddle and galloped off, and buried falchions from
the crown of their head to their girdle, as William of

Tyre informs us; but it was the wily veteran, Bohe-
mond, Prince of Tarentum, the son of Robert Guiscard
of more martial renown, with his cousin Tancred, the
flower of chivalry, that took and kept Antioch. Phirooz,
a renegade commander of three towers, was bought by
them, and opened the gates to the Knights of the Cross.
Kerboga, Emir of Mosul, next brought an army to
attack it, but the Crusaders sallied and defeated him.
During the siege, however, some of the most distinguished amongst them deserted the cause, Raymond
of Toulouse was too ill to remain, the Duke of Nor-
mandy went to Rome to ask the Pope's absolution from
his campaigning license, Hugh of Vermondoir simply
returned home, Stephen of Chartres ran away, William
of Melun left the army, and, finally, Peter the Hermit
himself sought a field, where penitential rather than
obligatory fasts prevailed, for it is recorded that he fled
from the famine. Knights and monks dropped from
the walls with the aid of cords; and the people of
Antioch—as incapable of refraining from a joke, even in
such extremities, as they were in the time of Julian—
called them rope-dancers.

A French writer attributes to the Crusades a civi-
lising tendency in Syria. I cannot take this view,
either of their motives or of their influence. When
Peter, the Hermit of Amiens, called Europe to re-
pentance and arms, and Christendom responded by
martial and pious zeal in favour of the deliverance of
the Holy Sepulchre, when the sword of destruction
was unsheathed in the name of the Prince of Peace to

recover Calvary and Bethlehem, his tomb and his cradle,
and thus atone for the general violation of the precepts
of his Gospel, a motley rabble of enthusiasts, on their
way to the Holy Land, under the guidance of a goat
and a goose, to which animals was ascribed an infusion
of the Divine Spirit, assailed, in an evil hour for them,
the western frontier of the kingdom of Room, then
ruled by Sultan Suleyman. Anna Comnena gives the
result in the graphic sentence, ' a very admirable mound
of bones, high, deep, and broad.' After them Europe's
best chivalry was arrayed under the banners of the
most renowned princes and knights. In the words of
the Byzantine historian-princess, Europe was upriven
from its roots, and hurled at Asia. The successful
siege of Nicea, the hard-won battle of Dorylæum in
Phrygia, and a long hungry march by Konia and Eregli
to Marash, brought the Crusaders on Syrian soil. Principalities and kingdoms were founded, and lost, after a
duration of about a century and a half. Jerusalem
was taken and retaken. Saladin, or Salaheddin, the
Koordish founder of an Arabian empire extending
from Tripoli in Africa to the banks of the Tigris, after
defeating the Crusaders, gave letters and knowledge to
the inhabitants of his dominions, which were superior
to the degree of enlightenment possessed by the Frank
invaders. Thus ended the Crusades, which Robertson
the historian calls, the most stupendous folly ever engendered by the human intellect; and nothing remained in
Syria to indicate that its soil had ever been trodden by
Western warriors, who could do nothing to advance

civilisation in the East because they were themselves
less civilised than the Greeks of the Lower Empire and
the Arabs under their greater Khalifs.   Indeed, the
distance now existing between the enlightenment of the
West and that of the East has been produced less by
the fall of the latter than by the rise of the former.
The improving tendencies of Christianity were unavailing to improve the East at that time, because the
Christianity of the West was unenlightened.   Since
then, Syria has not been carried forward as Europe has,
in consequence of the debasement of the Eastern Christian Churches and the incompatibility of Islam with
progress.

LETTER IX.

Tripoli: December 10, 1858.

IN spite of the advanced season, the weather was still
fine, and, having resumed my rambles, I found
myself, after a three days' ride over the very fertile but
scantily tilled plain of the Orontes, at the pretty little
town of Hama. What battles must have been fought
on that plain during the wars between Toi, king of
Hamath, and Hadadezer, king of Zobah; for I persist
in identifying the latter place with Aleppo, notwithstanding all arguments in favour of the other theory,
that it was in or near Edom. An Arab tradition makes
a bad pun on the name Haleb-es-Shahbah, Aleppo the
White, alleging that Abraham, on his way from Haran
to Palestine, stopped there to milk a famous white cow
he had, the words being also susceptible of translation
as having milked the white; and the first word is often
left out in naming Aleppo emphatically the White.
But it certainly looks white enough on a hot summer
day to warrant the name, without reference to Abraham
and the cow. The words Shahbah and Zobah being
the same, it is not improbable that Aleppo was called

the White in the times of Saul, David, and Solomon,
all of whom were engaged in war with Zobah. However this may be, there seems to exist no doubt as to
the identity of Hama, which is evidently Hamath the
Great of the Prophet Amos. It occupies a hollow
through which flows the river Orontes, whose banks,
converted into gardens, and gigantic water-wheels
render Hama a picturesque little place. Those wheels,
the largest of which is eighty feet in diameter, turn with
the stream, and raise water in their hollow circumfe-
rence to the highest parts of the town. The shrill
creaking of the smaller, with an occasional deep groan
from the larger ones, is not unmusical. Ibrahim Pasha
complained of their keeping him awake at night when
he was there, and had them stopped ; the whole population became sleepless for want of their accustomed
lullaby. Hama has thirty thousand inhabitants.

The officer in command of the troops had just returned
from an expedition against the Ansairi, who cover the
long screen of mountains shutting off the plain of the
Orontes from the sea. Ismael Khair Bey, a renowned
Ansairi chief, had gone to pay homage to the newly-
appointed Governor-General of Damascus, Ahmed
Pasha. Another high functionary took umbrage at
this, and sent a detachment to arrest him on his way
back in default of payment of arrears of taxes due by
his people. Khair Bey, when thus attacked, repulsed
his assailants, and escaped to his mountains. A military
force was then sent against him from Hama, infantry,
cavalry, and artillery. The troops entered a long

ravine defended by the Ansairi, who fired on them
from both sides, and obliged them to retreat with loss.
Before leaving the Ansairi country, however, they
went to a village which had taken no part in the affair
and attempted no resistance.   They plundered it, and
carried off several prisoners, amongst whom was a boy,
eleven years of age, related to Ismael Khair Bey.
These prisoners were escorted by dragoons to Damascus,
on foot, piuioned, and scantily fed ; the poor boy's shoes
soon wore out, and he had to trudge through the mud
barefoot, though brought up in such affluence as can be
found on those mountains.

From Hama we travelled southwards, crossing the
Orontes by a fine bridge of Saracenic construction at
Restan, the ancient Arethusa.   Late at night we arrived
at Homs, once the important city of Emesa, and now
possessing a population of twenty thousand, seven thousand being Christians.   The tomb of Khalid, the Sword
of God, is there, and receives much reverence from the
Mahometan inhabitants.   The Mussulmans of Homs
are not looked upon by the Christians of the place with
that dread which is noticed elsewhere.   The two classes
of the population live in perfect harmony.   There are
no foreign agents at Homs, whether ostensible or
otherwise.   This, in my opinion, points to the great
truth underlying all disturbances in Turkey. A striking
corroboration of my views is furnished at Homs.   The
Christians there have no officious protectors to make
them dissatisfied and insolent by telling them of their
rights and prospects ; the Mussulmans are not irritated

by the arrogant interference of strangers and the constant hostility of the Christians. People may descant
at any length on outbursts of Mussulman fanaticism,
but they leave the subject without conveying an idea,
even partially correct, of its real character, by omitting
the principal feature. There is a latent fallacy in the
appeal often made to one's natural feeling in favour of
Christians placed in an antagonistic position towards
Mussulmans. Nothing can be more erroneous than the
view thus taken of the question from the stand-point
of religion, while its essential element—foreign interference—is kept out of sight. It assumes a very different
aspect, however, when enquiry relates, not to the alleged frequency of conflicts, or the reality of their details
as facts, but to the hidden sources whence they arise.
The importance of the interest at stake is then found
not to lie merely in the preservation of life and religious
liberty in Turkey, but also in fidelity to treaty obligations elsewhere, and consequently in the maintenance
of peace in Europe. I am not one of those who ascribe
every act of undue protection of classes to secret
instructions, either special or general. I can well
believe that it is difficult to get out of an old-accustomed
groove now prohibited, and I am quite prepared to admit that it may not always be followed premeditatedly.
But the imputation of motives has nothing to do with
the proof of facts, and I wish only to define the practical origin of most disturbances in Turkey. According
to the best of my judgment, it is unfair to attribute
them summarily to Mussulman fanaticism without

further explanation; I conceive that they generally
arise from Mussulman fanaticism under a course of
systematic exasperation.   One is weary of the very
word fanaticism.   Mussulmans are fanatical, it is true;
and Eastern Christians are not less so ; nor are Roman
Catholics, nor Irish Protestants.   Only let the Mussulmans be left alone, and their fanaticism will remain a
religious prejudice, without ever becoming a political
difficulty.   In point of fact, the Turks are declining
from mere ignorance of the elementary principles
which lie at the root of the administrative science.
But they do try to recover their waning vigour.   This
is not to be allowed.   Discontent must be instilled in
the governed class, jealousy and hatred in the govern-
ing ; both are kept constantly oscillating between frantic
excitement and sullen apathy.   Outbreaks are the
natural culmination of the treatment they are subjected
to, and when outbreaks occur, then is pronounced
the hackneyed denunciation of Mussulman fanaticism,
which rings from one end of Europe to the other; then
is the bewilderment of the Porte, the opportunity of
such other Cabinets as seek what they respectively call
glory or aggrandisement through the sufferings of
nations.   During the Crimean war, French agitation
in Turkey sheathed its sword, furled its banner, and
retired from the field.   After the destruction of Sebastopol, the collapse of the long-prepared Russian system
of aggression gave Turkey a respite.   Both have now
resumed their previous attitude : Imperial France can-

not afford to keep quiet, and hyperborean Russia ne-
cessarily gravitates southwards.

Leaving Homs, we rode to the Orontes, whose course
we followed upwards for some way by the lake of Kedes,
formed artificially for irrigation by the Seleucidæ, towards what is called, in the books of Numbers and
Joshua, the entrance of Hamath, and the entering into
Hamath, which can be no other than the narrowing
valley of Cœle-Syria, now named Bukaa, lying between
the gigantic portals of Lebanon and Hermon, and being
the most ready channel of communication between the
land of Israel and the northern kingdoms of Hamath and
Zobah. We passed at some little distance from Baalbek,
which I did not visit on this occasion, and I need not
add a description of its glorious remains to those of
so many distinguished travellers. To me they appear a
perfect chronological table of the history of Syria: the
age of Joshua represented by the enormous blocks which
must then have supported some other edifice than their
actual superstructure; that of Solomon, seen in the
massive columns of the great temple; the Macedonian
sway in Syria recorded by the light Corinthian style of
the smaller monuments with their elaborate tracery;
and the heavy Saracenic towers and ramparts closing
the series. I cannot doubt, as some have done, that
Baalbek is identical with the Baalgad, in the valley of
Lebanon, under Mount Hermon, of the book of Joshua,
translated in its more recent name of Heliopolis, the
City of the Sun. Turning again westwards, round a
spur of Lebanon, and riding over the low mountains of

Akkar, a region entirely divested of cultivation, we
reached Kalaat-el-Hussun. This large fortress was
built by the Saracens to command the pass from the
coast to the interior between the ranges of Lebanon
and the Ansairi mountains. Its first garrison having
been Koords, it was called Hussun-el-Akrad, the castle
of the Koords, and, when it was taken by the Crusaders,
they corrupted Akrad into Krak, under which name it
is mentioned by William of Tyre as being in the hands
of the Knights Hospitallers of St. John of Jerusalem,
who capitulated after a siege of fifteen days by Bibars.
A small Turkish guard now occupies the place, which,
from its position, as well as from its works being still
in good repair, is defensible, although the purpose of
holding it can only be to prevent its being made a
stronghold of the revolted Ansairi or Bedaween, as
there is no trade by this route to protect. Descending
on a cold foggy morning to the valley of the Nahr-el-
Kebir, formerly the river Eleutherus, we passed a large
monastery belonging to the Greek Church, and dedicated to St. George, who is claimed as a native of this
part of the country. Below the convent we saw the
Sabbatical river of Josephus and Pliny, which is merely
an intermitting spring, whose irregular flow has no
reference, that our enquiries could corroborate, to the
Jewish Sabbath. At hot noon we were near the ruins
of Arka, the seat of the Arkites of early Canaan, which
was still strong enough at the end of the eleventh century to repulse the attack of Count Raymond of
Toulouse, but is now utterly desolate. After a long

gallop on the sands, we entered Tripoli, with a glorious
sun setting on the bright blue waves.

What remains of the three cities subject to Aradus,
Sidon, and Tyre, in which originated the name of
Tripoli, now hardly suffices to make one poor little
Turkish town. But the extensive orange groves
stretching along the beach, and up to the grey battlements of the castle overhanging the picturesque vale
of the river Kadisha, are worthy of all praise and admiration. During our stay of a fortnight here the
weather has been very fine, and we have taken many
charming walks and rides in the neighbourhood. The
most interesting of the latter was to the village of
Sgorta and the Maronite convent of Caftin in the Kesrawan district of Mount Lebanon. We were invited
by Yusuf Bey Karam to visit him in his village. Leaving
the town, we followed the course of the river to a
prettily-situated tekeb, or retreat of dervishes, passing
behind the fortified residence of Raymond III., Count
of Tripoli, who betrayed the last king of Jerusalem to
the victorious Saladin. It is now dismantled, but it
must have been an important position in the time of
the Crusades. The country above the valley is well
cultivated by the Maronites, who occupy exclusively
this part of the great mountain. They have extensive
plantations of mulberry and olive trees. After a pleasant ride of a couple of hours, we were received at
Sgorta by our host, a young man of prepossessing appearance and polished manners. He had been educated
at Paris, and spoke French fluently. His sympathies

also tend unmistakably towards France, as he is one of
the favoured and most influential chiefs of the Maronites. A copious repast awaited us in his seigneurial
tower, but there was a sort of restraint about the whole
affair which we attributed to the class feelings of a
French partisan when conversing with Englishmen.
We tried to make it understood that the welfare and
affections of our country are not exclusively bound up
in the cause of the Druzes, but it was in vain that we
talked of impartiality, and even of indifference; no such
ideas can enter a Maronite brain.

This people took its name from its first bishop,
John Maro. Like him, the Maronites were Monothe-
lites until they joined the Church of Rome in the end
of the twelfth century, after having assisted the Crusaders against the Saracens. They are inferior to the
Druzes in martial qualities, but are four times as
numerous; the latter being computed at only fifty
thousand, while the Maronites number two hundred
thousand. The Jesuits have schools and colleges
amongst them on Mount Lebanon, embittering thus
the more their political rancour by the gall of the *odium
theologicum*, into which all the poisonous dregs of past
conflicts are drained; changing bewildered Turks into
so many Neroes, ready to burn their respective Romes
for their pastime, and ranging Druzes and Mohamm-
medans, Arabs and Osmanlis, in one vast antagonism
to the oppressed nationality in favour for the day.
The plain truth of the Maronite controversy appears
to me to be no more than this: a few misguided

priests and pamphleteers of great polemical activity
try to make a noise in the world, and, their virulent
clamour being repeated in the circle of those whom it
suits, people are deluded into the belief that the Christian population of Mount Lebanon is often forced
to fight a brave and noble fight for the protection of
its hearth and creed, and, when unsuccessful, suffers
martyrdom. But if those who believe in the Turkey
of poets and travellers, monks and sensation-article
writers, would only take the trouble to disentangle
such statements from their confusion and clap-trap, to
sift the grounds on which they claim acceptance, no
sane man amongst them would fail to discern the truth.
Gibbon says that a single robber or murderer, or a
few associates in robbery or murder, are branded with
their genuine name; but that the repeated exploits of a
numerous band assume the character of a lawful and
honourable war. The collisions between the Maronites
and Druzes owe the latter character only to their
frequency and comprehensiveness.

LETTER X.

Dama; December 24, 1858.

WHEN leaving Tripoli, we found the tents of a
considerable Turkish force encamped outside
the town. It was under the command of Tahir Pasha,
an officer with whom I am well acquainted. He had
studied at Woolwich, and speaks English. On learning
the failure of the expedition from Hama against the
Ansairi, he had marched from Beyrout to attack them,
and was now returning, successful after a manner.
When Ismael Khair Bey heard of the advance of the
Turks, he prepared for an obstinate defence of his
residence at Safita, which is on a rugged part of the
Ansairi mountains, and further protected by a strong
tower. One of his cousins, a wily old man, who had
recently visited Beyrout, dissuaded him from fighting,
and induced him to retire with his two brothers to his
own village, situated on still more difficult ground. Suddenly Tahir Pasha appeared at break of day before this
village with his troops. Ismael and his brothers rushed
out in utter amazement, but, before they had gone
many yards from the house of their treacherous cousin,

a volley was fired upon them from the door and
windows, and they all three fell dead. The cousin
then went to meet the Pasha, and was installed in the
place of Ismael as chief of the Ansairi mountains.
The moral of the tale is obvious. I enquired about
the prisoners taken to Hama: they are in gaol at
Damascus. And the boy? The boy died on the road.

We pitched our tents at an old khan on the right
bank of the river Bered. In the night one of our
horses was stolen under the very eyes of our sentry;
the animal stumbled at a little distance, and the alarm
was given. We all ran out, but too late to catch the
thief, who made off, leaving the horse to walk quietly
back to his picket. Continuing along the shore on
the following day, and across a narrow plain without
villages or cultivation, a fair sprinkling of both being
visible on the mountains, we reached Tortosa, the
ancient Antaradus, whose extensive remains form a
rich field of research for the collectors of antiquities at
Beyrout. The modern town is still surrounded by the
ramparts of the Crusaders. Within it there are several
buildings of their time, displaying Gothic ornament;
and outside the wall stands, almost entire, the noble
cathedral of St. Giles, built by Raymond, who was
Count of St. Giles and Toulouse before he received
the fief of Tripoli under the King of Jerusalem. It
seemed strange that a fine Gothic structure should
have been transformed into a mosque: I have seen
many Greek temples and Byzantine churches thus
desecrated, but that Moslems should worship under

a groined roof and pointed arches was new to me, and
suggested some little respect for Charles Martel and
Sobieski, who perhaps kept them out of Westminster
Abbey.   The sea was calm, but a heavy surf rolled
in on the unsheltered shore after a westerly gale.   We
wished to visit the island of Ruad, formerly Arvad,
and Aradus, about two miles distant.   The only boat
in the place could not be got off without great
difficulty.   By dint of insisting and bakshish—all-
powerful bakshish, the open-sesame of every heart in
Syria—we found ourselves at last with an old man and
a small boy struggling to get a crazy craft through
the breakers.   A gigantic wave struck us down: the
old man was taken overboard by it, but he caught
a rope, and we pulled him into the boat again.
Another frantic plunge, almost a somersault, and we
were in comparatively smooth water, with a tattered
sail filling to the light breeze, which wafted us safely
to Ruad.   A strange little town it is, without an ounce
of earth in it; built on a rock, streets excavated, and
the spray dashing into the windows.   The whole
population is seafaring, like their ancestors in the
service of Tyre.   Nets hang on all the terraced roofs.
Boats are hauled upstairs.   The only vestiges of
antiquity to be seen are some large quadrangular
blocks with the Phœnician bevil, which must have
supported a wall round the towns.   The inhabitants
are four thousand, all Mussulmans, with the exception
of twenty families of Christians, who live in brotherly
love with them.   The island is never visited by

strangers, but the people seem to have brought back
from frequent voyages a salutary appreciation of its
own self-sufficiency. A good-natured old sailor has
been governor for many years, and he gives perfect
satisfaction without reference to higher authorities.
But the wind had increased meanwhile, and a formidable swell was spreading an ominous belt of white
foam on the opposite beach.   To try to go as we came
would have involved a certain ducking, if nothing
worse; besides, the good people of Ruad would not
hear of it.   They would show us what they could do.
A large boat was soon launched, and four broad-
shouldered oarsmen seated in it.   A weather-beaten
old steersman, with a venerable white beard, helped
us in, and shipped the rudder.   The long oars bent
under the lusty stroke, and the boat sprang forward,
now on the crest of a wave, now in the trough of a sea,
unbroken, perhaps, from Sicily and Malta to Syria.
Under skilful management we did not ship a drop of
water; the surf, however, looked awful when we
neared it.   They turned the boat with her stern to
the shore just outside the breakers.   The old man
unshipped the rudder, and dropped a fifth oar over the
bow. Then they waited for a wave they liked the
look of, and, suddenly giving way with all their might,
kept close behind it without letting another wave
overtake us.   We jumped out on the sand, and bade
adieu to the brave Arvadites, who, straining at the
oar, buried their boat in the spray as they drove it
through the surf, and, stopping beyond the breakers to

bale out the water they had shipped, waved their arms
to us, and pulled steadily back to their island.

When we mounted our horses next day, the strong
west wind had brought up heavy rain-clouds, which
began to discharge their burden upon us before we
had proceeded far on our northward course. We
found it impossible to get beyond Merkal, a curious
triangular fort of the Crusaders, at the most dangerous
point of our road. A few resolute men could stop an
army there, so easily is the defile commanded, and
travellers have also been stopped there, if the Ansairi
be not grossly maligned. Below the castle, there is
an old tower on the shore, and, finding a narrow winding stair that led to its flat roof, we pitched one of our
tents on it, as being the most defensible position. The
tent was blown down in the night, and torrents of rain
made a reservoir of the terrace with its parapets, which
was thus by no means the most dry of bedrooms, but
it was safe, which was a great comfort. Early morning saw us on the road again, deluged with rain, and
splashing in mud. We took a hasty lunch at Jebelah,
the Gabala of the Macedonian era, where we found a
noble amphitheatre in good preservation, and, fording
with difficulty the swollen river Meander, we reached
Lattakia in the evening, thoroughly drenched. The
weather became finer after our arrival, but we found
little to compensate for the discomfort of our journey.
The ancient Laodicea, founded by Seleucus Nicator in
honour of his mother, and to commemorate her name,
has left nothing but a ruined gate of some architectural

merit to the modern Lattakia. The Crusaders improved its small land-locked harbour, and built picturesque towers at its entrance; but the Turks have
allowed it to become so completely choked with sand
and mud, that it is useless to the trade of the place,
which consists chiefly in the exportation of a very
fragrant kind of tobacco grown in the neighbourhood.
Were the port dredged, it might well accommodate
forty or fifty vessels, which would amply suffice for
the demand; but, as it is, ships can only approach in
fine weather, and, when caught there by a gale, are
often lost on the rocks surrounding it. For the rest,
Lattakia is but a diminutive sample of the Syrian provincial town, with its Christians talking of their grievances, its native agents of foreign powers denouncing
Mussulman fanaticism, its pasha displaying a vast
amount of zeal, efficiency, and perseverance, in the
smoking of his chibook, and all of them assiduously
filling their pockets.

The Christians of Lattakia are chiefly a remnant of
the Greek Church, which has been numerically much
reduced by secession in Syria, consequent on the
missionary success of the Church of Rome from the
middle of the seventeenth century to the present day.
The schism of the Greek community created a new
one, calling itself the Greek Catholic Church, but it is
hardly entitled to that double name. It predominates
in most of the cities of Syria, but at Lattakia, the old
Church is still strong. The austere system of fasts had
something to do with the adoption of Roman Catholicism,

which is more indulgent in this respect. Then a quarrel about sacerdotal robes between a Bishop of Acre and the Patriarch of Alexandria induced the former, with his spiritual flock, to seek support at Rome. But the immediate grounds of the division arose out of a rivalry between two candidates for the patriarchal throne of Antioch, towards the end of the seventeenth century. The people favoured Cyril, and the Synod of Constantinople wished to appoint Neophytus. The former was elected, and almost immediately deposed to make room for the latter. The Roman Catholic missionaries espoused the cause of the malcontent, and, at the death of the successful candidate, obtained through the papist embassies at Constantinople his restoration to the see. This timely assistance secured his secret adherence to Rome. But his zeal for the Pope was not sufficiently fervid and manifest to satisfy the Roman Catholics, who succeeded in having him again deposed through the influence of the French ambassador at the Porte. So overwhelming a display of power alarmed the bishops of Tyre and Sidon, Beyrout, Heliopolis, and Tripoli, who had already been tampered with. They all sent a confession of faith to Rome, acknowledging the supremacy of the Pope. Cyril also made full submission, and was made Patriarch of the Greek Catholics at Antioch. On his death-bed, however, a Jesuit missionary attending him, required him to confess according to the Papal form, which he refused to do, declaring that he died a member of the Greek Church. This scandal was wiped out, according to the Greek

Catholics, by the consecration of another Cyril at Damascus, from whom was derived the ordination of all their clergy. The Greek Church impugns the validity of that ordination, on the plea that the consecration in question was not performed in a church, but in a cave on the roadside, and by three bishops of different communions, under compulsion by the Maronites, when the whole party were in a state bordering on intoxication. Scandals exist even to the present day among and between the Churches of the East, and, however painful may be the fact for the honour of Christendom, I should regard it as the mere fastidiousness of reverence to disguise that fact. Last year an Armenian bishop, nephew of another Armenian bishop who died, took possession of his episcopal vestments. The Church claimed them, and finally obtained a firman for the imprisonment of the contumacious prelate. Suddenly he declared himself a Roman Catholic, and took up his quarters in a Franciscan convent, which French protection secured from the execution of the firman. After a time the Armenian Church reflected that it was unnecessary to lose both the robes and the bishop, and an arrangement was concluded by which he should keep them and return to his flock. Then the Roman Catholics claimed their bishop, but the only satisfaction they obtained was the payment of their bill for his board and lodging in the convent. On another occasion, an Armenian bishop was on a tour of collection with a relic of the great St. Gregory the Illuminator. He kept the money, and declared himself a Protestant.

The Church argued, that as the saint was their property, the produce must return to them. The bishop replied that the relic was a bone of some animal he had picked up in the street. The want of education is, of course, the cause of such abominations; but Christianity on such a footing can hardly hope to be respected by the Moslems. A few children of the opulent classes are taught to read and write, but tuition does not extend further, and the clergy are generally taken from the poorer families, the chief qualifications for holy orders being the payment of a fee and some aptitude for chanting. The Greek Church of Syria has no national affinity with the Greek people, and are Arabs like the rest. They know nothing of the Greek language, and have their services in Arabic. The country is divided into two patriarchal dioceses, Antioch and Jerusalem, with eight episcopal sees in each. Both patriarchs and bishops are for the most part non-resident, and remain, with few exceptions, in their convents, leaving their duties to native priests. This is not disadvantageous, as the higher clergy are generally Greeks from Constantinople, who know nothing of the Syrian people or their language. The Greek Catholic sect forms an Oriental Papal Church, believing in the procession of the Holy Spirit from the Father and the Son, in purgatory, in the Pope's infallibility, and retaining only their services in Arabic instead of Latin. They receive the Holy Sacrament in both kinds, and their priesthood is unmarried. The name of Greek is thus inappropriate. They have a patriarch at Damascus, and eight bishoprics.

The Roman Catholics are distinguished in Syria by the appellation of Latins, being the only Church whose services are in that language. They rally round their convents in the different towns, and enjoy French protection. They have schools and give hospitality to travellers. In dress they are European, but under the monk's cowl they are generally found with bronzed Asiatic features, and the pure guttural Arabic dialect.

Leaving Lattakia, we ascended the Ansairi mountains, and rambled amongst them for several days, enjoying their Alpine scenery during the fine frosty forenoons, and seeking their clean white villages when the sun was low. A blazing fire of pine-wood in the centre of a large plastered cottage was more congenial than our tents in the cold winter nights, and we assembled, squatting on carpets, every evening round the large vaulted rooms forming the habitations of the people. One long ravine, in which we crossed a turbulent river no less than six times, kept us for two days in an untiring enthusiasm of admiration of its luxuriant variety of foliage. The scenery was most un-Syrian in its character: dense woods around us, sparkling streams beneath our horses' feet, and brawling cascades on the moss-grown rocks; then, rugged paths and lofty peaks imbedded in firs, moors of wild thyme, patches of cultivation in the least-expected nooks and corners, irreclaimable jungles and vineyards, vegetable gardens, and orchards, suddenly announcing our welcome proximity to the villages selected for our resting-places. In these we are always kindly received. The best to be

had is willingly given, and payment often refused.
This is one of the prettiest villages we have seen. The
white flat-roofed cottages scramble up one side of a
valley, in the centre of which there is a curious Gothic
chapel cut out of the soft rock, evidently a work of the
Crusaders. A gigantic solitary boulder had stood there,
and they had fashioned it inside and outside into a
highly ornamented place of worship. The name of the
village is said to have been taken from a lady who
owned it, the wife of a Count of Laodicea, and, from
being the property of the dame, it became plain Dama.
The family of our host, in telling this tale, seemed
thereby to establish a sort of claim on their Frank
guests.

The only subject we find them ill-disposed to make
a topic of conversation is their religion, and they art-
fully elude all questions relative to its mysteries. Of
the state of the country, however, they speak freely.
Their tribes cover the mountains extending from Mount
Casius southwards to Mount Lebanon. That they are
the last survivors of the primitive inhabitants of Syria,
Canaanites or Phœnicians, may be surmised from the
Pagan rites they still practise, though the exact nature
of these rites seems to be buried in hopeless obscurity.
Neither tradition amongst themselves, nor any distinctive dialect, throws the least light on their ethnological
origin. The Syriac, Arabic, and Hebrew languages
have so much affinity, that peculiarities of idiom or pro-
nunciation prove nothing. Their worship of the sun
and moon certainly looks very like vestiges of the ancient

K

idolatry of the followers of Baal and Ashtaroth of the book of Judges, while the licentious meetings of some of their sects may be traced to the mysteries of Astarte, the Syrian Venus. Ibrahim Pasha of Egypt, wishing to satisfy his curiosity on the subject, and set the question for ever at rest, selected one of his most faithful and attached servants to be located amongst the Ansairi, and become initiated in their religion. The mission was duly fulfilled; but, on the man's return after a two years' residence on this mountain, nothing could induce him, not even the appearance of the executioner, axe in hand, to reveal the secret. It is well kept, because a violent death always follows close on the slightest suspicion of intended betrayal, as it does, indeed, on most other grave offences among this people. This custom is said to have introduced the word 'assassin' in European languages, being the name of one of their sects brought from Syria by the Crusaders. Robbery is an institution of the Ansairi; they rob travellers, other villages, neighbours, even their father or brothers. Their number, in all two hundred thousand, is split up into many tribes, generally hostile to each other, the grounds of division being those of creed as well as of plunder. They are devoted equally to agricultural and pastoral pursuits, and do not disdain the manual labour of petty trades in the towns. At Lattakia there are not fewer than three thousand of them, and at Antioch twice as many. Though not so violent, nor perhaps so courageous, as the Turkomans and Bedaween, the Ansairi can nevertheless defy the power of the Turkish authorities, and though usually

affecting a nominal obedience, they are easily roused
by an act of injustice to unite in arms against the
Sultan's troops. They practise polygamy, and are
said to intermarry within the closest of all degrees of
consanguinity. Their women are regarded as mere
chattels, and bartered freely—two men exchanging
daughters, or one giving a sister for a donkey; and as
such the poor creatures seem to be used, carrying loads
great distances, in line with other beasts of burden.
They have no priests, and neither forms of prayer nor
fixed times and places of worship. What they seem to
revere the most is the tombs of eminent men. They
resort to these at night in great numbers, but what
ceremonies, if any, are there performed has not been
ascertained. I fancy it would be dangerous to watch
them. One of our party accidentally came to a cottage
in which some people were assembled before a fire
kindled at one end, but a man rushed out to order an
instant withdrawal: whether the fire was being wor-
shipped, or merely enjoyed on so cold a day, did not
appear. I examined one of the tombs held sacred, and
found it completely plastered over, and freshly white-
washed, that being a frequent attention paid to the
illustrious dead. There was no door by which to enter
the small mausoleum, but a hole in the wall, about six
inches square, seemed to penetrate, and an oil lamp is
kept always burning in it. The transmigration of souls
apparently plays a prominent part in their creed, whatever it be. The silly rhapsody attributed by Assemani
in his 'Bibliotheca Orientalis' to a nameless old man

of Cupha in Arabia, whom he calls the founder of their
religion in the end of the ninth century, is evidently
not deserving of consideration. The legend offers,
however, some curious associations, if they cannot be
regarded merely as coincidences. The old man was a
saint after the manner of the East, consisting in very
light attire, frequent fasting, and healing by a word or
touch. Of those who followed him, he selected twelve
to preach the doctrines he taught them. A sheikh
arrested him, and ordered that he should be crucified
next day. At night he kept the key of the old man's
prison beneath his pillow. A girl of his family pur-
loined the key when he was asleep, and released the
prisoner. In the morning a miracle was proclaimed.
The old man escaped to Syria, where he founded a sect
said to be one of those inhabiting the Ansairi mountains, if not the whole Ansairi persuasion. It appears
to me that the near proximity of this people to the
sites of Arka, Arvad, Zimra, Sin, and Hamath, which
were inhabited by the sons of Canaan when Abraham
entered Syria, gives a sufficient colour to the theory of
their descent from them, while the little that is known
of their worship, and their pure Semitic language, both
tend to corroborate it. We see, too, that in all conquered
countries, where descendants of their original population
continue to exist as a separate race, they are to be
found concentrated in the nearest mountainous regions,
to which they had retired to save something of their
independent state; and the Ansairi range, accordingly,
stands surrounded by the remains of those five Canaan-

itish cities known to have been inhabited by a people in many respects similar to the Ansairi of the present day.

The actual condition of this part of the country may be estimated by recent incidents, showing that little change has here taken place from the old times of rapine and bloodshed in Turkey. A village of worshippers of the sun refused to pay its taxes. A member of the provincial council of Tripoli was sent there to remonstrate a few days ago. Having failed in his mission, and not having ventured to proceed to extremities with so violent a people, he was returning home, when he passed through a Christian village. Village for village mattered little; he set fire to it. The panic-stricken inhabitants hurriedly conveyed their moveable property into their church, in the hope that it would be respected. The church was broken open and plundered by the followers of the functionary. Another village had been totally abandoned a few months ago on account of the unchecked depredations of a band of malefactors under a leader of infamous character named Issa. The villagers with their families took refuge at Antioch, where they remained in a state of the utmost destitution, while their crops were being publicly sold by Issa at the neighbouring small town of Jisr-Shogl. Efforts were made by the poor people to obtain protection from the Turkish authorities, but Issa found means of obtaining support amongst the members of the provincial council of Antioch. Last year the two Amamreh tribes, one of which bears the distinctive name of Beit-el-Shelf, the other Mohelbeh, together with the tribe of Beni-Ali,

determined to attack and subjugate at one blow the
hostile tribe of Cardaha. The latter, having discovered
the plan of attack, resolved on dividing into two bands ;
one to meet the assault, the other to destroy the villages
of their assailants. The second detachment burnt six
villages of the Beni-Ali, killed several persons, burnt
two villages of the Mohelbeh, and carried off all the
cattle they found, while the first detachment was driven
in, and the villages of Wady-Beit-Hassar, situated on
the high hills of the Cardaha, were destroyed. The
people of Beit-Tashoot, a portion of the Semet-Cobli
district, hastened to defend the villages of the Beni-Ali
and Boodi against the Cardaha, but the Crahleh tribe,
from another part of the Cardaha mountain, called
Carem-Ibalieh, attacked Beit-Tashoot. Taking advantage of this opportunity, Ahmed-Aga-el-Mohammed-
Adra, an enemy of the Crahleh, advanced from his castle
of Merkab with a large party of his followers, attacked
and burnt several of the Crahleh villages, and carried
off a great many of their cattle. The tribes of Darins,
the two Amamrehs, and Beni-Ali, united, and, negotiations for peace having been opened, hostilities ceased,
and have not been renewed as yet, but they will be,
as soon as a good opportunity offers. The Turkish
authorities were fully cognisant of all that passed, but
did not interfere further than by sending orders to preserve tranquillity. Mohammed-Aga-Haznadar, a chief
of irregular cavalry, however, casually met several
parties of armed men belonging to both sides, with
whom he exchanged a few shots ; three of his horsemen

were wounded, and he reported having killed four of
the Ansairi. The inhabitants of Beit-el-Shelf, who
are moon-worshippers, attacked lately El Harf, a part
of the Bahluli district, burnt two villages, and carried
off all their live stock. Three lives were lost on each
side. The assailants were subsequently routed in their
turn by the villagers of El Harf, who killed three more
of their number. The Scoobin worship the sun, and
are therefore immemorial foes of the Beit-el-Shelf. A
mere squabble among some children led to a whole
day's desultory fighting between the two tribes, during
which five men of the Beit-el-Shelf and one of the
Scoobin were killed, while another of the latter was
taken prisoner and burnt to death, after having his
hands and feet cut off. On this occasion twenty
mounted irregulars were sent to the spot, but they did
not interfere between the combatants, and returned
home with the head of an Ansairi, in no way connected
with the affair, whom they had met on the road, and
decapitated unquestioned. This brutal act was justified
by the statement that at the same place where the man
was met by his executioners, a Turkish officer had been
put to death by the Ansairi two years ago, and his
body left to rot by the roadside. So deplorable a state
of anarchy and conflict exists in a province, the chief
town of which contains three hundred regular and three
hundred and eighty irregular troops: of the former
none have been ordered out of Lattakia, and of the
latter none ever reached the scene of action, although
they left the town for the purpose of restoring tran-

quillity. The very presence of irregulars in the town
is an evil, for their frequent excesses prevent the industrious and peaceful portion of the Ansairi population
in the immediate vicinity from bringing provisions and
other commodities to market. When war rages on the
distant hills, a poor gardener living at the gate of
Lattakia may be dragged to prison for it by this police
force, which declares he was taken fighting against the
constituted authorities fifty miles off. The government
not only does nothing to remedy this, but also adds to
its bad results by a practice which, while it allows disorders to continue, impedes an honest livelihood, and
deprives the town of supplies; for a single act of violence,
sometimes even an accident, suffices to make it prohibit
all communication between the town and the villages,
the plain and the mountains, on the unreasonable idea
of holding a whole tribe responsible for the misdeed or
misfortune of an individual.

LETTER XI.

Jisr-Shogl — Jebel-el-Aâla — Ruined Convents — Druzes —
Metaweli—Waldi Settlement—Chalcis — Haji-Batran — Sheikh
Jrdaan—Agriculture—Trade.

Chalcis: March 19, 1859.

ON coming down from the Ansairi mountains, we
entered the valley of the Orontes, and reached
that river at the small town of Jisr-Shogl, whose fortified khan commands the only bridge in this district.
The hereditary chief of the place, which contains about
five thousand inhabitants, almost exclusively Mahometans, had on previous visits shown me some civility;
but I had recently heard of so many misdoings on his
part that I thought it right to let him understand how
distasteful they were to Englishmen, and I declined
his proffered hospitality on those grounds, which I explained to him. We therefore crossed the long bridge,
and proceeded on our way. This local tyrant, whose
name is Mehemed-Aga-Yansu, had been guilty of excesses, it would seem, which would hardly be believed
at Constantinople; and he has succeeded in establishing such a reign of terror around him that no complaints
are made. Extortion in the villages is the most venial
of his vices. Innocent men have been arrested on false
pretences, and kept chained in dungeons until a ransom

is paid; women carried off by force; plundering expeditions sent out without an attempt at secresy. Much
noise would have been made about all this if a Christian
had been wronged in a single instance. But Yansu is
an intelligent as well as a wicked man, and carefully
avoids molesting any but Mussulmans and Ansairi,
who, he knows, have no friends to make political capital of their sufferings. After traversing the broad and
fertile plain of the Orontes, here partially cultivated,
we had to climb the rocky hills, called Jebel-el-Aâla,
which form a broad belt of naked ruggedness, once
thickly peopled by monks and hermits. There is hardly
any soil in this whole stony region, and how so vast
a population of religious zealots was supported is a
riddle to me. Anchorites would not want much, but,
to judge by the spacious and highly ornate ruins of mo-
nasteries and convents, there must have been also other
occupants not on bad terms with the world. One of
the small plains surrounded by rocks was that of Immae,
where Zenobia took her stand against Aurelian, and
was defeated: it is now called Halka, or the Ring.
There are many Greek inscriptions on these ruins,
which are so numerous that one can count five-and-
twenty villages or large cloisters in sight at once; the
dates range from the third century to the time of the
Saracen conquest, when they abruptly terminate, and
the purport, being mostly sepulchral records, throws no
light on the history of the buildings. The few villages
still inhabited are occupied chiefly by Druzes, who are
in close communication with those of Mount Lebanon.

A secret post and police establishment of foot-messengers to convey verbal intelligence is kept up between the different branches of this sect with singular efficiency. The most minute circumstances of their frequent struggles with the Maronites are thus made known to all their brethren, without exaggeration as without attenuation. On Mount Lebanon, the open protection given by the French to the Maronites having encouraged a fanciful sympathy with England amongst the Druzes there, it is here also evinced with an unerring echo. As Englishmen, we were accordingly received very cordially by them.

The religion of the Druzes was for a time a mystery, and no enquiring traveller could make out what it was, but their books have now been read and commented on, proving that there was not any great secret to discover. It is merely a Mussulman heresy of the end of the tenth century, whose crazy founder, El Hakim, claimed the honours of divinity. Like the Coran, the sacred books of the Druzes contain plagiarisms from the Gospels and Pentateuch, beyond which little remains but a mystic jargon, whose obscurity seems to be its chief attraction to the initiated. They quote, in support of their tenet of the transmigration of souls, our Saviour's statement that John the Baptist was Elijah. Consciousness of a previous existence they assert to be frequent. They tell a story of a child of Jebel-el-Aâla, who complained to his parents of the hardship of being born a peasant, after having lived as a rich man on Mount Lebanon, and begged them to take him to his former

home. They did so, and he mentioned the names of
the places they passed. He guided them straight to a
house, where he called a woman and told her he was
her dead husband, asked after their children, and requested that the neighbours should be assembled to
greet his return. In their presence he enquired if
some money that he had concealed had ever been found.
On a reply in the negative, he went to the place, and
produced his hoard. A compromise then took place;
and his new parents accepted a share of the treasure
on the condition of taking him back to Jebel-el-Aâla,
and keeping him there. The Druzes have secret signs
of recognition, like the Freemasons, and they ask
strangers questions without apparent meaning, to which
the conventional answers must be given before they are
received as brother Druzes. They are temperate in
their habits, and in some respects moral. Dignified
in their deportment under all circumstances, they bear
affliction with the greatest fortitude. The particulars
of the death of Jumblat, by order of Abdulla Pasha of
Acre, which have been minutely recorded, equal in
grandeur the last moments of Socrates. What that
lofty principle is which raises the Druzes above all sub-
lunary sorrows has not been defined, but certain it is
that, whatever it may be, its effects are hardly surpassed by the holy resignation and sublime faith of
Christian martyrs. Self-mortification is a favourite exercise with them, many having passed their whole lives
in a state of voluntary penance, altogether eclipsing
the asceticism of Romish and Greek monks. Charity

is an essential part of their piety; not merely almsgiving, but the largest development of brotherly love:
confined, however, to those of their own sect. Their
worst trait of character is a profound dissimulation
towards other communities, apparently inbred in their
race. Religion absolves them from every fraud on
those in the position of infidels towards them. Thurs-
day is their weekly day of prayer. The whole evening
is then passed in chanting portions of their sacred
books. Their supplications, which go on during the
night, are chiefly for purity of heart and tongue, pardon before death, a sufficiency of worldly provision,
and a final translation to a holy tabernacle. They add
that they do not pray for a reversal of divine decrees,
but that grace may accompany them when awarded as
chastisements. Their praises are eloquent as Oriental
languages and diction alone can make them; God is
addressed as the High, the Great, whose grace is in-
visible, whose power is illimitable, the most generous
of hearers, whose commands none can gainsay, whose
designs none can frustrate. After chanting, prayer,
and praise, at their religious meetings, they discuss
until a late hour the politics of the day, which they
regard as an important branch of religion; and only
the initiated of the highest grade are allowed to remain
during these debates. All information received by
each of their number is then stated; the character of
persons in authority, whose position may exercise an
influence on the welfare and destiny of their race, is
scrutinised; and arrangements are made for communi-

cating the results of their deliberation to the most
distant branches of the sect. Thus, when they are
engaged in war with the Maronites, or when attacked
by the Turks, there is a degree of unity in their action
which is quite surprising. One spirit pervades the
whole body of the Druzes, scattered, though it be, over
districts, often hundreds of miles apart, which fact may
in some measure account for the frequent successes of
this sagacious people under the assault of superior
numbers. They have a supreme contempt for all other
creeds, with the sole exception of the Metaweli, who
are in close contact with them. We slept in two villages of the Jebel-el-Aâla belonging to this sect, which
is a branch of the Sheite heresy of Islam. The differences in practical matters between these and the orthodox Sunnites are very trifling. They keep, for
instance, a small cake of earth from the spot where the
martyr of the sect of Ali, El Hosain, was killed, and
touch it with their foreheads when prostrate in prayer.
They divest themselves, during prayer, of every ornament or garment worked with gold or silver, even their
watches, when they have them, with the idea that they
are not consistent with humility. The Metaweli, like
the Sheites of Persia, contract marriage for predeter-
mined periods, at the expiration of which they are renewed if desired. They are computed at fifty thousand
in Syria; a small number, fortunately for the Sultan,
as there is no more disaffected people in his dominions
than the Metaweli, who show all the hostility of sec-
tarianism against the Sunnite Turks.

I have now come here to visit the Arab sheikh whom
I advised to settle, as formerly mentioned. Mehemed-
al-Ganim, with his tribe of Weldi, have adopted that
suggestion, and the government has allotted to them
this site for cultivation. His people go freely to Aleppo
to make their necessary purchases; and their example
is followed by many of the other Bedaween, who now
appear for the first time in the bazaars. It is said that
an unusual degree of activity in the sale of British
manufactured goods has arisen in consequence of the
novel feeling of security on the part of the Arabs. The
Bedaween population, occupying a vast territory, on
the western boundary of which lie the towns of Urfa,
Aleppo, Hama, Homs, and Damascus, and numbering
at the lowest computation, with the inhabitants of Arabia
Proper, four millions, possesses a great amount of wealth
yielded by their herds of camels and flocks of sheep.
The cotton stuffs and colonial produce, which they require in large quantities, have hitherto reached them
after passing through many hands, with a proportionate
increase of price, while the importers received only a
small part of the profit. The Bedaween being now
encouraged to go to the towns, and deal directly with
the merchants—the latter being also enabled to forward
their wares to the desert for sale, without incurring the
risks previously apprehended, through the protection
given by the sheikhs to persons recommended by them
—both the purchasers and the sellers are considerably
benefited. On the other hand, the locating of the
nomads is not without its dangers and inconveniences.

A too numerous concourse of tribes on plains heretofore
unpeopled may give rise to disputes for pasturage, or
wells, or defensible positions. Judicious and active
measures will become necessary, and one can only hope
that the Turkish authorities will not be found wanting.
What they have done in the matter thus far is good.
They will surely not be blind to their obvious interest,
for it would form no unimportant element for the consolidation of Turkish power, were the wandering and
predatory habits of the Arab tribes thus modified, and
so wide an expanse of country, almost all of which is
arable, inhabited by a peaceful and productive population. I find about three hundred tents here, and a
good deal of land sown. Mares and lances have been
sold; oxen and ploughs purchased. I cannot say the
furrows look very straight, but the soil is extremely
fertile, and a fair harvest may reward their labour,
unskilled though it be. Haji-Batran is here with a
strong detachment of his Hanadi horsemen, to protect
the crops from the Anezi. The ground is well chosen
for the experiment; a boundless plain of black loam
extending eastwards, with a lower valley of rich alluvial
earth on the banks of a small stream. On the north
and south there are ranges of low hills to cover the
plain from incursions of the nomads, who are not fond
of ground where they can be seen from a distance.
This place thus becomes a sort of entrance of the desert,
and the settlement of a tribe here will be a defence to
the villages on the west. That it was formerly a commanding position, is proved by the remains of the ancient

fortified city of Chalcis, which still stand on the western slope of the valley. Its whole line of ramparts, and the gates, can be traced in grass-grown mounds with large cut stones fallen down their outer sides, where there seems to have been a broad moat. In the centre of the enclosure there are larger mounds, which might be interesting to excavate, as Chalcis was a wealthy city, if one may judge by the ransom it paid to Chosroes, king of Persia, when he successfully besieged it in the middle of the fifth century.

As I sat one afternoon in Mehemed-al-Ganim's tent, discussing with him the all-important subject of the crops, Haji Batran came in with a strange tale of an Anezi force in the neighbourhood. The Weldi Sheikh started up, and ran to the summit of a tumulus which served him as a watch-tower. I said to Batran that, of course, the Weldi would not suffer by any attack of the Anezi while he was here with his Hanadi for their protection. He replied that the Anezi would not hurt them, but that it would not be so easy to prevent their turning their mares in to graze where they find cornfields. I began to think I understood, and I enquired what sheikh or aghid was leading the Anezi; Batran could not know; it might be Jedaan himself. I left the tent, and sent one of my own Arabs to look for the Anezi, and to ask their leader, whoever he might be, to come and speak with me. Mehemed-al-Ganim then came down from the mound, plucking his beard with vexation, his great eyes rolling wildly, and uttering lamentations with all the picturesque vehemence of his

L

race. Hundreds of Anezi were guarding their mares
while feeding on his crops. I remarked to Batran that
it was surely time for him to do his duty. He ac-
quiesced, but with no very remarkable alacrity, and,
mounting, proceeded with several hundred Hanadi in
the direction pointed out by Mehemed-al-Ganim as
being the scene of his disaster. The latter then opened
his full heart; he even wept over the loss of his first
agricultural produce. He could not be mistaken; Haji
Batran must be at the bottom of it all; he never would
let the tribes settle; he would lose his bread if they
settled; the services of the Hanadi were well paid by
the government; if the work were better done by
settled Bedaween, the Hanadi would no longer be required; they would have to settle too; they are too
lazy to work; and Batran would no longer be the
governor of the desert; it was no use; the Weldi must
get back their mares and their lances; they must rove
and plunder as before. Such was the burden of the
poor Sheikh's excited wailing, which continued till long
after dark. Next morning my Arab messenger returned.
He had passed the night with the Anezi. Batran had
never gone near them. Jedaan, who was there, would
be here immediately. He soon appeared. We talked
awhile on his own affairs, skirmishes with the Shammar
and the like, and then I asked him what had brought
him to the Weldi settlement. He answered quickly
that Batran had sent to tell him he would find here
plenty of green forage; that the mares of his tribe were
starving; and that he had brought some of them to get

fat on the barley of these fools who had settled. I
alluded to the government, but he cut me short by
saying that Batran is the government, and that I, who
was always urging him to obey the government, ought
not to find fault with his having done so on this occasion.
I remarked that he would probably find out his mistake
when he applied for the annual permission to trade,
which the government could not consistently grant,
after having proved their wish that the Weldi should
settle by condoning the tithes of their produce for two
years. The Anezi Sheikh opened his eyes wide with
astonishment, whistled a long low note, and said that he
was himself the fool. He then jumped up, hoped I
might be eternal, and sprang on his mare. In another
half-hour all the Anezi were on their way back to the
Euphrates, with their long swinging gallop and occasional halt to breathe their mares, which takes them
over the ground with so much rapidity and so little
fatigue. Haji Batran did not return to the camp.
Mehemed-al-Ganim appeared all smiles and thanks;
Jedaan had sworn to him to compensate for all damage
done, and to spare and protect the Weldi for the future,
and Jedaan's word is better than any bond.

The prospects of the settled Arabs seem encouraging.
The price of grain is high, and, if in this first year
there is a fair profit, the example may be followed by
other tribes. What chiefly depresses agricultural produce in the market is the want of means of conveyance at a remunerative rate. The country grows
more than it consumes, but the surplus reaches foreign

ports only when there are famine prices. The extent
of cultivation would be increased if there were a
demand for produce, and improvements would also be
introduced in its practice. Implements have not been
altered since the days of Abraham, and are of the
worst description. The advantage of a rotation of
crops being unknown, land lies fallow after one
crop. No manure is used; marshes remain undrained;
irrigable fields unwatered, excepting near the towns.
Mechanical power and appliances, especially adapted
to a thinly peopled country, have not been resorted to.
For these reasons the exportation of grain from Syria,
which might become extensive and lucrative, is merely
a casual and doubtful resource for the corn-merchant,
when there is a failure of crops in other countries. If
properly protected, the settlement of some of the Arab
tribes might soon convert these desert plains into
fruitful cornfields and vineyards. If, instead of kind-
ling dissensions amongst the Bedaween, the government were to inspire confidence, a located population
might be formed; at first in detached positions, to
serve as nuclei, whose growing strength would power-
fully impress the surrounding nomads, and bring them,
from coveting the wealth and welfare of villagers, to
adopting the same means of acquiring them. Then
there are so many other species of culture suitable to
the soil and climate, which might become a source of
prosperity to the settlers and the country. Cotton,
for instance, is indigenous here. There is no lack of
land, light, friable, and dry, such as is, in a high

degree, calculated to produce it in abundance. The summer is hot, it is true, but strong westerly breezes prevail, which render it generally more temperate in autumn, when the cotton plant is in flower. Little of the land sown with cotton is irrigable, but the young plants are watered once or twice by hand when a long drought tends to stop their growth. The yield is excellent. Land is measured by what is called in Arabic a feddan, the area which a pair of oxen can plough in a day, that is, about a third of an acre; this requires 15 lbs. of seed, and yields on an average 12 cwt. in the husk, or 266 lbs. of cleaned cotton wool. Its cultivation could be greatly extended, were the proper steps taken. Twenty years ago, three times as much cotton was grown in Syria, but the importation of English twist has enabled the local manufacturers to work more profitably with it, and they do not use the native produce so much as formerly. It has consequently decreased nearly to the level of the supply required for making wicks and stuffing furniture. Its increase, like that of every other branch of agriculture in this country, has hitherto been checked by the insecurity of property. The periodical inroads and plundering expeditions of the nomadic tribes lay the whole rural population under a burden, which alone suffices to frustrate their endeavours to attain prosperity. Without this one paramount drawback, cultivation of many kinds might enrich these wretched peasants, and cover the broad expanse of the Syrian plains, which now only show a

few scattered patches of tillage amidst wildernesses of
fertile land. This location of tribes seems to be the
only possible remedy for the evil. Traditions exist
amongst them of a former state of intellectual culture
and national power, and a vague presentiment is occasionally expressed by them that a change will at some
future time restore it. The physical and mental
faculties of these descendants from one of the most
noble stocks of the human race, are not inferior to
those of their Palmyrenian and Babylonian ancestors.
The history of the intercourse of nations, which Mon-
tesquieu identifies with the history of the development
of agriculture and trade, shows that their decline,
while accounting for the present obscurity and isolation
of this once great people, is not irremediable. With
the rise of cultivation and commerce, that fallen greatness might be revived. The vicissitudes of Asiatic
nations have always been more decisive than those of
European countries. The growth of a state in the
East is rapid as its decay. Syria fell before the
advance of the Turks. Unlike the warlike races
which people the West, the effeminate inhabitants of
Asia, when vanquished, become subject in fact and in
spirit. No love of liberty, no pride of independence,
takes up arms after defeat. In this case, moreover,
success in war on the part of the Turks was not followed by the advantages which the conquerors of the
Gauls and Britons conferred on those subjected to the
Roman yoke. New arts were not introduced, agriculture not encouraged, commerce not maintained.

Here, ruined cities, countries laid waste, still record
the havoc of wars long past. The invasion of the
Turks was devastation for its own sake, the wild
beast's thirst of blood, the barbarian's lust of mere
dominion. We now see in the state of this country
the necessary effects of such causes. But the clouds,
which have threatened the Turkish domination since
the commencement of the present century, have not
blown over. If they do not burst in a storm, as has
been so often predicted, though such is not my opinion,
they cannot be dissipated without leaving a changed
atmosphere. Then will arise a question of difficult
solution, amongst many others equally or more so, in
the disposal of several millions of nomadic Arabs,
Koords, and Turkomans. The plains of Western
Asia, from the Euxine and the Caucasus to the Red
Sea, the Indian Ocean, and the Persian Gulf, are
peopled by these races, each of them capable of aspiring
at national independence, and none of them advanced
enough to form a state ; while on their northern frontier
stands a compact body of over sixty millions, feeling
the concentrating and invigorating influences in favour
of conquest wielded by an absolute despotism, with a
formidable military system to bring these lawless
nations beneath its yoke. They must either be subjugated by that Russian sword, or saved by the pacific
weapons of agriculture, industry, and trade, which can
alone give them strength to withstand its inevitable
thrust. Without pursuing further a discursive range
over the bright domains of a possible future, the car-

dinal fact of the matter seems to be that, if Western
Asia is not to be left to the unresisted encroachments
of Russia, the best chance for its escape lies in the
extension of those arts, and the development of those
resources, which no other foreign power can so well
foster as Great Britain, and which will also bring wealth
to our own shores.

LETTER XII.

Beroea : August 29, 1859.

A SHOOTING party was organised a week ago
to try the hills of Haas, where red-legged par-
tridges were said to be abundant. Though no sports-
man, I joined it for the sake of exercise. Fifteen miles
to the south of Aleppo we came to the large village of
Sfiri, which was made the head-quarters of the expedition. Guns and dogs and game-bags were got ready;
a donkey laden with provisions, followed by another carrying two large skins full of water, opened the march;
a motley crowd in shooting-jackets and gaiters of many
cuts and hues filed off in animated discussion on the
merits of breech-loaders and patent cartridges, and
narrating marvellous exploits to prove their theories.
All this was not in my line, and I soon got tired of it.
Strolling back to the village, I met an Arab of the
Mowali tribe, and asked him where their camp was.
At Irjil; that was nothing, just four hours' ride from
Sfiri. I engaged him to guide me to his sheikh, with
whom I had sworn the oath of brotherhood two years

ago. Two villagers volunteered to accompany me, and
I took one of my own Arabs: we were thus a party of
five. We cantered along gaily for some time, then
pulled up, and cantered on again, according to Bedaween rule, until the close of evening, when we found
ourselves at Irjil, the site of the ancient city of Re-
gillum, but now a series of foundations of buildings
without a stone above the surface, and a large well
at the foot of a conical hill on which the citadel had
stood. Lines of cut stones and green mounds were
plentiful, but no tents were to be seen. The tribe we
sought had left. An examination of the cinders where
their fires had been, and of the footprints of their camels,
showed that they had not been gone long, and that
they had moved in a southerly direction. To return
as one came is always disagreeable. The Mowali guide
said his people must be at Hara Iji Sheham, a camping-
place at about the same distance from where we then
were as we were from Sfiri, but in the opposite quarter
of the compass. There was no moon; we could steer by
the stars. A short council of war was held, and we decided on going to the camp rather than the village,
hoping to finish the night, if we could not commence it,
in bed. It was a weary ride, over a naked plain, without road or path. Shortly after midnight, the Mowali
halted, saying we had reached Hara Iji Sheham. Here
also were cinders and camels' footprints, but no tents.
My four companions began talking all together, each
giving an opinion which no other listened to. I took
off my mare's bridle to let her crop the short grass in

default of her accustomed feed of barley, and, tying the
halter-rope to my wrist, lay down beside her, and was
soon fast asleep.

The sun shining on my eyes awoke me, much re-
freshed, but very hungry. The plain around offered
not a single object to relieve its inhospitable aspect;
all was flat, stale, and unprofitable. One was not in
the best of humours for consultation, either; one felt
forcibly what a benevolent institution one's breakfast
is. There was nothing for it, however, but to make
the best of a bad bargain, and the best was a moderate
draught of muddy water in the palm of one's hand.
No well or spring was there, but the grass, still green
on one spot when all around was burnt up by the summer sun, proved that water was near the surface, and
holes had been dug by the tribes that were in the habit
of encamping at Hara Iji Sheham to procure a limited
and unwholesome supply for their use and that of their
flocks and herds. Round one of these holes we all sat
down, each holding his horse's bridle, and looking at
the other. Nothing seemed to occur to any of us.
Matters looked too serious for much conversation.
One fact, however, was suggested by the Mowali for
consideration, and was fully appreciated: we should
have to ride the whole day to return to the village,
whereas a tribe might be within a short distance of us.
The unanimous resolve, and of course the least rational,
was to go from camping-place to camping-place until
we should find a tribe. That day passed without food,
but not altogether without water. We stopped at

three different wells, where traces of recent camps remained, and we saw two large wild boars near one of
them. But we were travelling fast to the south-east—
that is, away from the border of the desert, where villages can alone be expected—and we were beginning to
wonder how we should get back. At nightfall we saw
three Bedaween boys, from six to ten years old, tend-
ing a flock of sheep. They told us the Mowali, to
which tribe they belonged, were only a few hours' ride
to the south of us. They gave us some milk with a
few crusts of coarse hard bread, and we lay down by
them to sleep, our mares grazing peacefully with the
sheep. Nothing but the best Arab blood could have
stood such work, and fortunately we had the best.
I was surprised at dawn to find that I had slept very
well, and did not suffer so much from hunger as on
the previous morning. Our anxiety was, moreover,
relieved by the prospect of soon coming up with the
Mowali, for we had, until we met these boys, penetrated
into the heart of the desert without any information of
the position of the tribes, and two risks were thereby
incurred—first, that we should neither fall in with one
to receive us kindly, nor have the means of returning;
secondly, that we should cross the path of some marauding expedition, neither belonging to the tribe of
our guide, nor to any other with whose sheikh I had
the bond of fraternity. In the latter case we should
simply have been robbed of our animals, stripped almost entirely of our clothes, and left to wander about
on foot and helpless till starvation should definitively

settle the question of our 'to be or not to be.' Last
year a caravan of three thousand camels with six
hundred men perished near where we were. It was
bound from Damascus to Bagdad, and lost the way.
No Bedaween happened to be within reach, and a tribe
came upon their remains long after their death. They
would have given assistance had they been in time, but
to restore the goods to the merchants would have been
too much to expect, and that tribe has become rich by
the spoil.

The little boys gave us some more of their ewes'
milk, but they had no more crusts to give. We then
mounted, and followed the direction pointed out by
them. They would follow leisurely with the sheep to
replenish their provisions. The good-natured fellows
said they could not want for much, so long as they
could share the food provided for their lambs, which
seemed to be plentifully supplied by a couple of hundred ewes. We rode the whole of that day, cantering
as much as we could with due regard to the strength of
the mares, on whose lasting quality our lives depended :
luckily for us, that quality was of the highest order. In
the afternoon we passed the ruins of a fine old castle
on the summit of a conical hill, called by the Bedaweens,
Shuemis. Its architecture was neither Saracenic nor
of the time of the Crusaders, and it must have owed its
origin to the period of the commercial greatness of
Palmyra, as it stands midway between Hama and the
glorious remains of Zenobia's City of Palms. Not far
from the castle was the site of the ancient Irenopolis,

now Selamieh, boasting of a few cottages built so as to
form a sort of fort within the area of the previous town.
We had then the hope of soon reaching the Mowali
camp, and did not care to turn westwards out of our
course to seek rest and refreshment. We still kept
advancing as fast as we could, sometimes at a good
gallop when we thought we were near our journey's
end. An hour after dark we saw a fire ahead of us,
and pressed on to the camp as we thought; it was only
a caravan of camels laden with soda on its way from
Sokhua to Hama. From the drivers we learnt that
the Mowali had moved that day from the spot indicated
by the shepherd-boys to one several hours' ride to the
south-east. We had passed their abandoned camping-
ground during the day without recognising it, and we
still held on our course, husbanding the strength of our
mares. About midnight we came to another fire, from
which some Arabs came out to beat us off, supposing
we were a plundering party. After a few words of explanation they told us they were an outpost of the
Mowali camp, which was only a couple of hours' ride
to the east, and gave us some bread. Following their
directions, we rode on till the dawn was beginning to
break, when a horseman galloped towards us, chal-
lenging quite in military style ; on our replying that
we were friends, he approached, and I distinguished
the features of a cousin of Ahmed Bey, sheikh of the
Mowali. This man's history was curious. He had
been taken prisoner ten years ago by the government
irregulars, and brought to Hama, where he was

forcibly enlisted as a private soldier in a regular
cavalry regiment, then marching to Kars. After
several years' service, his intelligence and efficiency
earned promotion, and finally he attained the rank of
lieutenant. His regiment having returned to Syria,
the temptation was irresistible; he deserted, and
rejoined his Bedaween brethren. When our arrival
was announced by the quondam officer of dragoons,
Ahmed Bey came forth with the warmest welcome.
We were not sorry to find ourselves at last comfortably
installed in his hospitable tent.

The Mowali are a Syrian tribe of Bedaween, generally to be found within a triangle formed by Aleppo,
Palmyra, and Damascus. Their country was once
much more extensive, but they have been driven westwards during a long series of years of vain resistance
to the advance of the Anezi. Even now they only
succeed in holding their ground by means of alliances
with the Hadideen, Lehep, Ferdoon, and various other
tribes. Their proximity to the Anezi brings them into
frequent collisions with the great desert tribe, but
their number is too limited, only two thousand tents, to
permit their unquestionable bravery to be of much
avail. They bear a worse character than the Anezi,
and have fewer of the virtues supposed to belong to
the Bedaween. Their bad name in the desert originated
in their having treacherously murdered, about fifty years
ago, some of the Anezi sheikhs when assembled in a
Mowali tent to conclude a peace; and it has become a
proverb amongst the other tribes that the tent of the

Mowali is the tent of shame. A tradition assigns their
rise to the journey of a youth, the last descendant of
the Ommiad Khalifs, to Constantinople, where Sultan
Amurath took compassion on his reduced state, and
purchased all the slaves that could be found in the
desert to make a tribe of which he was appointed sheikh.
The sheikh being Mowla, or prince, his tribe took the
name of the Arabic plural of that word, Mowali, and
his successors, alone amongst all the sheikhs of the
desert, have consequently borne the title of Bey. The
present chief, Ahmed Bey, is thus the representative
of the most ancient aristocracy amongst the Arabs, that
of the Khalifs. He is renowned for his bravery, and,
notwithstanding what is thought of his tribe, he is himself much respected. In comparison with other sheikhs,
he is certainly an enlightened young man, and disposed
to keep his people from committing excesses. In
appearance he is very tall and athletic, with a dark
commanding countenance.

A day of rest was no small satisfaction to us after
such a gallop, and our trusty mares seemed to be quite
of the same opinion. They looked just a little drawn
in about the flanks, but there was no diminution of
muscle, nor of appetite. We did nothing that day, but
strolled about the camp, which I found was pitched on
the outer plain of Palmyra. The ancient site itself is
screened from the west by a wall of low hills as a
garden, whose every tree is a Corinthian pillar, and
noble temples for its arbours, but all dried up and
lying dead with its wreaths of marble colonnades and

porticoes glittering in the evening sun like Byron's gilded halo hovering round decay.

It had been agreed with Ahmed Bey that the camp should be moved westwards next morning. I therefore got up before sunrise, and found the Sheikh's tent already struck. This is the signal, and no other warning is ever given of a march. The tribe was all soon busily engaged. The chief labour seemed to fall on the women. Taking away the poles, and rolling up the long tent-coverings, was concluded in a very few minutes. Camels were laden with pots and bags of grain. On the top of the load, a parapet was formed of rolled carpets, and children were hurriedly thrown into the hollow space. Girls mounted in front to guide the stately animals; women climbed up by the camels' hind legs when they were in motion; others walked humbly after them. The Bedaween make a point of always moving their camps in the shortest possible time in order to keep their women in practice for all emergencies. The horsemen, lance in hand, proceeded to the front and flanks of the line, some on their mares, others on dromedaries with their mares led behind them. The order of march was abreast, the laden camels in the centre. As the sun rose over the level horizon, it was a singular sight, this tribe in motion, covering at least a mile of ground, with the long uncouth shadows of the camels stretching out on the naked yellow desert before us. We rode for about four hours in a perfectly unvarying direction, and at last we came to some undulating grassy land. Ahmed

M

Bey got from his dromedary to his mare, and, galloping
on, disappeared amongst the low mounds. In a quarter
of an hour he returned slowly without his lance, which
he had stuck into the earth where he meant the camp to
be pitched. Suddenly all the horsemen left us, and we
soon came to the spot, now a forest of spears. The men,
dismounted, were sitting on the ground in circles at a
short distance, while their mares grazed at will around
them. Each woman, recognising her husband's lance,
pitched his tent where he had planted it. Young
girls, carrying skins to fill with water, ran to a small
stream. Children spread in all directions, gathering
wild thyme and other woody herbs to burn. In an
incredibly brief space we were established as if we had
been stationary there for months.

Near us was a large camp of the Sebaa Anezi, with
whom the Mowali are at present in alliance. This is
the wealthiest and most numerous of the Anezi tribes;
not so warlike as the Fedan, but fearing no enemy,
as they can muster ten or twelve thousand horsemen
with ease at any time. They have enormous herds of
camels and flocks of sheep, and their mares are of the
purest blood to be found in the desert. They trade
largely; and rarely suffer much hardship, being possessed of money, which can hardly be said of any
other tribe. Their name is taken from the Arabic
word Seba, or seven, that being the number of their
subdivisions, which remain, however, almost always
together. The names of these sections are Duam,
Abideh, Ishfoaieh, Mooeneh, Gmassa, Mooajeh, and

Besieh, with the two smaller bodies of adherents
called Pteinat and Roosali. I do not think anyone
else has had the opportunity of drawing up a correct
list of the Bedaween tribes and subdivisions, and, as I
have given myself some trouble to ascertain them
with accuracy, I now record the result. The Fedan
Anezi are subdivided into nine tribes, which are
Mehed the people of Jedaan, Fooeris, Ajajara, Roos,
Shmeilat, Greibat, Roaba, Hrisa the followers of
Deham, and Omeir. The other Anezi tribes are Jelas,
of which the numerous family of its sheikh, Faissal
Ibn Shalan, form a distinct tribe called Roala; Seloot,
Erfuddi, Shumlan, Hayaza, and Ibn Haddal, which
generally roam in the neighbourhood of Hilla, the
ancient Babylon, and Bagdad; Fooenis, Amarat, Majin,
Serdyeh, Tiar, and Hesenneh, rarely leaving the southern
regions of the Syrian desert, and the Nejd or Central
Arabia; Weled Ali, encamping almost always to the
east of Damascus; and Beni Sachar, and Salbaan, to the
east of Jerusalem, and occasionally on the plains of the
Jordan and Esdraelon. The Shammar, who confine
their wanderings to Mesopotamia, are subdivided into
the tribes of Abdeh, Amud, Assareh, and Jerban.
The Mowali, Weldi, Lehep, Ferdoon, and Hadideen,
on the western skirts of the desert, and the Obeideh
and Montefik, on the eastern, low tribes, more or less
numerous, and the Sokhni, Aghel, and Aghedat, also
not of high repute, are all dependent on the greater
tribes for protection. The sheikh of the Sebaa is
Fares Ibn Hedeb, a fine old man of eighty, much

respected for his justice and kind nature. I went over
to see him when our camp had assumed the routine of
desert life. He received me unwillingly, and it was
evident there was something unfavourable on his mind.
After a short interchange of ceremonious enquiries about
each other's health, I rose to leave, saying I had learnt
for the first time that he was capricious, as we met on
different terms now from those of our previous intercourse, without any cause that I was aware of. He
begged me to sit down, and then asked if all Franks
were of the same tribe. I replied that certainly it was
not so. He hoped I did not belong to the same tribe
as a person whom he named. Nothing could be further
from the fact; we did not even speak the same language.
This seemed to please the old man, who at once opened
his heart. Some men of his tribe had made a bargain
with the person in question for the safe conveyance of
some travellers to Palmyra; the Bedaween conveyed
them safely thither and back, but the money was not
paid. When I told Fares that I knew the travellers he
alluded to, and that they also were natives of a country
far distant from my own, where no gentleman ever behaved so, he said simply that he was very glad to hear it,
because he had come to the conclusion that all Franks
were contemptible rascals. Future travellers may suffer
for this, I fear. The Sheikh then mentioned several
occasions on which his tribe had escorted travellers,
and asked me if I knew what country they belonged
to. I diverted this scrutiny by putting the question
whether any of them had ever been guilty of such

conduct. He answered, with a sonorous but not irre-
verent oath, that none had, and admitted the force of
my argument, that one black sheep does not prevent
the remainder of the flock from being white. We then
talked very cordially, and he showed me his mares and
one horse, which he boasted that no money could buy,
and such as probably never left the desert.

When I returned late to the Mowali camp, I found
it in a state of uproar. Fifteen laden camels had just
been brought in from a caravan plundered between
Hama and Homs by a party of Mowali. Ahmed Bey is
a great fighter and plunderer in the wars of the tribes,
but he has no taste for the road. As I entered his
tent, he was beating the robbers unmercifully with a big
stick. He desisted on seeing me, and I remarked that
it was all very well to inflict punishment, but that
restitution seemed to me not less urgent. To this he at
once assented, and, ordering some of his own family to
mount immediately, he sent the laden camels back un-
touched. One of the relatives of Fares had accompanied
me home, and I suggested that, if he went with them,
the authorities would have an additional guarantee for
the safe delivery of the goods. This was also done
most faithfully, as I afterwards learnt from the Hadideen who were with the caravan that had been robbed.

After another day's march in a north-westerly direction with the Mowali, we encamped on a fine plain,
well supplied with water, where the Sheikh announced
his intention of remaining a week at least. In the
middle of the first night, however, I was roughly aroused,

and told to mount, for the regular troops were on us.
A quarter of an hour had not elapsed before all the
tents were struck and loaded on the camels, ready to
follow the flocks and herds which were being driven
rapidly eastwards. Ahmed Bey asked me if I was
going with him, and, on my replying in the negative,
he took a hurried leave, gave the word to march, and
galloped out of sight. I was thus left with my own
Arab and the two villagers of Sfiri, each holding his
mare, and wondering what would happen next. To
go towards Hama or Homs might prove unsatisfactory,
inasmuch as we should meet the troops, and either have
to betray the Arabs by telling which way they had
gone, or appear to take their part against the government by refusing to give that information. The great
bear pointed to the best course we had to follow, and I
led on, steering directly for the polestar. When the
day broke, the troops became visible far behind us, infantry, cavalry, and artillery, marching steadily towards
the east, but without the most remote chance of over-
taking the Mowali. We rode all day, and rested at
night on a tumulus where we found good water and
grass, but we had no food for ourselves, as, in the hurry
of leaving, Ahmed Bey had not thought of offering us
any, or we of asking him for it. The mares were fresh,
and we went on gaily next morning, still keeping their
heads to the north. I do not attempt to describe the
country, for two reasons—first, because I thought only
of writing about the state of its population when I
began these letters, so many books full of descriptions

having already been published; and.secondly, because
the sameness of the scenery in the desert leaves me
without an object to describe. Suffice it to say that
we advanced as fast as we could, tightening our respective waist-belts from time to time for obvious reasons.
We arrived in the evening at a spring called Arooneh,
where we hailed with delight the appearance of a few
Hadideen tents. After a two days' fast with violent
exercise, the mess of half-baked balls of unleavened
bread swimming in melted butter, which was placed
before us in a wooden platter one foot deep and three
in diameter, seemed to have reached the perfection of
culinary art.

The Hadideen are a quiet kindly tribe of shepherds,
who never enjoyed any reputation for martial qualities
until quite lately. They are not well mounted, and, to
enable them to defend themselves, they had been for
some time gradually and secretly procuring fire-arms.
A quarrel between the Mowali and Hadideen for pasturage occurred last year, just when the troops were
sent from Hama against the Ansairi of Ismael Khair
Bey. The first attack of the Mowali was met, to their
utter surprise, by a volley from upwards of a thousand
muskets. Ahmed Bey, talking of it to me, said he
could not make out what the Hadideen meant when he
saw them sally forth from their camp on foot with big
sticks in their hands; but, when fire issued from the
sticks, and bullets whizzed about his ears unhorsing
several of his men, he exclaimed that they had turned
Turks with guns, and he led off his lancers at their best

pace. The Mowali had not retreated many hours when
they met about a thousand Metaweli horsemen armed
with carbines, who said they had come to assist them.
No great friendship had ever existed between the two
tribes, and Ahmed Bey, not understanding the motive
of the offer, declined their aid. His cousin, Mehemed
el Harfan, had personal grievances, however, against
the Hadideen, and, taking three hundred and fifty
volunteers from the Mowali, he joined the Metaweli,
who consented to attack the Hadideen with him. Mehemed el Harfan had carried off and married a young
girl of the Hadideen. She had escaped to her tribe
after having lived a couple of years with him; and, when
he claimed her from her family, as the mother of his son,
they had rejected his demand. His honour, as well as
his affection, was at stake. He thirsted for revenge on
his enemy, while he sighed for love of his wife. A
battle took place near Arooneh. The Hadideen were
defeated. Mehemed el Harfan called on the Metaweli
to accompany him in the pursuit, that he might recover
his wife. At that moment a messenger arrived in hot
haste to give the Metaweli some tidings, on hearing
which they turned back, and left the Mowali alone.
The Hadideen rallied on seeing this, and assailed the
Mowali, who succumbed to their superior numbers
and weapons. Two hundred of them were killed and
wounded. Mehemed el Harfan received several balls.
He succeeded in reaching the spring of Arooneh, where
we enjoyed the hospitality of the Hadideen ; lay down,
and tried to drink, but was stabbed to death by those

pursuing him. They cut his body into small pieces, and sent them round the camp to prove that the honour of the family, whose daughter had been taken, was avenged. The strange conduct of the Metaweli in this affair was afterwards explained by themselves. They were in alliance with the Ansairi. On hearing of the advance of Tahir Pasha from Beyrout, Ismael Khair Bey sent to beg the Metaweli to create a diversion in his favour in the vicinity of Hama, which might prevent the garrison there from attacking him on the other side. They did so, and caused such a fight that the small Turkish force could not show itself. But, when they received intelligence that Khair Bey and his two brothers had been killed, they had no further motive for fighting, and returned home.

While we were still on the field of battle, and the scene of Mehemed el Harfan's death, some of the Hadideen tribe, who had been at Hama, reached the tents. They told us they had been with the caravan robbed by the Mowali, and that the fifteen loaded camels sent back by Ahmed Bey had been handed over near the town to a party of government irregulars, who had boasted of having recaptured them by force. They also said that the regulars had marched home when they found that the Mowali were gone; and that reports had been spread—not by themselves, it is to be hoped—of a battle having been fought, in which the Mowali had been totally routed with great loss.

Towards the evening we continued our journey, but no longer impelled by any urgent motive for haste after

partaking of Hadideen hospitality. With the polestar
before us, we rode through the night, which was not
very dark, and much safer.   I had nothing to fear from
Anezi, Mowali, or Hadideen, but I had no claim on the
forbearance of any Shammar who might be out, and I
knew that they often cross the Euphrates, and go great
distances after plunder.   About midnight we heard
voices behind us.   We were fortunately near a small
tumulus, and got behind it.   Then, creeping to the top,
I could distinguish against the horizon a large party of
Bedaween coming after us at a gallop.   Mares do not
neigh at the approach of other mares, which is one of
the reasons why the Bedaween prefer them to horses
for their own use.   The horsemen passed close to the
mound, but we kept moving round it, so that our
proximity was not suspected.   The sounds grew faint
in the distance, then ceased altogether, and, mounting
again, we altered our course several points of the compass towards the west, in order to describe diverging
lines with the marauding expedition, whoever they
might be.   At dawn the horizon was clear all round us,
and the appearance of a great marsh, which I had visited
before, proved that my steering had not been wild, as
sailors say.   A solitary old tomb with some pretensions
to Saracenic architecture, revered under the name of
Sheikh Abraca, suggested that we could not be more
than a few miles from a village lying to the west of our
course; and our two villagers of Sfiri, being somewhat
damaged by hard riding and spare diet, preferred seced-
ing in that direction to persevering in the regimen.   I

was thus reduced to a single follower, who was staunch.
A sudden charge of several hundred gazelles in a close
troop was a beautiful sight, but they seemed to run
towards us instead of from us; their flight was soon
explained by the spectacle of a huge wolf in full chase
behind them. We charged the wolf, revolver in hand,
but he made off as hard as he could. Not wishing to
be unjust to our good mares, we pulled up, satisfied
with having spoiled his sport, and we made for the
marsh, where I knew there was a spring of fine water.
This marsh, called Midih, is formed by the river
Chalus, which flows from the hills of Aintab, through
Aleppo, to lose itself on the plain. There must be some
underground channel for the escape of so much water,
especially as the marsh is always at the same level,
while the river swells and recedes. The Chalus is still
as full of fish as when described by Xenophon. I lay on
the ground for half an hour at the spring to let my mare
have her breakfast in the long grass beside me. My
Arab was less wisely tiring his by galloping furiously
after a large wild boar, which had come trotting con-
fidently along the plain to drink at the spring, and had
turned sharp off when he saw me there. It is astonishing how swift are those unwieldy-looking animals, and
my man returned without his game. We have now
come on here, where some Hadideen tents invite us to
rest until my companion's mare is able to proceed, for
that last gallop quite finished her. I while away the
time by writing.

Gibbon says that Berœa and Aleppo were one. He

is mistaken. They were two cities, some fifteen or
sixteen miles apart, and, at the time when he supposes
Aleppo was called Berœa, its name was Chalybon.
The remains of Berœa are very extensive. Though no
buildings are still standing, one can trace their foundations, which show that it must have possessed some fine
edifices. The acropolis is as large as that of Aleppo,
and seems to have been very similar to it in construction. It is, however, like the town, in a completely
ruined state.

LETTER XIII

Airkeh: September 26, 1859.

AN unusually dry season has told sadly on the crops,
and wheat is up to famine prices. Much distress
will, it is feared, ensue. The settled Arabs may not
suffer; because, if there is a diminution of quantity, it
may be made up to them by the increased price. But
those who are disposed to settle may be deterred by
the expense of buying seed. The difficulties were
already too great to bear any addition. The want of
protection on the part of the government forces agriculture to decline. The tiller of the soil has to take
his chance of reaping his crop, or of seeing it carried off
or destroyed. When unfavourable weather comes to
swell the obstacles, there can be but little hope. The
existing resources of the art of husbandry in this
country are altogether incompetent to meet such a
contingency. The alternations of rain and sunshine,
so necessary to vegetation, are not often subject to
irregularity in this climate; and the husbandman can
therefore calculate with some degree of certainty on
the growth to maturity of the seed he consigns to the

soil, without seeking to use any of those precautions
which a more advanced state of knowledge and a less
propitious climate have introduced. A most primitive
species of plough is his only implement, and, after the
field is prepared by furrows only four or five inches
deep, and the seed is covered by crossing them, nothing
further is done, no care taken, until the grain is ripe.
This poor culture generally succeeds, however, when
the season is not very bad; but the cultivator is helpless, and the crop is lost, if he is not aided by the
weather. The latter alternative having befallen the
country now, apprehensions of great scarcity are entertained. A mob of several hundred Mussulmans and
Christians accordingly assembled a few days ago in the
streets of Aleppo, complaining loudly of the high price
of wheat, which they attributed to culpable speculations
on the part of the members of the provincial council,
in monopolising the produce of the country to sell it at
their own rate, and to the want of energy and zeal on
the part of the Governor-General in adopting remedial
measures. On hearing what was going on, the Pasha
proceeded to enquire into the nature of a movement
which appeared seriously to threaten the tranquillity
of the town. Placards, full of seditious expressions
and personal abuse of the authorities, had meanwhile
been posted up on the walls of the bazaars. Some of
the rioters were arrested. The first examined declared
that he and his family had been without food for two
days, because wheat was so dear. His house was
immediately searched: ten bushels of wheat, two sacks

of flour, and a sufficient quantity of bread for present
use, were found.   This, and subsequent discoveries of
a similar character, gave a different turn to the enquiry,
which resulted in the convicting of two notables of the
town, with several other persons less conspicuous, of
having incited the disturbance.   They were all put on
horseback, and exiled.   For once, the Turkish authorities were active and resolute.

At Aintab, also, there have been some disturbances.   A crowd gathered round a house whence
sounds of festivity were proceeding, and, after breaking
open the door, reproached its owner, a member of the
provincial council, with his enjoyment of abundance
while the people were starving.   The Governor repaired to the spot, and succeeded in dispersing the mob.
On the following day, a man of well-known turbulent
character, who had been present at the previous riot,
assembled a number of vagabonds, and plundered the
Mufti's house of all the corn stored in it.   That of the
most influential notable of the place was next assailed,
but he saved it by distributing loaves of bread among
the crowd, and thus pacifying them for a time.   The
tumult soon recommenced, however, and more violently
than ever; for almost the whole population of the town
attacked the Governor's residence.   That dignitary
barricaded himself in his private room, and nothing
could induce him to come out of it.   The same notable
who had given bread to the mob diverted their fury by
conducting them to the principal corn-store of Aintab,
which he opened and placed at their disposal, telling

the owner that he would pay the value of its contents.
The whole of the grain was at once carried off by the
insurgents. The Mufti also took an active part in
quelling the affray. He emptied a mosque used by
the government as a flour-magazine, sending the flour
in it to the public ovens, to be baked and given to the
poor. An outcry was then raised against the Governor
for not having taken previous steps to relieve the wants
of the people; and the notable, who had become so
prominent, was proclaimed Governor. The chief of
the police attempted to restore order; two men were
killed, and several wounded. Finally, the ex-Governor,
with his retinue and officials, left the place to the
notable, who was perhaps at the bottom of the whole
affair. The government, however, has not allowed
him to enjoy the position in which he had been placed
by the will of his fellow-townsmen; for a new Governor has been sent to Aintab.

At Marash, there is a considerable degree of excitement amongst the Armenians on account of the
wholesale proselytising of their church by the Protestant missionaries. One of the converts to the latter
persuasion has been stripped, fastened to a tree, and
nearly strangled by the Armenians on the road to
Zeitoon; they finally banished him and his family from
their district, on his persisting in his fidelity to his
new faith. They have threatened to kill any missionary venturing to tamper with their allegiance to their
church, and have offered a reward for the denouncing
of each convert. This persecution, as in the early ages

of Christianity, produces only enthusiasm on the part
of the proselytes, who glory in what they call their
martyrdom.

Disorders continue among the Ansairi. Last week
three hundred of them went from near Lattakia to the
district of Caair, lying between Antioch and Jisr Shogl,
where they attacked the villages of Miredj and Meset-
beh, and carried off all the grain they could find. A
Dehlibash with ten horsemen was sent by the government
to protect the villages, but did not venture within five
miles of those which had been plundered. The motive
attributed to the assailants was a blood feud of eighteen
years' standing. The Governor of Jisr Shogl, whom
I mentioned in a previous letter, took this opportunity of playing the robber himself. He accused a man
of the district of Caair of murder in the conflict, and
attacked and plundered the two villages of Ferfereh
and Kerbiaz for concealing him.

A curious instance of the mode of conducting public
business in this country has just occurred at Aleppo.
The farmer of the customs of Northern Syria had given
general satisfaction in the administration of his department. Besides the customs he had farmed the tithes of
a part of the province for two years. His contract was
considered too advantageous to him by the provincial
council, which summarily cancelled it on learning the
probable profit, notwithstanding that the same council
had previously sanctioned it. The farmer had collected
a portion of the tithes, and had made payments to the
treasury. It proved that the two amounts did not

N

counterbalance each other; he was a debtor of about a
thousand pounds, and a creditor for two thousand. The
council ordered payment of the debt without taking the
credit into account, on the plea that the two sums
belonged to two different years. In vain the farmer
combated this mode of proceeding, and, finding that he
must pay or go to prison, he abandoned all hope of recovering the balance due to him, and absconded.

Halaf-es-Shehemi, sheikh of the tribe of Ferdoon, is
one of the Bedaween in a state of transition between
nomadism and location. He also has obtained exemp-
tion from tithes for two years, and is preparing land for
sowing. I have come here to see his embryo settlement, situated between the shore of the Salt Lake and
a stream bearing the encouraging name of Nahr Dehab,
the Golden River. Whence the epithet is derived, I
cannot say, but I think the stream must be identical
with the Daradax, which Xenophon mentions as running
near the palace of Belesis destroyed with its large and
beautiful park by Cyrus. I believe its site to have
been where I was last year when with the Fedan
Anezi, and this river takes that course. The Ferdoon
are still under tents, but they say they will build
cottages next year if their agricultural experiment
should succeed. I have not a doubt that it will,
if they can surmount the first obstacle in their way,
the exorbitant price of seed-corn. This position will
then form the second in a proposed cordon of settled
tribes from Chalcis, held by the Weldi, to Beroea,
where the Hadideen seem disposed to remain; which

will protect the plains behind them from the inroads of
the nomadic tribes, and gradually extend in width into
the desert. The Weldi are satisfied with the result of
their first year. The Ferdoon are sanguine of success.
The Hadideen were never an unruly tribe, and have
always been faithful and useful as the shepherds of the
towns. Their location, now that they are well provided
with fire-arms, and have proved their bravery in war,
will greatly strengthen and further the scheme in pro-
cess of realisation. Haji Batran has done all he could
to frustrate it, and, being backed by his official authority
as agent for the government in the desert, his opposition has been very formidable. It would, to be sure,
have been more so, were it not perfectly understood
that its motive is entirely personal, for I have difficulty
in giving credence to the report he assiduously spreads
of his being instructed by the government to follow the
course he has adopted. The settlers see through his
artifices, which they attribute to the fact that his services
would be supplanted by the cultivating tribes ; and, on
several occasions when they have talked of abandoning
their fields and returning to their former habits, they
have been kept to their work by their desire not to let
him triumph over them. Seeing that he was getting
the worst of it, Haji Batran went lately to the Governor-
General of Aleppo, who understands little of the complicated politics of the desert, and so bewildered him
with ominous forebodings of disorders about to arise
from the unusual concourse of Bedaween in this province, that he obtained the exclusive and supreme

control over the tribes and their interests in exchange
for an unrealisable engagement to hold himself responsible for all losses by depredation. Batran thus secured
to himself the power of persecuting the settlers, and
bringing them back to their former condition, while he
could deter other tribes from settling, as they are disposed to do. Good luck, or rather the blessing attendant
on a good cause, shaped his course otherwise than he
had rough-hewn it. When returning to the desert
with a large party of his followers, he found a caravan
of forty-two remarkably fine mules grazing without a
guard; the temptation was too much for him; he sent
them off to Asia Minor for sale. He had been seen,
however, and recognised. The mules, unfortunately
for him, were the property of an influential merchant.
The evidence against him was complete. He is, therefore, in prison, waiting the decision of his fate; and the
settled Arabs have time to breathe.

Another portion of the Weldi tribe, numbering about
five hundred tents, has just crossed the Euphrates
from Mesopotamia, to join Mehemed-al-Ganim. They
will probably become cultivators also, if they like what
they see of his new condition. Trade is deriving pal-
pable advantages from the presence of so numerous a
class of consumers of manufactured and colonial goods.
A new species of cloth has been introduced. The
Arab women wear only a common blue dress of native
manufacture; a cheaper and stronger unbleached stuff
from Manchester is being bought up, and dyed with
the coarse indigo sold in the market, for the purpose of

underselling the manufacturers of the Syrian towns,
which proves an excellent speculation.   The handker-
chiefs worn by both men and women on their heads,
are also now exclusively of British manufacture.   No
such movement has taken place among the Bedaween
since the year 1809 when a person of the name of Lascaris de Vintimille was employed by the first Napoleon
to introduce French goods in the desert, which he
sold to the Arabs under cost price, with the view of
gaining influence over them to facilitate his designs on
British India.   M. Lascaris spent three years with the
Bedaween, and formed a confederation of tribes ready
to march on condition of being provisioned by France.
He died at Cairo before transmitting his papers to his
government, and it is said that they fell into the hands
of the late Mr. Salt, our Consul-General in Egypt at
that time.   The Arabs still talk of M. Lascaris in a
way which leaves no doubt of his having succeeded in
his mission, and they perfectly understood that the importation of French wares, sold to them so cheap, was
not his primary object.   The present more legitimate
endeavour to check the overlapping of the agricultural
by the pastoral territory of Syria, is not so congenial
to their ideas as a military expedition at foreign expense, but it has also the advantage of having been
prepared by similar means, as many of the Bedaween
served in the irregular troops raised by England in
Turkey during the Crimean war, and they have
brought home with them a lively sense of the justice
and even generosity with which they were treated.

The British goods they now purchase so freely are,
moreover, cheap and substantial, and the Arabs feel
the benefit to them of this new trade, while those who
have settled do not fail to vaunt their gain by cultivation.   It was full time that some defence should be
raised against the nomads, who have pushed their predatory incursions as far west as the banks of the
Orontes, and the tide of whose devastation has even
reached the sea in two places, near Acre, and between
Tripoli and Lattakia; while the villagers have gradually
receded before it, and more rapidly of late years on account of the great increase of the flocks and herds of
the Arabs, who impede cultivation for the purpose of
securing pasture.   The agricultural class of the population has thus been driven into the towns, and the
Turks have boasted of the increase of their inhabitants.
But political economists regard the migration of the rural
population to towns as one of the worst symptoms of
the state of a country.   The Turks do not like statistics, and they are right.   They have less to gain by
that science in the conviction it would give them of
their decline, than they would lose in that conviction
being imparted to others.   It is notorious that they do
not allow even a common statement of imports and exports to be made from the registers of their custom-
houses.   Those who would know the real state of
Turkey, must wear out their lives in the country, la-
boriously adding fact to fact until sufficient data are
amassed.   In Europe, a careful examination of a few
figures and totals in published tables shows where the

greatest material development is to be found in states, for we cannot now form an opinion of their relative power by mere intellectual superiority, and the world is no longer divided between Greek and barbarian. When one quotes statistics to Turkish politicians, they reply by talking of reforms. In the island of Cyprus, there were, thirty years ago, eighty thousand Mussulmans and forty thousand Christians; reforms have not prevented there being now sixty thousand Christians and forty thousand Mussulmans. Mr. David Urquhart once answered a grand vizier, who boasted of Turkish reforms, that their only reforms were in the cut of their pantaloons and tie of their cravats. They have certainly reformed their army, which, with all its shortcomings, is preferable to janissaries and irregulars; but look at the loss it has entailed on the country. At the lowest computation, three hundred thousand young men, future fathers of families had they lived, have perished in the ranks of that army during the last twenty years. There is no such drain on the Christian population. Things are not in a worse state, however, than might be expected under the circumstances. The expectations entertained were exaggerated. On the accession of Sultan Abd-ul-Mejid a new era opened for Turkey, and an improved system of government was inaugurated by the Edict of Gulhaneh. More was expected from this enunciation of good intentions than was warranted by the state of the country generally, estimated by appearances in the capital, while the provinces were incapable of keeping pace with it in the

career of improvement. Old vices of the administration
could be more or less eradicated under the eye of a
well-meaning sovereign and an enlightened ministry,
with the vigilance of foreign representatives to watch
over their efforts, whether it be to assist or to expose
weakness.   Some little advance in the same direction
may doubtless have been made also in the management of provincial affairs, but it is far from being such
as could meet the expectations of those who believed in
the regeneration of the Ottoman Empire.   I consider
the origin of their disappointment to lie in the facts,
that the provinces were judged by the capital, that
their capability to receive reforms was overrated, and
that the reforms attempted were not compatible with
their actual condition.

LETTER XIV.

Damascus: January 20, 1860.

I HAVE been here about three weeks, having come
leisurely in eight days by Hama and Homs. This
is certainly a charming place in winter, when it is not
too hot for the enjoyment of long rides over its richly
wooded plain, or on the banks of the Barrada, whose
clear waters ripple pleasantly on their pebbly bed, so
different from the muddy rivers I have as yet seen in
Syria. The spot of St. Paul's conversion is shown to
travellers as that now occupied by a small Protestant
cemetery, but I suppose it has no better title to acceptance as such than other fanciful sites of historical and
sacred events in Palestine. One of the resorts of pilgrims is the village of Abraham, which I too visited of
course, but without much faith in its identity. Abraham
became king of Damascus, if one may believe the Damascene historian Nicolaüs, on whose authority rests the
claim of the village; as king, he would scarcely have
more connection with one village than another, and the
town existed at the time of his migration this way from
Haran to Hebron, if Josephus be not in error in attri-

buting its foundation to Uz, the son of Aram and
grandson of Shem. However all this may be, it is
certainly one of the most ancient cities in the world.
Its population is now about a hundred and ten thousand, of whom fourteen thousand are Christians. The
latter inhabit the quarter in which the street called
'straight' of the Acts of the Apostles may still be recognised, as well as the part of the town-wall where St.
Paul was let down from a window; such features of
the place being not unlikely to retain their outward
appearance and traditional record. The houses of the
wealthy inhabitants, whether Mussulmans, Christians,
or Jews, are exceedingly spacious and cool, and covered
with lavish decoration in oriental taste.

I have seen Ahmed and Tahir Pashas several times,
the Governor-General and the Military Commandant.
After the fate of the Ansairi prisoners, whom I mentioned in my letter from Hama, I can scarcely refrain
from strong language about those functionaries. The
prisoners were avowedly in no way implicated in the
affair of Ismael Khair Bey, itself an abominable affair
on the part of the Pashas, but they have nevertheless
been kept here in gaol for upwards of a year, and finally
they were all publicly executed last week. Ahmed
Pasha especially was quite determined to have them
put to death.

I find here two sources of alarm for the tranquillity
of Syria, the animosity of the feuds of Lebanon, and
the pride of national achievements. The Moslems of
Damascus brood sullenly over their fallen greatness,

There are men amongst them, learned in Arab history, who maintain an irritating sense of their past glory. The Druzes come here frequently from the mountain, and from their district in the Hauran, to seek the patronage of high Turkish authorities. The Christians, chiefly Maronites, oppose countermines to every mine undertaken against them, and find foreign agents willing to encourage them, and foment the discord existing between the different sects. Damascus is thus not only one of the hotbeds of strife amongst the different branches of the modern Arab race, but is also the centre of a dangerous recalling to memory of its ancient renown under the Ommiad Khalifa.

From the days of Kahtan Ibn A'bir, as the Arabs call Joktan, son of Eber, of the books of Genesis and Chronicles, and their two other progenitors, Ishmael, who, they believe, married one of his descendants, and Esau, to the seventh century of our era, when Mahomet organised them as a nation, the Arabs seem to have been in the same divided and pastoral state in which they are now to be found in the Syrian desert. One of the laws of their ancient Nabatean confederation, formed at the time of Alexander's invasion of Asia, made it a capital crime to sow corn, build a house, or plant a tree, for they thought man prone to sacrifice his liberty to preserve immovable property. They were then strong enough to defy the Greek power of Antigonus and Demetrius, the Ptolemies and the Seleucidæ, as later they successfully resisted the attempts of Pompey to bring them under the Roman yoke.

Towards the middle of the fourth century, they were
so far under the influence of ideas of progress, that
the Gassanide tribe was converted to Christianity in a
body, and retained their creed until the year 637, when
they were subjugated by the growing power of the
Mussulman system, and their sheikh Jabala became a
renegade with all his followers. When the prophet of
Islam and his immediate successors raised the Arabs to
the dignity of a race of conquerors in the world's history, they extended their frontiers to the Indus on the
east and Caucasus on the north in Asia, to the Great
Desert on the south and the Atlantic on the west in
Africa, and to the Pyrenees in Europe. These vast
dominions, more comprehensive than those of Alexander
the Great, and nearly equal to the Roman Empire, had
their first capital at Damascus. The wealth of the
khalifs ruling over them was so great that Zobeideh,
the wife of Harun al Rashid, is described as wearing
robes of silk lined with ermine and slippers embroidered
with pearls, while her dishes and drinking cups were
of massive gold studded with precious stones; and
Almamun had thirty-eight thousand pieces of tapestry
in his palace, and twenty-two thousand Persian carpets,
while he presented a Greek ambassador with a tree of
pure gold bearing enormous pearls as fruit. In arts
and sciences they surpassed Europe. Thus, amongst
the offerings brought by the ambassador of Harun al
Rashid to Charlemagne, who was in vain struggling to
raise his subjects from their state of barbarism, was a
watch manufactured at Racca on the Euphrates, which

called forth the admiration of the French court, where
nothing so wonderful had ever been seen. Painting
and sculpture, being contrary to the doctrines of the
Coran, were neglected, but poetry, music, architecture,
astronomy, and mathematics, were highly cultivated
by the Arabs, and in a manner above all parallel with
other nations of the time. Military ardour had given
place to the love of letters. The ancient literature of
the Greeks was studied at Damascus, Bagdad, Cairo,
Racca, Ispahan, Morocco, and Toledo. The works of
their historians and philosophers were translated into
Arabic, through which language alone some of them
were preserved before the recovery of the original
text. Grammar became a science amongst the Arabs,
and they invented the most perfect system in existence. Libraries and colleges were instituted; in one
of the latter six thousand students were maintained
gratuitously. Observatories, furnished with gigantic
instruments, arose. Laboratories were devoted to che-
mical experiments. Hospitals offered a field for medical
study. The Arabs, who are called by Humboldt the
real founders of the physical sciences, were thus the
only guardians of civilisation in the middle ages when
barbarian invaders from the north had darkened their
light in Europe. The first centuries of the Hegira were
taken up with triumphant wars; when Charles Martel
checked further conquest, and the Ommiad Khalifs had
fallen, the era of intellectual culture commenced; it
lasted until the middle of the fifteenth century after
Christ, when we received the rays of knowledge which

had set on the East. Darkness fell on Asia, and enlightenment dawned in Europe. After their glorious
series of military successes under the Ommiad Khalifs
of Damascus and Cordova, and after their mental superiority under the Abbasside and Fatimite Khalifs of
Bagdad and Egypt, the Arabs were destined to see
their vast empire dismembered by the Tartar and Mongolian invaders, who founded new states on its ruins,
now concentrated in the Ottoman Empire, falling in
its turn. Such are the lessons taught, and reminiscences vaunted, by the learned sheikhs of Damascus,
amongst whom is Abd-el-Kader, the Algerian prisoner
of France, since pensioned by her and allowed to reside
in this city.

The other danger impending at Damascus—that which
may arise from the Druze and Maronite controversy—
has been grossly misrepresented as regards its origin
and respective rights. In the year of the Hegira 386,
Abu Ali el Hakim, the sixth of the Fatimite Khalifs,
not the third as has been erroneously stated, ascended
the throne of Egypt at the early age of eleven. By
cursing publicly in the mosques his predecessors the
companions of Mahomet, forcing Christians and Jews
to become Mussulmans, then insisting on their resuming
their former faith, he soon established a name for madness. In the East, madness is tantamount to inspira-
tion. Hakim was thus a prophet. He declared himself
a god. All did not believe in him, however, and, while
holding converse with angels, he was suddenly assailed
and put to death. His followers were dispersed.

Hunted down by the true believers, many of them found their way into Syria, and, seeking safety from persecution, united to make a stand against their enemies by occupying the least accessible heights of Mount Lebanon. From them are descended the Druzes. They took their name from Mohammed Ibn Ismael el Dorazi, or Durzi, or Druzi. This man was the author of a book to prove the divinity of Hakim, and the believers in the book received the surname of its writer.

Towards the close of the sixth century of the Christian era, the small port of Jebail, the ancient Byblos, situated between Beyrout and Tripoli, was inhabited by a population addicted to predatory practices. A monk from the banks of the Orontes, named John Maro, visited them in the hope of reclaiming them from those vices, and making good Christians of them. In this he seems to have failed, but he remained with them as their bishop. John Maro was a man of genius. He acquired such influence and respect all over Syria, that his people, who were called Maronites after him, were able to circumvent all endeavours to bring them into submission to the constituted authorities of the country, and even to give an asylum to refugees from other districts. Outlaws, brigands, rebels, flocked to the growing sect, which thus became more powerful without becoming less disorderly. Like other proscribed persons before them, the Druzes were well received by the Maronites. The two tribes lived together in peace, and were united in all the wars that

swept over Syria; retaining thus their common independence, and descending from their rugged mountains
only to plunder the surrounding country.

Sultan Amurath III., towards the end of the six-
teenth century, being moved by complaints from the
inhabitants of Damascus, Sidon, Beyrout, and Tripoli,
forced their last retreats; and they were then first reduced
to obedience and the payment of tribute. A governor
was appointed, but, as was the case in all the Turkish
provinces at that time, he was allowed to rule without control. One of his successors became celebrated
in the beginning of the seventeenth century under
the name of Fakir ed Din. He was a Druze. The
state of the empire then enabled an ambitious and
resolute man to extend his power; and this governor
encroached on that of the governors of Damascus,
Tripoli, and Sidon. An expedition was prepared to
overthrow him, but the wily Druze conceived a singular
plan of defence. He went to Europe, declared himself a descendant of Godfrey of Bouillon, and represented the Druzes to have originated in the retreat of
some crusaders to Mount Lebanon when Saladin took
Jerusalem, and asserted that their name was derived
from that of the principal knight amongst them, the
Count of Dreux. The fable took, and interest was
made in his favour. He returned to his government,
a greater man than he went from it, for it was made to
include the cities on the coast. But his tyranny and
depredations were such that he was again attacked.
After a long and obstinate resistance to Sultan Amu-

rath IV., he was taken and put to death at Constantinople. Then came the governors of the Shehab family,
who were Mussulmans from Mecca, and claimed kindred with the Prophet. At the time when the Turkish
provinces were farmed out to speculators who sublet
districts to local chiefs, and before the system of
centralisation was adopted in the last reign, Beshir
Shehab became the first of that line of governors of
Mount Lebanon through a pecuniary arrangement of
this kind. He was a man of some ability, and possessed
of much determination. Inflamed by ambition, he bethought him of supplanting his immediate superior,
Abdulla Pasha of Acre, from whom he had received
his appointment. Beshir Jumblat, the principal Druze,
was his abettor in this insurrection. A battle was
fought near Sidon, and the rebels were defeated.
Shehab escaped to Egypt; Jumblat to the desert,
where the Bedaween made him a prisoner, and gave
him up to Abdulla Pasha. A man of rare intellect
ruled in Egypt, Mehemed Ali, who had raised himself
from the ranks of the Albanian irregular troops to a
position almost equal to that of the Sultan, and was
then inaugurating a policy of reform superior to the
feeble efforts of his sovereign towards a similar end.
Mehemed Ali aspired at the revival of an Arab throne.
He received the refugee with eager hopes of making
him of use to his great design. They soon came to
an understanding, in pursuance of which Mehemed Ali
negotiated a peace between his new confederate and
Abdulla Pasha, by casting all blame for the past on

Jumblat. The latter was accordingly strangled in
prison, and the Emir Beshir Shehab returned to the
government of Mount Lebanon, which he held from
the Porte on the recommendation of the Governor-
General of Acre. The attack on Syria by Mehemed
Ali, in 1831, brought thirty thousand men under the
best general of the East, his adopted son Ibrahim, to
besiege Acre. Abdulla Pasha defended his post for
six months, and surrendered. The Emir Beshir was
active in the cause of his Egyptian patron, from
whom, when victorious, he hoped to obtain the supreme
government of Syria. France encouraged the rebellious vassal, Mehemed Ali, in his attempt to wrest a
province from his sovereign ; and the Maronites, to
gain support abroad, espoused the same cause. This
combination of interests opened a new vista of ambition to the time-serving Emir, who declared himself
a Christian for the double purpose of attaching the
Maronites to his fortunes, and of placing himself with
them under the protection of a great European power.
The battle of Konia was fought, and lost by the Sultan.
Syria was annexed to Egypt. During nine years
Ibrahim Pasha governed this country, and common
justice obliges even the enemies of his usurpation to
admit that it derived great material advantages from
this period of its history. The Emir Beshir, meanwhile, had been deceived by Mehemed Ali, who declined to reward the traitor, though he accepted the
benefits of the treachery. Mount Lebanon became
again disturbed, through the machinations of its dis-

appointed governor. Ibrahim suppressed the revolt
easily enough, but in a way which called the attention
of Europe to his system of administration of public
affairs in Syria, which was successful, but ferocious.
A conference was held in London in 1840; Syria was
signed back to the Sultan; the government of Egypt
was made hereditary in the family of Mehemed Ali
under the mere suzeraineté of the Porte. When this
arrangement was opposed in its execution, Beyrout,
Sidon, and Acre were taken by the British fleet with
a few Austrian and Turkish vessels, and the Egyptians
were driven out of Syria. The Emir Beshir was
removed to Malta, whence he proceeded to Constantinople, and there died.

Beshir Kassem, his nephew, was appointed by the
Porte governor of Mount Lebanon. He was a quiet,
good sort of man, without energy as without ambition,
but possessing a sense of justice. Some Druzes quar-
relled with some Maronites; some villages were burnt.
A Turkish pasha was sent to take the thing in hand.
He soon found out that it would be impossible to get
the Druzes to submit to the authority of a family
whose founder, the Emir Beshir Shehab, had betrayed
and caused the violent and ignominious death of their
most revered chief, Beshir Jumblat. Omer Pasha, the
future commander-in-chief of the Turkish army on the
Danube and in the Crimea, was made governor over
both the Druzes and the Maronites. He was efficient
and popular. For a time the mountain enjoyed tranquillity. The cry of Maronite privileges was now

raised for the first time. The right to choose their own
governor of their own religion was claimed for them.
The Porte tried in vain to reason with the foreign
cabinets enouncing this novel idea, but was obliged
to yield; faintly murmuring that the Sultan had never
conferred any privileges whatsoever on the Maronites,
and that, if he had not, no one else could.   France
wanted a Shehab; persisted even in representing that
family as Christian, and as elected governors by the
Maronites; whereas it was notorious that they were
Moslems, had then feigned conversion, and reassumed
Mahometanism after the fall of the Emir Beshir, though
occasionally again pretending to be Christians when it
suited their purpose; and anyone who looks into the
case will see that they were first raised to power by
the Pasha of Acre, and next by the Pasha of Egypt.
Prince Metternich, not fully cognisant of the subject
in all its bearings, proposed a middle course, out of
which, when adopted, have grown all the evils of the
last twenty years on Mount Lebanon.   Two adminis-
trations were formed, one for the Druzes, and the other
for the Maronites, with Turkish garrisons in the large
villages, but without any authority vested in their
commanders—divided government and divided responsibility resolving themselves as usual into no government and no responsibility. The Maronites and Druzes,
let it be remembered, do not everywhere occupy separate districts, but form in many places a mixed population.   The choice of persons was also curious.   The
Maronite governor, the Emir Haydar, was of a Druze

family converted to Christianity, or feigning conversion; and the Druze governor, Ahmed Roslan, did not belong at all to the influential classes, which are confined to the Jumblatieh and the Wezbekieh, both of those powerful clans being thus opposed to his authority. After a long continuance of disorders arising from the defects of the arrangement, the Emir Haydar died. This happened during the Crimean war, when Turkey was under great obligations to Europe, and could not but adopt the suggestion of an ally in arms. France took advantage of that circumstance to obtain the nomination of an adherent of her own. The Emir Beshir Ahmed, whose antecedents were not his best recommendation, was brought forward. He had changed his religion several times, and no one knew when he was Maronite, Druze, or Mussulman. Complete anarchy prevailed during his administration. Pillage and murder were of daily occurrence. Three years ago, this deplorable state of matters came to a head in a general insurrection of the Maronites. The Emir Beshir Ahmed was deposed. Athanasius Shaïn took his place. Foreign patronage was openly avowed. The governor himself hoisted the French flag, declaring Mount Lebanon a province of France. Robbery and carnage reigned over the country. Women were horribly ill-treated, and then massacred, by the Maronites; amongst whom were the wife and two daughters of Diab Kassem, whose bodies were left, by order of Shaïn, exposed for several days on a public road without any covering, and finally dragged to the foot of an old

wall, which was thrown down upon them. Last year,
a quarrel about a sheep that had strayed caused a fight
between the Maronites and the Druzes, ending in the
burning of the village of Beit Mari where it commenced. The Maronites were the aggressors. Since
then, there has been no renewal of conflicts, but people
think that the priests of the Maronite Church are
forming an extensive conspiracy, and distributing arms
and ammunition for a future war of extermination
against the Druzes.

These are the leading facts of the case, which I have
carefully verified on the spot. How far they are consistent with the version accepted in Europe is another
matter.

LETTER XV.

Jerusalem: February 6, 1860.

ON leaving Damascus, we kept far to the east of the usual route by Cesarea Philippi, and entered the ancient Ituræa, formerly a country of the greatest possible fertility, now a naked desert, lying between the lofty Hermon and the low range of hills traversing that part of Bashan which received the name of Batanæa after the Captivity. Ituræa is now called Yedoor, bringing the name nearer to that of its first settler, Jetur, the son of Ishmael. We crossed the river Pharpar, and slept at Kesweh, a wretched village on the site apparently of one of the ancient towns in the tetrarchy of Philip, I know not which. Rising early, I strolled about, and questioned the villagers on their condition. It is the same as I have always found on the margin of the desert. This illustration of it, however, is almost more remarkable than any other can be. A district of rich soil, which possessed a hundred villages twenty years ago, now tenanted by only a few lingering peasants, destined soon to follow their kindred to the hills ranging

along the seaboard, driven westwards by the Bedaween. Mounting our horses, we took a still more
easterly course, which brought us to the Leja, the ancient Trachonitis, and still more ancient Argob. This
is the stronghold of the Druzes of the Hauran when
they rebel against the government, for no troops can
follow them through the intricacies of its wonderful
formation of basalt cropping up, as far as the eye can
reach, in rugged boulders of fantastic shape from ten to
twenty feet above the plain, and so thickset that there
is not anywhere a path of fifty yards without obstacles
difficult even to climb and scramble over. The land
around this singular region is splendid, and may have
well sufficed to support the many small towns and villages whose ruins occupy its impregnable recesses. We
visited one of them called Musmeih, the ancient Phæno,
and found fine architectural remains of low Greek art,
with many inscriptions in that language, highly ornamented temples almost entire, well-paved streets, houses
still roofed with great slabs of stone, and their massive
doors of single blocks of basalt swinging on their pi-
vots, ready to be inhabited. Within sight were many
such fallen cities, with thousands of acres of fine arable
land spread around the Leja, showing tracks of water-
courses for irrigation, and now yielding only pasture
for the sheep and camels of the Bedaween. Returning
westwards to seek shelter for the night, we came to a
Druze village called Jebab, where we were received
with enthusiasm as soon as it was known that we were
English, and frequently assured by the assembled vil-

lagers, as we passed our evening round a blazing fire,
that there is no place in the world like England.

Early dawn found us again in the saddle, and following the line of the great Moslem pilgrimage through
the ancient district of Gaulanitis, now Jaulan, to Esh-
miskin, one of its stations, where we slept. The traffic
created by the annual passage of thousands of pilgrims
has made a prosperous place of that and many others
of their halting-places, where enormous profits are
realised on what is sold to them. Next day we passed
into Auranitis, the Hauran of proverbial fertility, but
altogether uncultivated. Passing Edrei, one of the
capitals of Bashan, whose ruins are now scarcely dis-
tinguishable, we reached the fortified village of Mezarib,
identified by some topographers with Ashtaroth Karnaim. If, as is said, the epithet of the Horned applies
to two peaks, it must be sought elsewhere, for there
are none such at Mezarib; but the theory of attributing
the horns to the moon, whose worship was practised at
the place, seems preferable. It has all the appearance
of having been an important place, and, if it was not
Ashtaroth Karnaim, there is no other recorded city
near the spot. A castle, built three centuries and a
half ago by Sultan Selim I. for the accommoda-
tion and protection of the pilgrims, is the only considerable edifice now standing at this once renowned
shrine of the Syrian Venus. There is a small lake,
containing an island covered with ruins, perhaps of her
temple; and a stream issuing from it, and flowing
westwards, is now called Yarmuk, formerly Hieromax,

one of the tributaries of the Jordan. We struck off
due south over mountains clothed with the oaks of
Bashan, and a long day brought us to Hawara, an
Arab village plunged in the utmost destitution by a
recent attack of Bedaween. The huts were absolutely
empty, even their doors and shutters gone, and the inhabitants had neither clothes enough to keep them
from suffering greatly from the bitter cold of the
nights, nor food to eat, in so far as we could ascertain
by questioning them. They told us that twenty-five
villages, of which theirs was one, had thus been plundered, a few days before we came, by a single incursion
of Sheikh Mehemed Doohi with a couple of thousand
Weled Ali and Beni Sachar horsemen.   .

We had an agreeable ride next day through the
forest of Ephraim. Why it was called by the name of a
tribe whose lot was on the other side of the Jordan, is
more than I have been able to comprehend. It is a
picturesque hilly country, covered with noble timber.
Joab's military skill in manœuvring Absalom into it, is
fully illustrated by the thickness of the wood and the
ruggedness of the ground. By almost any one of the great
oaks, a fugitive might be knocked from his horse, and
left on the low branches, which in many places give no
passage of any height between two trees. The evening
found us at Soof, where Arabs live in huts in winter,
and under tents in summer, on the produce of numerous
flocks of goats. Being the only site of an ancient town
we saw in that region, and having all the appearance of
former greatness, while the track we had followed was

evidently the main artery of an almost impenetrable
district, and would not probably avoid any other place
of past importance, the thought struck me that Soof
might be Mahanaim, which has not yet been identified.
However this may be, we had no reason to carry away
an agreeable impression of it, for we passed a wretched
night, pestered for money by several hundred Arabs,
showing an unmistakably Jewish cast of features, as
well as instincts.   Before leaving next morning, the
controversy became a scuffle.   A captain and two
sergeants of the Sultan's regular cavalry had been sent
with us by Ahmed Pasha of Damascus, but, on the
proposal being made to them to draw their swords and
clear a way for us out of the screaming mob, they
evinced no sympathy for the *ultima ratio regum*, and
we were obliged to purchase, at an exorbitant price, the
freedom of the Sultan's highway.   A couple of hours
of descent from the wooded mountains of Ephraim, arrayed before us a spectacle capable of making us look
kindly even on a party of rascally Arabs, who had escorted us from Soof to give a colour to their extortion.
We were soon surrounded by the gorgeous remains of
Gerasa.   While rambling, amazed and delighted, along
the great portico a mile in length, at one end the circular forum adorned with columns, at the other the
fine temple of the sun, with the two theatres and other
massive edifices, scarcely injured by time and earthquakes, studding the large area of the town, I could
not repress the reflection that, if the Decapolis reared
such cities under the pagan government of the Anto-

nines, after Vespasian had subjugated it, what is to be
said of the Mussulman government of the Sultans,
under which they have been mere ruins in a desert
during so many centuries?

When we moved on from Gerasa, our path led us
down the right bank of the river Jabbok, enclosed in a
narrow and very deep ravine. We came to a small
village called Burmeh, occupying the site of an ancient fortified town, possibly another candidate for the
honours of Mahanaim. This was more like the description of Peniel, where Jacob wrestled with the
angel, and more likely than Soof to have an opportunity
of offending Gideon, by refusing help to his troops in
pursuit of the Midianites. That Burmeh was Mahanaim
is, I think, a theory worthy of the consideration of com-
petent judges. We crossed the clear stream of the
Jabbok, probably by the same ford which Jacob's family
and flocks traversed when he sent them to meet Esau,
for this seemed to be the natural line of route towards
the south. Passing thus from the territory of Og, king
of Bashan, to that of Sihon, king of the Amorites, we
climbed a high and steep mountain, on which at nightfall we came to a camp of the Salhaan tribe of Bedaween. The Sheikh seemed much surprised to see us,
but his reception was not unkind. When seated together
in his tent, he addressed a number of questions to us
with regard to our having penetrated unannounced into
that part of the country ; and, finally, having apparently
abandoned the attempt to understand how we came to
be there, he rose, mounted his mare, and disappeared

in the darkness around us. The position was high, the
winter was severe, and, one whole side of the tent
being open, we spent rather an airy night. As the
sun, rising over the eastern heights, began to dispel the
chilly gloom in which we were steeped, our host was
to be seen riding down the face of the hill towards us,
accompanied by three or four Bedaween horsemen.
They came straight to the tent in which we were
sitting, and, dismounting, took their places beside us.
After the usual salutations, we were emphatically told
that the principal figure, a sulky-looking Arab in a red
embroidered cloak, was Goblan, the great sheikh of all
the Salhaan. Repressing the impulse to reply that we had
never said he was n't, we made some desultory remark
about the pleasure of his acquaintance. He then enquired of us whether we were aware that no one could
pass those mountains without his permission, and quoted
precedents to prove his postulate. We answered that
it might all be very true, but that we had come up one
side of the mountains, and must go down the other.
Goblan did not appreciate our mode of reasoning, said
it was useless wasting time in conversation, and invited
us civilly enough to mount and follow him. We rode
for a couple of hours, over beautifully wooded hills, to
a sheltered spot, where we found the ruins of a walled
city. In an open space stood the tents of Goblan and
his immediate retinue, and, alighting, we entered the
principal one. On enquiring, we were told that the
name of the place was Jilad, and that it had never before been visited by travellers. We had been led off

the usual road from Gerasa to Jerusalem, which passes
some ten miles farther west by the modern town of
Es Salt, which has been thought to represent Ramoth
Gilead. It appears more natural that the ancient strong
place, still bearing the name of Jilad, and displaying in
perfection the character of Ramoth heights, to complete
the title, should be the real site; while Es Salt may
be, as it was once supposed to be, Machærus, where
John the Baptist was beheaded.   While I was deep in
the study of our map, Bible in hand, Goblan interrupted
me by broaching another subject of some delicacy. He
had given, he said, hospitable orders, fatal to the arrival at maturity of a lamb cropping the grass before
the tent, but, before the sacrifice was performed, and a
bond of amity thereby concluded between us, we must
distinctly understand each other.   Being invited to
proceed, he told us we were going to rest an hour, then
regale ourselves on the lamb, take a dozen of his best
horsemen as a guard as far as the Jordan, and give
him the honour of showing us the way himself; but
. . . . . But what ? Hitherto he had conducted the
negotiation with all the polish and ability of an accom-
plished diplomatist.   Now his manner descended to the
coarse laconism of a garotting ticket-of-leave man, and
he told us simply to hand over our money. Knowing
the exact amount of authority vested in the Sultan's
dragoons, and feeling that we were entirely in the
power of the Sheikh, we soon made up our minds to
give the money and proceed on our journey. We took
an unprofitable satisfaction, however, in refusing the

offer of coffee, and in saving the life of the lamb. We
mounted, and, escorted by Goblan and his Arabs,
whether we would or not, we scaled the remaining
heights of Gilead. The descent into the valley of the
Jordan, which wound its way like a silver thread to
the distant molten-lead-like surface of the Dead Sea,
encased in the rugged cliffs of Moab, was magnificent
as we crept along the precipitous brows of the mountain, then plunged into deep ravines encumbered by
huge masses of rock. We had little intercourse with
our escort, whose company, after all, may not have been
quite unavailing, for we saw some wild-looking Bedaween on the way, who glanced wistfully as we passed
with Goblan's people. When we were nearing the
plain, and the daylight was waning fast, the Sheikh
pulled up, and rode alongside of us. He remarked
that we must naturally be much pleased with his
guidance over the mountains and guardianship of our
personal safety. The remark did not elicit any very
lively expression of enthusiasm on our part. That
seemed to be a good revolver in our belt—a very good
tabanja. We would surely give him a tabanja for the
trouble he had taken. No answer having been vouch-
safed, Goblan rode on. After another mile or two, he
reined in again, and the word tabanja was suggestively
muttered from beneath his cloak. Still no answer;
this was more than Salhaan patience could brook. A
few hurried words to his followers, and half a dozen
lances crossed our path. The Turkish captain expos-
tulated mildly. Goblan told him he would eat six

dragoons any morning for his breakfast, and the captain
subsided.   There we stood a full half-hour, on a fine
night in the valley of the Jordan, with Anglo-Saxon
obstinacy listening to the everlasting tabanja.   The
Arabs would not attack us now, for we were well
mounted and armed, and the difference of respective
numerical strength was not so great as in the camp.
At last the lances were raised with a threat that justice
would be done at Jericho.   We pushed on rapidly
through the rich tropical vegetation of the plain, here
thirteen hundred feet below the level of the Mediterranean; reached Bethabara, and forded the Jordan,
whose waters reached our saddle-bows, at the spot
where Christ was baptised by John.   After another
hour's riding, we found ourselves trying to sleep in a
filthy mud hut at Jericho, with the faint echo of tabanja
meeting our ears from the opposite side of the fire,
where the disconsolate Goblan sat sighing over the
coveted object.   I dropped asleep, and, when I awoke
in the morning, he was gone.

When our horses were being prepared, we walked
through the miserable assemblage of hovels called
Jericho, with a single square tower bearing the spurious
title of the house of Zaccheus.   The ancient city stood
more than a mile from the spot, as indicated by an extensive field of mounds.   The road to Jerusalem is one
long ascent over a dreary region supposed to be the
scene of our Lord's fasting and temptation.   To one
part of it is assigned the charitable act of the good
Samaritan.   Robbers are said still to lie occasionally

concealed by the roadside; and our captain and sergeants,
unmindful now of Soof and Goblan, made a gallant
display of chivalry, charging on in front, firing off their
carbines, and swearing they had put to flight I know
not how many men in buckram suits and Kendal green.
Late in the afternoon we came to Bethany, and, turning the flank of the Mount of Olives, suddenly opened
out the striking panorama of the City of David—finer
by far from the east than that which hails the pilgrim's
approach by the ordinary road from Jaffa. Crossing
the Valley of Jehoshaphat with its many tombs, we entered the Gate of St. Stephen, and soon suffered the
bathos of alighting at the door of a respectable hotel.

I have now been a week at Jerusalem, going the
round of the sights, some of absorbing interest, others
of revolting absurdity. The first was, of course, the
Holy Sepulchre, then King David's tomb, the Mount
of Olives and the Chapel of the Ascension, Gethsemane,
the village of Emmaus, and finally Bethlehem. They
are all too well known from books for me to attempt
description. It was far from my purpose, in writing
about this country, to tread feebly in the footsteps
of the many learned authors on it, but merely to give
my impression of its present state as a part of the
Turkish Empire. I cannot, however, pass over Jerusalem without saying how painful it was to me to
listen to the desecrating tales of guides at the sacred
shrines. The Church of the Holy Sepulchre is neces-
sarily of surpassing interest; but the doubt of the identity of the tomb—the flight of steps leading from it to

P

Calvary, which is also in the church, and the monkish
triviality with which every detail is pointed out—the
sockets of the three crosses—the rock riven by the earthquake during the crucifixion—the stone on which the
Lord's body was prepared for burial—that on which the
Empress Helen sat when she found the true cross —
finishing off with the sword of Godfrey of Bouillon—and
all this seen under a guard of Turkish policemen—drive
reverence from the mind most bent on simply believing
that Christ died there.   On Easter-eve it is still worse,
I am told.   The Greeks and Armenians assert that fire
descends miraculously from heaven to light the lustres
and tapers round the Holy Sepulchre, as the altar was
burnt at the prayer of Elijah in the First Book of
Kings.   Strange antics are then performed, ludicrous
were they not profane.   People rush wildly shouting
round the tomb; and so mad is the frenzy excited, that
persons have even recently been trampled to death in
these superstitious orgies when the struggle to light
tapers at the holy flame is raging.   Formerly a white
pigeon was thrown from the cupola into the sanctuary,
to represent the descent of the Holy Ghost; but this
gross aggravation is happily now discontinued.   And
we expect Christianity to be respected by Mussulmans
who witness such degrading mummeries; for there are
always some Turks in the church to guard it, and on
great festivals there are large bodies of soldiers and
police, to tell the tale of Christian inferiority to the
purity of their own form of worship and that of the
Jews.   The noble Mosque of Omar is very different in

its general effect. Impressed by its grave repose, one
rejoices to recognise the undoubted features of the
threshing-floor of Araunah, a bare rock unadorned with
priestly gewgaws, and precisely in the same state in
which it was when Abraham bound Isaac on the altar he
had erected on it—when Melchizedek or Shem (if they
were really the same person) offered bread and wine to
Abraham on it, receiving a tithe of his spoil—when the
angel stood there to threaten Jerusalem with pestilence,
and when David built his altar on it. Then this was
the court of the Temple of Solomon, whose vaulted foundations I visited, while pilgrim Jews from Germany
and Poland wept outside, in all simple grief for its fall,
at the Place of Wailing. It is truly a grand monu-
ment, eclipsing, both as a Jewish temple and as a
mosque of Islam, the tawdry finery of the Christian
Church of the Holy Sepulchre. One can well comprehend the enthusiasm of Saladin when he said, as
recorded by the historian Emad ed Din, that it was
the abode of a prophet, the resting-place of saints, the
goal of pilgrimage of angels, the future scene of the
general resurrection and judgment, the spotless and
beautiful pavement whence Mahomet ascended to heaven, and whence the lightning flashed on that night of
mystery, illuminating every point of the universe.

One cannot stay a day at Jerusalem without hearing more than one cares to hear of the squabbles of
the rival churches. They are, it is true, paltry and
spiteful, but, under them, political interests move the
world. Never were such important results so little

understood in their primary causes and pretexts.
People say that questions of church keys are unworthy
of serious notice: they would be so, were they not
fraught with consequences whose gravity cannot easily
be estimated in more enlightened and rational countries.
In Turkey, preponderance of influence confers material
as well as political advantages on the foreign power possessing it. Foreign influence in Turkey rests chiefly
on questions of religion. Creed and nationality are
here convertible terms. A native is asked if he is an
Arab, and replies that he is a Latin or a Greek.
Though of the Armenian nation, he will call himself a
Catholic, not an Armenian, if he belong to the sect
acknowledging the supremacy of the Pope. Jerusalem
is the first battle-field, Constantinople being the second,
of religious rivalries, which take the place, and play
the part, of the patriotic nationalities of Europe. The
Greek and Romish Churches, cheered on by the voice
of temporal policy, and marshalled under their respective patrons, Russia and France, fight out their unholy
struggle for the mastery on this holy ground: when
victory is declared on one side or the other, the case
goes to Constantinople, and may culminate in a European war. England has a church and a bishop at
Jerusalem; but mark the difference: they preach only
on the subject of religion, supply the population with
translated Scriptures, and found schools for the education of their children. To England the question,
whether the right of Rome and France to the keys of
the Holy Sepulchre confided to Charlemagne as the

champion of Catholicism, or that of Constantinople
and Russia by the confirmation of Khalif Omar, is
the more valid right, is interesting only in the consequences of the controversy.   England does not seek to
obtain in the East that species of influence on which
some other countries found their hopes of advantage, if
evil befall the Turks.   She requires only to watch and
to understand the various phases of the controversy, in
order that she may not be taken by surprise when it
produces great practical results.   The position of England as the first of liberal and commercial states suffices
her, and she will probably find, as such, more sympathy
in an Eastern crisis than those who build upon the sand
of time-serving priestly attachment.

When the seat of the Roman Empire was trans-
ferred to Byzantium, a political rivalry arose between
the two capitals; both fell, and their rivalry became
ecclesiastical instead of political.   Photius, in his ambition to become a Byzantine pope, laid the train of
scandals in Christendom.   Certain savages, meanwhile,
appeared in the Bosphorus, paddling canoes of hol-
lowed trees, clothed in the skins of wild beasts, and
worshipping cruel gods to whom they offered human
sacrifices.   Some of these barbarians, prostrate before
Byzantine civilisation, became converts to Christianity,
and, returning to their northern steppes, were accompanied by a Greek priest.   Russia, in her infancy,
thus received the so-called Orthodox Christian Faith !
When her full growth was attained, and the rude
vigour of her age as a state gave her the strength

inherent in that period of national life, she turned to
her parent Church, now decrepid in its senility, and
gave it protection and support.

When two centuries of distant warfare had worn out
the crusading spirit, there remained open to European
pilgrims at Jerusalem only the hospitals of St. John
and St. Lazarus. After the withdrawal of the knights
in charge of these receptacles of foreign Christians to
Rhodes, and thence to Malta, the Minor friars, imitating
their founder, St. Francis of Assisi, who had braved
the Soldan Malek Kamel at Damietta, raised a monastery at Jerusalem for the protection of pious strangers
visiting the tomb of Jesus. The Franciscans thus
became the representatives of Catholicism in Syria,
and, being chiefly French, the protection of that denomination devolved on France.

Officially, the protectorate of France first appeared
in the treaty concluded between Francis I. and the
great Sultan Suleyman II. That of Russia commenced
a century and a half later, when the Czar Fedor III.
made peace with the Turks after driving them from the
banks of the Dniester, and opening the Black Sea to his
incipient trade. With how much courtesy and mode-
ration France has exercised this function may be in-
ferred from the facts that one of her ambassadors, M. de
Marcheville, was sent out of the country, and a native
dragoman of her embassy was impaled, by Sultan
Amurath IV., for their imperious insistance. The
arrogance of Russia did not appear on the political
stage of the East before the decline of the Ottoman

power. The treaty of Carlowicz first announced that
the period of Turkish conquest was at an end; that of
Passarowicz confirmed the fact. The military successes
of John Sobieski, the Duke of Lorraine, and Prince
Eugene, were followed up by the exploits of Roma-
noff and Suwarrow in the reign of Catherine II. The
treaty of Kainarjik was imposed by Russia. Then
came the wars of the present century: under Kaminski
and Kutusow, terminating in the treaty of Bucharest;
with the Emperor Nicholas in person, and Diebitsch,
resulting in the treaty of Adrianople; and, finally, the
officious aid given to the Sultan against the Pasha of
Egypt, producing the treaty of Hunkiar Skelessi; all
of which treaties struck repeated blows at the root of
the Turkish domination, and called into progressive
existence the disaffection and ambition of the Greek
Church in Turkey. Encouraged by unvarying good
fortune, the Emperor Nicholas sent Prince Mentschicoff
to clinch the nail now driven home, but a new antago-
nist took the field. As Russia was the champion of the
Greek Church, so was France of Roman Catholicism
in the East. England was dragged into the quarrel.
Russia, in her turn, saw her career of conquest closed—
for a time. The last phasis of the religious controversy
commenced at Jerusalem, ripened into war at Constantinople, and was concluded at Sebastopol.

This controversy forms the staple of the archives of
the French and Russian embassies at the Porte. The
Church of the Holy Sepulchre was built by the Greek
Empress Helen; the Saracens took it from the Greeks;

the crusaders from the Saracens; and the Saracens from the crusaders, to yield it to the Turks. The Chapel of the Grotto of the Nativity, and the Church of Bethlehem, also owe their origin to the piety of Helen; the crusaders repaired them; and it was in the latter church that King Baldwin was crowned. The Russo-Greek claim rests on the original erection of the buildings, and on the recognition of both the Saracens and the Turks; the Franco-Roman claim is founded on the period of occupation by the crusaders. When Jerusalem fell into the hands of Saladin, it was seriously contemplated to annihilate its attraction to foreigners by destroying the churches and ploughing up their sites. Had the purpose been carried out, real religion would have lost nothing, and the lever now moved by the enemies of Turkey would have had to seek another fulcrum. In 1808 the Church of the Holy Sepulchre was destroyed by fire: it was said that the tombs of Godfrey and Baldwin, under the rock of Calvary, had been rifled, and the heroic dust of the great crusading and Roman Catholic kings thrown to the winds, by malignant Greeks. When the Bourbons returned to Paris, they revived the French protectorate at Jerusalem, abandoned by the impiety of the great revolution, and endeavoured to come to an amicable arrangement with Russia. Baron Strogonoff and the Marquis de la Rivière, the respective plenipotentiaries, were on the point of concluding it when the ebullition of Greek ambition in 1821 broke off the negotiations, which were never resumed. The Roman Catholics have ever since been reduced to the possession of two small chapels in the Church of the Holy Sepulchre, of which they had previously held the whole. They have had to suffer many most indecorous insults on the part of the Greeks—such as the cutting of ropes by which lustres were suspended over the heads of priests while officiating, and the like. On Good Friday, in the year 1846, a carpet of the Greeks was moved by the Latins during mass; an unseemly altercation ensued, and a quarrel in which blood was shed before the very altar. In 1847, a silver star inlaid in a marble slab of the Chapel of the Nativity, was cut out and carried off by the Greeks, to resent the alleged insult conveyed by an inscription stating that it belonged to the Latins. A firman, ordering that it should be restored, was obtained from the Porte after a year of negotiation on the part of the papist embassies at Constantinople; but it was not put into execution. The dome of the Church of the Holy Sepulchre is now the bone of contention. Each sect having hitherto prevented the other from keeping it in repair, the whole of one side has fallen in, and the sacred tomb is open to wind and rain. The Sultan should himself repair it, and thus cut the Gordian knot which priestcraft and diplomacy have so elaborately tied.

LETTER XVI.

Jacob's Well—Shechem—Plain of Esdraelon—Nazareth—Acre
—Russian Steamers—Scala Tyriorum—Tyre— The Leontes—
Sarepta—Sidon- Said Bey Jumblat—Fakir ed Din's Cave—Lady
Hester Stanhope's Grave—Tomb of Jonah—Beyrout—Politics of
Mount Lebanon.

Beyrout: February 24, 1860.

WE have come here by land. From Jerusalem we
went to Nabloos by Gibeah, Bethel, and Shiloh,
passing a night at the romantic village of Ain Yebrood.
Of all these localities renowned in ancient Jewish history, the most interesting is the scene of Jonathan's
daring exploit against the Philistines, which minutely
corresponds with the description in the First Book of
Samuel. The country around is rocky and barren.
Here no Bedaween molest the villagers, and, in spite
of the difficulty of making the little soil there is productive, an air of well-being exists which one rarely
sees in Syria. The notables of the towns, and the
tax-gatherers, do not find enough to tempt their cu-
pidity, and the other great drain on cultivation does
not exist. Jacob's Well is a complete illusion. I expected more from it than from any other of the sacred
sites, and hoped to find it such as would fill up the picture drawn by imagination of our Saviour conversing
with the astonished woman of Samaria. But buildings

had been subsequently erected over it; they have fallen,
and no trace of a well remains. Shechem, with its
double rampart, Ebal and Gerizim, surpassed my ideal
of its beautiful situation in a well-wooded and watered
valley of gardens. We were received in the house of
the chief priest of the Samaritans, who told us that
there were now only a hundred and fifty persons of his
ancient faith in the world. This town, on the whole,
has a charm not often met with in this country, the
houses being well-built, the streets shady, and the population thriving. A Protestant community has been
formed under the auspices of our distinguished Bishop
of Jerusalem, and a school opened. The teacher, a
very intelligent young man, brought up by the establishment at Jerusalem, spoke hopefully of missionary
labour at Shechem. On leaving it, we had first an
agreeable hour's ride along its lovely vale; then rugged
hills to cross in a northerly direction; and another long
valley with several large villages on its steep sides to
follow past Dothan, where Joseph was feeding his
father's flocks when his brothers sold him to the Ish-
maelites on their way from Gilead to Egypt. There
were two places recommended for our halt, Jenneen
and Birkeen. The latter was a few miles farther on
our way, but then we should enjoy the comfort of a
better house, that of a worthy Greek priest. On this
information we decided to go there. The few additional miles let us in for a thorough drenching, as the
rain soon fell in torrents; and we passed the most
wretched night we had yet encountered in the cold

dirty hovel of the priest; while our Turkish captain,
who, not being with us when we left the straight road,
had gone to Jenneen, told us afterwards that he had
prepared an excellent Turkish house for our reception.
Our adviser, like all Christians in the East, had considered the hospitality of a Mussulman more to be
avoided than any other evil. We took about six hours
to ride across the great plain of Esdraelon, which presents the usual spectacle of unemployed fertility. The
depredations of the nomadic Arabs are there altogether
without a check, and they may be said to be perfectly
successful in their system of preventing cultivation in
order to enjoy pasture. A branch of the Hanadi tribe
is stationed at the north end of the plain under a sheikh
of the name of Akil, but he seems, like his kindred
near Aleppo, to be on too good terms with the Anezi
to be of any use to the government which pays him to
oppose them. The tribe commanding that part of the
country is called Ben-i-Sachar, which name struck me
as sounding very like Ben Issachar; and, the territory
of Issachar having been there, the association may not
be altogether fanciful. I do not know if the lost tribes
of Israel have ever been looked for in the Syrian
desert. The Bedaween often show decidedly Jewish
features, and I see no reason why some of the Israelites
should not have become nomadic, their Hebrew tongue
merging in its kindred Arabic. All the Jews of Syria,
moreover, speak Arabic amongst themselves; and only
their learned men know Hebrew as a dead language.
Advancing over the field of battle where the French

under Kleber, though victorious, thought it wise to
withdraw from a contest with the Arabs, we approached
the hills of Nazareth, with Mount Tabor and Mount
Carmel on our right and left. A long and winding
ascent with a sudden turn to the east brought us into
the secluded valley in which Jesus passed his childhood
and youth.

It seemed congenial to find the home of Mary in a
quiet little town, uninfested by professional showmen.
At Jerusalem sacred localities are paraded in crowded
streets by cicerones paid by the job, who hound one on
from tomb to shrine, from the shop of the Wandering
Jew, who told our Saviour to walk when staggering
under the cross in the street now called Via Dolorosa,
to the door of the house whence Veronica came to wipe
his brows, and the mark on the stone produced by the
fall of the cross when Simon the Cyrenian was made
to bear it, with a degree of technical skill and bustle
that jars on the impressions derived from the real scene
of his sufferings. Repose is the predominant character
of Nazareth. Shut out from the world by a girdle of
hills encircling its narrow plain, it lies concealed with
an air of that humility which Christ preached and
practised on earth. There are no thronged hotels, no
busy Frank shops—nothing but the homely simplicity
it presented twenty centuries ago. A Franciscan convent guards the chapel built over what was supposed
to be the house of Joseph and Mary; and the kind
monks receive travellers in a separate suite of rooms
on condition of each not taxing their hospitality for

more than three days. We should probably not have
stayed more than a night, had not heavy rain kept us
there the full allotted time. On the fourth morning
the dark clouds cleared away, and a bright sun invited
us to resume our saddles. The fine air, redolent with
the fragrance of mountain shrubs, our path meandering
from dale to dale, over rounded undulations clothed
with coppice, and winding gradually down deep ravines
overhung by noble timber, made our journey more like
a forenoon excursion than the serious task of getting
to our next halting-place. Passing the large village of
Shefa 'Amar, with its Saracenic castle, ruined church,
and picturesque woods, we descended in the afternoon
to the plain of Acre. Still the same indications of
misgovernment greet the traveller's eye as elsewhere
in Syria; the elements of agricultural prosperity, fine
land and an industrious population, are not deficient,
but the want of protection and encouragement prevents
their being turned to account. In other countries, the
tax-payer gets something for his money; here the government collects taxes, and does nothing in return for
them. No hope is entertained by the peasantry of
assistance against the Bedaween; and they are forced
by the exactions of the collectors to borrow at a ruinous
rate of interest. The maintenance of their families
requires that the threshing of their corn should not be
delayed; permission can only be obtained on the condition of twenty or thirty per cent. being given up
instead of the tithe. Very little thus remains to the
cultivator beyond what is necessary for his support,

and he ceases to sow a greater quantity of seed than
will suffice to produce it. One consequently sees on
the noble plain of Acre, as in most other parts of the
country, a rich black loam extending as far as the eye
can reach, and yielding, with the exception of a few
patches of cultivation, only a heavy crop of docks and
thistles. Around the scanty villages, stout oxen graze
in happy inactivity, and within them sturdy boors
lounge about with the utmost indifference to the value
of time, labour, and opportunities.

A long ride on the hard sand stretching round the
bay between Mount Carmel and Acre, and through a
grove of date-trees gracefully waving their feathery
boughs to the sea-breeze, with a wilderness of reedy
downs on our right, the reputed haunt of prowling
robbers, and the surf rolling over many black wrecks
of coasting vessels on our left, driven by westerly gales
on that dangerous shore, and now half buried in the
shingle, concluded our day's journey. We forded the
Belus—to whose vitreous sand Pliny attributes the
invention of glass by some sailors who cooked their
dinner on it—and reached the single gate of Acca, the
Accho of the Book of Judges, the Ptolemais of Ptolemy
Soter, and the St. Jean d'Acre of the crusaders, as the
sun was gliding below the western horizon in a yellow
blaze of sea and sky. Acre is still a mere military
post, as it has been during the whole of its eventful
history. Taken by the crusaders, and from them again
by its former Saracen holders, it was finally surrendered
by the Knights of St. John, who thence went to Rhodes,

and subsequently became the Knights of Malta, closing
thus the strange career of the Franks in the Levant.
Sultan Selim I. took Acre with the rest of Syria,
and it became a seat of successive Turkish governors. In the middle of the last century an Arab
sheikh called Daher suddenly entered the town at the
head of his Bedaween, and gained possession of it. He
improved it in every way, and the Porte thought it
better to let him keep it, and confirm his successor in
the post of governor. This was Jezzar Pasha, so
notorious for his cruelty, and known even in Europe
for having joined Sir Sidney Smith and made a gallant
defence against the attack of Buonaparte. Abdulla,
the next Pasha of Acre, was one of the semi-independent satraps who weakened Turkey so much during
the reign of Sultan Mahmoud, and from whom Acre
was wrested by the Pasha of Egypt. To restore it to
the Sultan, England was obliged to bombard the town;
Admiral Stopford avenging thus Richard Cœur de
Lion. Since then it has been used by the Turks as a
garrison town to keep their state prisoners in. These are
to be seen in the streets by hundreds, many of them
with chains from the ankles to the waist. Acre has,
therefore, never had any existence otherwise than as a
stronghold. Trade cannot live without a harbour, and
productive prosperity is not the privilege of any Turkish
town. The population, amounting to ten or eleven
thousand, is steeped in abject poverty, dependent for a
livelihood on what is expended for and by the garrison
and prisoners, while a rigid military rule prevails in

every particular of its condition. When walking next
morning on the flat roof of the house we occupied, I
saw a large steamer approach. It passed, as the want
of a port prevents Acre from deriving even the advantage of being included in any of the lines of steam
navigation along the Syrian coast. She showed her
colours to the Turkish flag on the fort: they were
Russian. The treaty of Paris reduced the Black Sea
squadron within narrower limits than were agreeable
to Russia or consistent with her policy: immediately a
numerous fleet of fine steamers, manned and officered
by the imperial navy, commenced running round the
Black Sea and down the coast of the Levant. They
belong to a commercial company, but the returns do
not come near the outlay. The steamers touch at the
several ports to keep up appearances, leaving an easy
competition for cargo and passengers to bonâ-fide
companies; and the line is continued in spite of all
losses. Russia has never yet been known to abandon
views which have become a part of her history, or to
overlook any detail which to her long-sighted vigilance
appears capable of contributing, be it ever so little,
towards the success of those views. The theory that the
results of the Crimean war, and of the change of reign,
have altered the policy of Russia, may be plausible;
but, to my mind, it wants the only thing that could
give it weight, which is truth.

After starting from Acre on our northward course,
we left on our right the palace of Behajeh, with its
extensive garden and plantations, the work of Abdulla

Pasha, and recently purchased for only four hundred
pounds by a Christian of the town. Our road lay
along the plain, not without cultivation as the mountains close in on the shore, and agreeably diversified
with occasional orange groves and orchards of apricot
and plum trees. At noon we wound along the Scala
Tyriorum, a path of a mile in length cut in the face of
a cliff whose base is in the sea two hundred feet below.
A precipitous mountain rises above it, ending in a bluff
headland called Promontorium Album by ancient geo-
graphers, from its composition of indurated marl veined
with flint. It seems to have been the only pass known
in history, and must therefore have been trodden by
Israelites, Assyrians, and Macedonians; but to which
of these conquering hosts it owes its origin does not
appear to have yet been ascertained. There is an
inscription on a rock beneath the path, which is said
to be in an unknown language; but it is so difficult
of access that no one has been able to examine it
and discover what light it may throw on the work.
Towards evening we came to Ras el Ain, a copious
spring, turning some mills, finely situated near the
shore, where European-looking houses had recently
been erected by the late Grand Vizier, Reshid Pasha,
for the purpose of establishing a colony. He had
bought a considerable tract of arable land on the plain
extending to the mountains behind it, and sent a Polish
refugee to take charge of his property; but the un-
healthiness of the climate frustrated the scheme, and,
like everything of this kind in Turkey, it was soon

abandoned. The doors and window-shutters of the
deserted buildings now flap mournfully in the wind.
At a late hour we arrived at the remains of Tyre, and
followed the sand-covered causeway built during the
Macedonian siege of the insular part of the ancient
city. Either ancient history is full of Oriental hyper-
bole, or modern ideas are greater than ancient facts;
for one is generally doomed to disappointment on the
sites of past renown. What Joshua called a strong
city—what baffled for thirteen years the power of
Nebuchadnezzar, and so long resisted the vigorous
attack of Alexander the Great—could at best have been
but a moderate fortress. That the merchants trading
there were princes and the honourable of the earth, as
Isaiah records, is quite intelligible, as the commerce of
those days would amply find its requirements in the
small port and open road to the east; and the abundance of the peculiar shell-fish producing the Tyrian
purple still shows how prosperous may have been that
local industry. But one looks around in vain for the
natural advantages which are said to have favoured
the great Phœnician capital—for the elements of that
military supremacy described by Ezekiel, the ramparts
manned by Arvad, the Gammadims in the towers, and
their shields hung on the walls round about. The
fallen city of Tyre has now a population of barely four
thousand, nearly equally divided between Christians
and Mussulmans. The former belong almost exclusively to the sect of Greek Catholics, and have a bishop
resident amongst them. The port, though small and

choked with sand, is safe, and encourages the inhabitants to devote themselves to the coasting trade and
to fishing. They also export tobacco, grown on the
mountains, to Egypt. But there is no life in the
place; and it must gradually become a mere village,
if inhabited at all.

A good night's rest—no slight benefit to one riding
daily through an ague fit—enabled us to take an early
departure on our way; having first walked awhile
about the ruins of the vast cathedral, best known by
the consecration-speech of Eusebius, of which the historian of the Crusades, William of Tyre, was officiating
bishop. We crossed the Leontes, second in Syria to
the Orontes, by a bold arch of no great antiquity.
These two rivers rise not far from each other in the
valley of Cœle-Syria, between Lebanon and Hermon—
the one flowing northwards to Hama, Antioch, and
Seleucia; the other southwards, to water the plain between Tyre and Sidon, before falling into the sea. We
passed the ruins of Zarephath or Sarepta, which, judged
by their extent, must have been a considerable city.
No building now remains above the ground, and the
foundations are being dug out and shipped for Beyrout,
whose best quarry is there. A cave is shown by travelling dragomans as the abode of Elijah—apocryphal
of course, for the widow is expressly stated to have
given the prophet a loft or upper chamber in her house.
The rest of our day was spent on the great Phœnician
plain, now scarcely cultivated; and in the evening we
entered the gate of the Phœnician capital. Sidon lay

smiling beneath the setting sun, with foaming breakers,
driven in from the west, falling in wild gambols at the
feet of bright green tamarisks. Noah's great-grandson, who gave his name to the future city, charmed
with the fairness of the spot, pitched his tent on the
height now occupied by the castle, according to a tradition not yet forgotten. There he formed his plan of
building arks on the flood that stretched away before
him to the distant horizon. Soon his city became the
metropolis of the young world's trade. Long lines of
laden camels wound down the hills from the interior,
and white sails were spread to the breeze, wafting the
produce of the far East to Western shores. But the
Assyrian, the Greek, the Roman, and, more than all,
the Turk, have dragged Sidon down to that low level
of small provincial towns where we now found it. The
crusaders tried to raise it again to importance, when
King Baldwin took the town and gave it as a fief to the
French knight Eustace Grenier; but they were unable
to hold it long, and it was retaken by Saladin after the
battle of Hattin had sealed the fate of the Franks in
Syria. The Templars purchased Sidon, but were soon
obliged to retire to Tortosa, and finally to Cyprus. The
town now contains many good houses. The inhabitants
are about seven thousand in number, of whom two-
thirds are Moslem, and one-third Greek Catholics and
Maronites in nearly equal proportions. The port was
once capable of sheltering fifty vessels, but it was
blocked up with stones by Fakir ed Din, the Druze
usurper of the government in the beginning of the

seventeenth century, to defend himself against the
Turks, and it can now be entered only by boats. The
chief trade of Sidon is the exportation of raw silk;
mulberry-trees being extensively cultivated in the
gardens which occupy the whole space between the
town and the hills.   Fruit of different kinds, reputed
the finest in Syria, is also shipped in great quantities.

We left Sidon on a lovely morning; and a most
charming ride we had with two much-esteemed American missionaries through the fresh luxuriant vegetation of
those gardens, orchards, and orange-groves. Emerging
from them, we suddenly found ourselves surrounded
by a troop of armed horsemen, while a pale-faced, in-
telligent-looking young man, in a Turkish frock-coat,
rose from a carpet spread under a large tree, and
advanced towards us. He was accompanied by an
exceedingly stout person in the Egyptian jacket and
bags. Recognition was not slow, and we sat down
with the great Druze chief, Said Bey Jumblat, and his
kehaia or lieutenant. He had inherited from his father,
Beshir Jumblat, who was strangled by Abdulla Pasha
of Acre, a whole district of the mountains above us, and
he was now visiting a part of his property. Half an
hour's conversation over pipes and coffee, with fre-
quently-recurring professions of attachment to England,
having disposed of this incident, we mounted again and
rode to the banks of the river Oweli, formerly Bostre-
nus, which we crossed by an excellent bridge of a single
arch erected by Fakir ed Din. A more ancient one
had probably preceded it, for the Phœnician level was

discernible on some of the blocks of stone irregularly
built into the buttresses.   This limpid stream descends
from the mountain by a gorge of the greatest beauty,
passing below Mukhtara, where the Jumblat family
has a picturesque residence almost deserving the name
of a palace, and plunging down a precipice of two
hundred feet in a noble cascade, with pine-clad cliffs
rising above it higher and higher till they tower aloft
in the one grand summit of Lebanon.   Beneath one of
those rocky ramparts is a cave, in which the rebel
Fakir ed Din held out against the Sultan's troops.
They undermined it, and it was not until the sapper's
chisel had pierced the carpet on which he sat, that the
brave old Druze surrendered, and carried his head to
the Seraglio Gate of Stambul.   The path follows the
coast for many miles.   Indeed, it could hardly do otherwise without getting embarrassed amongst the hills
which come down to the water's edge, deeply indented
with ravines, the uneasy beds of stormy winter torrents.
The remains of an ancient Roman road show that this
must always have been the trunk line of Syrian trade.
It is in some places cut out of the rock ; none of the
crust of pavement and macadamising, which I have
seen well preserved elsewhere, having resisted the wear
and tear of time, weather, and traffic.   On one of the
heights stand the ruins of Juni, the scene of Lady
Hester Stanhope's eccentric retreat from the toil and
turmoil of London life.   The once brilliant niece of
William Pitt lies there, without epitaph or head-stone,
amid a wilderness of rubbish around.   A singular

coincidence is recorded of her burial, which took place
by torchlight and in silence, like that of her early love
at Corunna, while Moore was the name of the only
Englishman present—our Consul-General at Beyrout.
We rested an hour at Nebbi Yunas, the Prophet Jonah
—a delightful halt, with its cool fountain and shady
trees, which few travellers despise, whether they believe
or not that the prophet was there cast on shore by the
whale, and that his remains still sleep in the mausoleum
visited by pilgrims, chiefly Mahometan, who pray so
devoutly at the shrine dedicated to his memory. A
couple of hours' ride farther along the coast, winding
round its little bays and creeks, on a bridle-path pushed
almost into them by the hills whose feet they bathe,
made us fain to rest again under the grateful shade of
a solitary carub-tree that spread its gnarled boughs and
dark glossy foliage over a rude pavement, evidently a
pious foundation in favour of weary wayfarers. Quarti-
dian ague is not the most agreeable of travelling companions, and I was beginning to feel how futile was
my effort to ride away from it. On the contrary, its
atra cura clung tighter *post equitem* as we advanced,
and it was now becoming evident that it must soon
succeed in unhorsing me altogether. But we were not
far from Beyrout and assistance. Another hour and a
half over heavy sand sufficed, and at nightfall, passing
through the pinewood above the town, we dismounted
at the door of an hotel, and I quickly put myself on the
sick-list.

Thirty years ago Beyrout was a mere haven with a

few warehouses, for the trade of Damascus. Ibrahim
Pasha of Egypt made it the capital of Syria, to spite
the people of Sidon, where he had not been well received; and Damascus sank in proportion as Beyrout
rose. It has now sixty thousand inhabitants, scarcely
the half of whom are Moslem, the remainder being
Europeans and native Christians. The winter here is
milder than in any other part of Syria. There are
occasional heavy rains, but one is never deprived of
exercise by bad weather. Since I have got rid of my
country fever, I ride or walk daily in terraced gardens,
decked with villas of the wealthy merchants, and showing here and there broken columns and fallen archi-
traves, dating from the reign of Augustus when Berytus
became a Roman colony, or from the time of Agrippa,
who adorned it with those theatres in which Titus,
rejoicing over the destruction of Jerusalem, sacrificed
so many Jewish prisoners by making them fight with
wild beasts. Built into the quays, and lying in the sea
near them, are numerous fragments of sculptured gra-
nite, both grey and red, giving evidence of more remote
antiquity—possibly vestiges of the Phœnician worshippers of Baal Berith mentioned in the Book of
Judges. The casting up of sand from the sea by every
gale, and the washing down of soil from the mountains, have formed a plain whose south-eastern side
rises to their lower slopes, while its northern and
western limits sweep along the shore with the port and
town imbedded in a clump of gardens, and meet in a
rocky cape crowned by the Ras Beyrout hotel—in the

verandah of which I sit enjoying the lovely prospect
as the sun rises over the rugged peaks of Lebanon.
An old friend appears, well versed in all the intricacies
of Druze and Maronite politics, and corroborates, in our
conversation on the subject, all my foregone conclusions
about these storms in a glass of water.

In a few words, the matter seems to stand thus:—
A small portion of the Ottoman dominions, neither so
powerful as the Danubian Principalities, nor so much
detached from the empire as the island of Samos, was
endowed with institutions which foster a spirit of independence without furthering the material well-being
of its population, and encourage enmities amongst its
inhabitants, as well as sedition towards their sovereign,
rather than progress in the common path of improvement. The Druzes and Maronites are thus in a position
at variance with all possibility of good government.
They do not prosper. Some lay the blame on Turkish
governors, some on foreign agents. Special causes are
assigned for every new collision. I imagine the truth
to lie chiefly in the conflict between their actual condition as a *quasi* state and the natural requirements of a
province. The first leads them in one direction, the
second in another. Their two phases of political existence clash, and the shock produces that confusion of
duties and rights which so often calls in vain for a
remedy. The only remedy applicable to the circumstances of the case, as I think, is the withdrawal of
nominal advantages and the conferring of real ones.
Their so-called immunities might be modified so as to

belong to the sects collectively instead of individually, with a better form of native participation in local government, not aristocratic as heretofore, but representative; while possible disorders, both internal and international, should be repressed by a strong hand more immediately over them, and more exclusively occupied by their affairs, than that of the Governor-General of Beyrout. Above all, no foreign agents should be accredited to that mountain authority, or allowed even to reside within his jurisdiction on the footing of an emissary, from any European government whatsoever.

The system of the Turks has generally been to make the most of dissensions, and to create two parties where none previously existed. They rarely depart from this immemorial policy of fomenting discord, pitting the different sects and creeds against each other, maintaining each contest as long as possible, and starting another when it is exhausted, on the *divide et impera* principle. Little could therefore be expected from the appointment of a Turkish governor of Lebanon. The Druzes are too subtle and designing, too methodically dishonest and unjust in their relations with both Turks and Christians, and too uneducated and unenlightened, to admit of a good governor being found amongst them. The native Christians are not in a state to offer any choice, on account of the influence exercised over them by foreign agents. The only eligible person, in my opinion, would therefore be a Christian, non-Roman Catholic—an Ottoman subject, and having enjoyed the advantages of European training.

The Roman Catholics and Maronites, with the sections of the Greek, Syrian, and Armenian Churches acknowledging the supremacy of the Pope, have completely eclipsed on Mount Lebanon the remaining portions of these latter communities which have fallen into comparative obscurity. The open protection given by France to all who look towards Rome has been mainly instrumental in producing this effect. Russia protects the small remnant of the Greek Church as co-religionist, and also the Armenians on the plea that their metropolitan see of Echmiazin is in Russia. The protection of Russia has somewhat differed of late from that of France, and from its own previous practice in its means of action. France is still overbearing and arrogant: Russia is no longer so much so. She gives now to her interference and encouragement the form of pecuniary grants attributed to private piety. No rivalry seems to be felt. Crimean recollections are apparently obliterated. Both would willingly hurt Turkey, if their actions furnish any key to their thoughts; but, while France retains her triumphant tone, Russia merely sulks: the one has long since thrown off the mask in Syria, the other wears it now for the first time. These may be reasons why Mount Lebanon might not be well governed by adherents of foreign powers, and especially of France; but I confess that it cannot enter my mind that the cabinets of great European states will ever derive any advantage for their own countries from petty endeavours to befriend insignificant sects inhabiting a few districts in Syria.

We have seen that an appeal to arms for the settlement
of differences arising out of conflicting interests in
Turkey was in no way influenced, during the whole
course of the contest, by the self-interested sympathies
of Oriental Churches.   The Roman Catholics and the
Greeks, when they had got France and Russia fairly
embarked in a war, thought only of themselves, and,
fawning on the Turks, left line-of-battle ships and
bayonets to do all the work for them.   Yet, notwithstanding that practical lesson afforded by interference
resulting in that struggle of nations, and in spite of a
treaty of peace establishing a contrary policy, still are
the Roman Catholics and Maronites assiduously protected by France, and the Greeks and Armenians a
Russian as ever.

LETTER XVII

Druze and Maronite War—Tahir Pasha—Massacres—General
Kmeti — Northern Syria — Massacres — Riots — Mussulman
Prophecy—Massacre at Damascus—Ahmed Pasha—Danger of
Aleppo—Fuad Pasha.

Aleppo : July 20, 1860.

A MORE general conflict has taken place between
the Druzes and Maronites of Mount Lebanon than
has occurred for many years, and it has been followed
by frightful disturbances at Damascus. It appears
that a couple of hundred Maronites went in the beginning of last month to attack the Druzes in the village
of Beit Mari. A stronger force of Druzes sallied forth
from the neighbouring village of Abadieh, and completely routed the assailants. Ten other villages were
destroyed that day by fire.

The disturbed state of some parts of European Turkey had unfortunately obliged the Porte to move thither
most of the regular troops stationed in Syria, and the
authorities had not a sufficient force at their disposal
to put down at once this insurrection, which bears the
character of an organised attempt to annihilate the
Druzes. Strange reports are spread of the Maronite
bishops having sent priests, and circulated written ex-
hortations, to induce the people to rise. The Christians
of Deir el Kamar were the next to attack the Druzes.

This is one of the largest and most important places on
Mount Lebanon, having about ten thousand inhabitants, and being almost deserving of the rank of a
capital town. The Druzes of Munassif routed the
Christians of Deir el Kamar. In revenge the latter
burnt some Druze houses in their town. Two small
villages, Kafi Hamal and Kafi Katrei, occupied by
Druzes alone, were assaulted, but the Maronites were
finally repulsed at both. The Druzes then attacked
Deir el Kamar. Twenty-five lives were lost on both
sides in the previous fights, which were allowed to go
on for several days without any interference on the
part of the government, although some of the few
troops they had were at Deir el Kamar itself.

Tahir Pasha, hearing of the attack commenced on
that place, proceeded to Beteddin, the ruined palace of
the Emir Beshir, which is within a short mile of Deir
el Kamar. He proclaimed to the assailants and the
assailed that he had come to restore order. They both
replied that they would make peace without his trou-
bling himself. A negotiation was accordingly brought
to a favourable conclusion, and, believing all danger
past, the Pasha returned to Beyrout. It was not so,
however, and the worst was to come. After peace was
ratified, and arms laid down, the Druzes entered Deir
el Kamar with all outward appearance of pacific intentions. No sooner in the streets than they fell upon
the Maronites, who took refuge in the quarters of the
detachment of Turkish soldiers. There, by an act
which has been called treachery, and which I believe

to have been mere stupidity on the part of the latter,
the Druzes were allowed to massacre the Maronites
without an effort being made to save them.   At Hasbeya and Rasheya, two other considerable places of
Mount Lebanon, events almost precisely similar took
place.   The three towns were destroyed by fire, after
having been plundered.   Zahleh, a large Christian
village, was also attacked; but the defence was successful there, in so far as to save the greater part of the
population, which escaped to the district of Kesrawan,
near Tripoli, while their houses were being sacked and
burnt.   Six hundred Maronites were thus butchered
at Deir el Kamar, and upwards of three thousand at
Hasbeya, Rasheya, and Zahleh.   About a thousand
Druzes fell.   The extraordinary conduct of the Turks
can, I think, be explained only by the theory that the
wily Druzes had convinced them of the Maronites
being rebels against the Sultan, insurgents in the pay
of a foreign power to overthrow his throne, and per-
suaded them to allow of a summary execution, which
they undertook as faithful subjects of the Porte.

  Great alarm was felt at Beyrout and Damascus.
The arrival of Ismael Pasha, the brave and honest
Hungarian General Kmeti, with troops which he
marched at once to the mountain, and the appearance
of British, French, and Russian ships of war on the
coast, restored confidence for a time.

  The Maronites were the aggressors, and in number
they were as three to one.   The Druzes were merciless
when victorious; but the same may be said of the

Maronites when fortune favoured their arms on previous occasions, when they had not the merit of sparing women and children, as the Druzes did now, and do habitually.

At Aleppo, Druze and Maronite quarrels find little echo; but a question between Mussulman and Christian invariably arouses angry feelings on both sides. The massacre at Jedda, two years ago, was thus a source of more apprehension here than these more extensive murders on Mount Lebanon. Only nine years and a half have passed since the Christian quarter of Aleppo was sacked, and Christian blood was shed by the Mahometan population on the most trivial provocation. A Greek bishop had been unwisely ostentatious in his sacerdotal pomp and retinue. A gold-embroidered saddle-cloth on the episcopal mule was too much for Islam to bear. The military conscription, too, had exasperated the more turbulent class of the population, on which it was purposely made to fall. Worst of all, a rich Christian had dared to refuse a loan to a needy notable. The obnoxious bishop fled from Aleppo, disguised as a Turkish woman, when the disorders commenced; but another prelate, the Armenian bishop, was taken for him, and so ill-treated that he died of his wounds and his fright. The wealthy Christian merchant was killed, others followed, and for three weeks the work of pillage and destruction continued without any check on the part of the authorities. Several Hungarian officers were here as political refugees at the time, and amongst them the well-known

R

General Bem; they finally contrived to get the troops
to move, and a battle was fought against the townspeople, who were dispersed, having a thousand killed.
So severe a lesson has not been lost on Aleppo; and
though frequent apprehensions have been entertained,
and occasional riots have occurred, nothing of so serious
a character has taken place since then. Two months
ago danger seemed imminent, but passed off. A ruined
building in the possession of an Austrian Jew was
claimed by the Ullema as having once been a mosque.
Evidence was taken by the Cadi. Old men swore that
they had attended Mussulman worship in it when
children. The Jew produced documents to show that
his father and grandfather had lived in it before and
during the period sworn to. All was of no avail;
mosque it was, and should be again. On the award of
the Cadi, the faithful commenced rebuilding the walls.
The Jew, enraged, pulled them down in the night.
Such a profanation of a holy place brought together
an infuriated mob in the morning. Three thousand
zealous Mahometans crowded the streets, calling loudly
for revenge on the person who had ventured to insult
Islam. One or two of the leading Mussulmans of the
town, who considered themselves aggrieved in their
private interests by the local authorities, had taken
this opportunity of raising a feeling of hostility between
the different classes of the population, as well as a
seditious spirit against the government, which they
accused of weakness and apathy in the cause of their
religion. Firearms and ammunition were immediately

bought up wherever they could be found. Young men of all creeds and of bad character rushed about inciting those they met to fight and defend themselves. Some of the Mussulmans secretly announced to respectable European families, with whom they were on friendly terms, that a general massacre was going to ensue, advising them to take refuge in the towns on the coast, where they could be saved by the ships of war. Fortunately, a firm and intelligent officer was in command of the garrison—a Mussulman of Russia, who had left the Russian army before Kars, and offered his services to the Sultan in favour of his religion. The town was patrolled, the sale of arms prohibited, and some of the most dangerous persons arrested. This Pasha appeared alone in the streets, assuring the Mussulmans that they would get justice if they would only keep quiet. The Austrian agent was applied to, and he settled the question by exiling the offending Jew from Syria; which measure certainly saved the Jew's life, and possibly that of many others. A few days afterwards, without any very conspicuous motive, placards were posted on the doors of the mosques calling upon the Moslems to attack and exterminate the Christians. The garrison was kept under arms for several nights, and numerous patrols guarded the streets. The Christians concealed their valuables in cellars, or conveyed them to the houses of Mussulmans in whom they had confidence. The streets were deserted, and the shops closed. Amongst other incendiary statements in the placards, it was announced that last time was the turn

of the Moslems, and that now the Christians are preparing to rise against them; which is explained by
certain rumours current of an insurrection of the
Christians of European Turkey. About a week later,
crowds of small traders and artisans, both Mussulman
and Christian, assembled in the streets for the purpose
of going in a body to the governor's residence to com-
plain of a reduction of the currency now giving rise to
much dissatisfaction in all classes, and to some suffering
on the part of the poor. Suddenly a couple of hundred
policemen appeared and began beating them indiscri-
minately. The tumult soon took the form of a conflict
between Mahometans and Christians; and many of the
latter were dragged to prison, kicked and cuffed by
soldiers on the way. The governor shut himself up in
his harem, alleging sickness. The members of the
provincial council were in a panic, and nowhere to be
found. Omar Pasha, the Russian, did his duty, and
succeeded in preventing matters from going further.
Nearly at the same time, some Mussulmans of Antioch
made a strange religious demonstration by repeatedly
entering the Christian churches during divine service,
and uttering aloud Mahometan prayers with their backs
turned to the altar. The Christian congregations had
the forbearance on each occasion to take no notice
of the offensive proceeding, and continue their own
worship. Great uneasiness pervades all classes of the
population. This has neither taken its rise in any
definite cause for alarm, nor has it been evinced by
violent outbreaks. Yet its existence is evident in a

general expectation of great events affecting the Turkish domination in Syria—in anxious enquiries about
the disasters on Mount Lebanon—in muttered threats
of one community against another, and in the stagnation
of trade consequent on the winding-up of commercial
affairs and departure from Syria of many respectable
merchants, both native and foreign. This disordered
state into which Syria has fallen recalls to the memory
of the conservative Mussulmans a curious prophecy,
generally though reluctantly believed. It was predicted in the beginning of the present century by a
much-revered sheikh that, when the first of the sevens
falls, the ruin of Islam will commence, and, when the
second falls, it will have been completed. We are
now in the year of the Hegira 1277; the year about
to open will invert the first of the two Arabic sevens
read from right to left—V becoming Λ; that is, 7
becoming 8; and in the year 1280 of the Hegira, the
second 7 will also be inverted. This prophecy, supported as it is by the reality of the troubles now
arising in various quarters, has naturally exercised a
great influence on the fatalist tendencies of the Mussulmans, and increased their ill-will towards other sects.
It is certain that feelings of animosity exist in a high
degree on the part of the Moslems against European
and native Christians on account of their superior
commercial prosperity and growing ascendency; and
on the part of the latter against the Mahometans—in
general, for their unmistakable indications of hatred
against the Turkish authorities,—in particular, for the

losses and insecurity arising from bad government.
How readily that reciprocal animosity, harboured by
the different sects, bursts forth when an opportunity
offers, and foreign machinations are at work, is seen
from year to year.   The silly finery of a Greek bishop,
with the refusal of a Christian to invest money in the
hands of an embarrassed Moslem, produced the massacre of Aleppo in 1850; the shifting of a flag on
board a coasting vessel which had changed owners,
sufficed at Jedda; a dispute regarding a right of water
in a garden, sent a raving rabble through the streets of
Tripoli last year with shouts of ' Death to the Infidels !
The time has come !'   And it required all the prudence of a cool and energetic officer to prevent a claim
for an old mosque, and a complaint against an alteration
of the currency, from leading now to rapine and bloodshed.   It is worthy of remark, that the endeavour to
keep up this state of feeling comprises also the encouragement of rancour and aversion against the Turks
on the part of Arab Mussulmans, who regard the
former as degenerate sons of Islam.   The Turkish
regular troops, too, are despised in Syria as mongrel
Franks.   The garrisons are not strong enough to face
these feelings on an emergency.   Each Turk in the
country would have thirty Syrians opposed to him
were an insurrection to occur; and, to quell it, he
would have to overpower an organisation and military
efficiency little inferior to those of the Sultan's army ;
for the survivors of the Janissaries, who numbered
no less than five-and-thirty thousand men affiliated at

Aleppo and Damascus when that force was suppressed in 1826, have kept up a species of secret union among themselves. They are all more or less inured to arms, young men recently affiliated, as well as old men belonging to the original corps. They look upon the Osmanli as a national enemy, and the persecutor of their banner; and they harbour hopes of a separation of Syria from the Ottoman Empire, by the formation of a new Arabian State under the sovereignty of the Shereef of Mecca.

Such was the temper of the people in this part of the country when the tragedies of Deir-el-Kamar, Hasbeya, Rasheya, and Zahleh, were repeated on a still larger and more horrible scale at Damascus; not by the Druzes alone, but, what makes it ominous to the whole empire, by the Mussulman population of the town. The origin of this appalling misfortune seems to have been an offence committed by a Christian in a Mahometan family. He was accused before the authorities, and put in prison to take his trial. Protection obtained his liberation without punishment. Several young Mussulmans entered the Christian quarter, and told those they met, with violent curses and threats, that they would take the administration of justice into their own hands. They also marked signs of the cross with chalk on the pavements, and trod on them with imprecations and vows of vengeance. Finally they tied small pieces of wood in the form of crosses round the necks and on the tails of street dogs. Being personally known, these Moslem lads were denounced to the

Governor-General of Damascus, still Ahmed Pasha, by a native Christian attached as dragoman to the Russian Consulate. The Pasha had them arrested, and, having been weak enough to consult the dragoman as to the punishment he should inflict, unfortunately adopted that person's suggestion that they should be made to sweep the streets of the Christian quarter in chains. The sight of such an indignity inflamed the pride of the people on both sides; the one enraged and humiliated, the other exulting and triumphant. Altercations took place in the streets between Mussulmans and Christians. An affray ensued, in which the prisoners were violently rescued from their guards, some Christian houses were set fire to, and thirty Christians and twenty Moslems were killed.

On the following day, Christian refugees from Hasbeya, Rasheya, and Zahleh, flocked into Damascus. They were followed by Druzes from Mount Lebanon, and met by Druzes from the Haurân, attracted to the mountain by the news of bloodshed, and the hope of plunder. Finding the Mussulmans of Damascus in a state of insurrection, both these bodies of Druzes cunningly joined them in order to make common cause with them in the event of the massacres on Lebanon being punished. The Christian quarter was assailed by thousands. The Russian Consulate was the first house destroyed; the consul sought safety in flight, under the disguise of a Turkish woman. The French Consulate was plundered, but not burnt. The Franciscan monks were almost all killed, as also the Rev. Mr. Graham, a

Missionary from Belfast. The French sisters of St. Joseph were saved by the Algerine Abd-el-Kader, who exerted himself nobly in behalf of the Christians. Many of the latter found an asylum at the British Consulate, which was respected, and in the houses of some of the respectable Moslem merchants. Several of the latter were murdered for their humanity. The massacre, pillage, and conflagration lasted three days. In all, twelve hundred and eighty Christians were killed. Many women, young girls, and little children were taken to the harems, and abominably ill-used. Ahmed Pasha sent some troops, under the command of two colonels, into the streets when the outbreak commenced. They soon applied to him for instructions, under the impossibility of keeping the peace without resorting to violence. He ordered them in writing to fire upon the people. One of the colonels, in command of the regulars, obeyed his order, and dispersed the mob ; proving thus that the evil might have been checked. The other colonel, who had charge of the irregulars, was won over by a Mussulman sheikh, who adjured him, in the name of the Prophet and their common religion, to join them, and clear the holy city of Damascus from the defiling presence of infidels ; he went over to the insurgents with his troops, who became the most sanguinary and cruelly licentious of the monsters who disgraced the name of man on those three awful days. Organised gangs rushed about the streets, with the butchers of the town behind them ; they dragged the men from their houses, and handed them over to those execu-

tioners; few of the women survived their shame, or
dared to make known that they were still alive when
carried off by the spoilers; and the houses, many of
which were richly furnished in the oriental style, were
completely emptied, then set on fire. Ahmed Pasha,
meanwhile, thought of nothing better to do than to as-
semble the provincial council; instead of taking his
sword and all his troops to the streets, where he might
have stemmed the torrent of destruction, or done his
duty by dying in the attempt, he satisfied himself with
a written statement, signed by all the members of the
council, that nothing could be done. The court of his
residence was filled with thousands of screaming women
and children; and he had the merit, though somewhat
negative, of closing the gates and protecting them from
their pursuers. During the three days many Christians
found refuge there; and their number having at last
reached between seven and eight thousand, they suffered greatly from exposure to the midsummer sun,
want of food, and insufficient covering at night. The
mortality was thus considerable, especially amongst the
children, in the palace-yard.

You may well suppose that the Mussulmans of
Aleppo did not hear of these abominable crimes with
indifference; and, had they been disposed to do so, the
panic felt by the Christians of this town would have
suggested an application of the circumstances to their
own case. For several days the most wealthy and respected Christian merchants of the place were made to
walk in the gutter when they met a Mussulman in the

streets; a conventional word was even adopted as an
order to admit their inferiority in this way, and little
boys called it out on sight of a Christian with unvarying success. Some Christians have been beaten, others
only vituperated. Shop-keepers were obliged to give
their wares without payment. False debts were
claimed, and paid. Still the Christians offered no resistance, and those who endeavoured to foment quarrels
and disturbances found all their attempts frustrated by
patience and submission. Finally, as at Damascus, the
street dogs appeared with wooden crosses tied round
their necks. Affairs were becoming serious. The ordinary police was no longer considered sufficient to
check the impending disorders. Perhaps no great confidence was felt in their zeal for the maintenance of
tranquillity, and in their impartial spirit. When the
military commandant was giving them instructions, and
asking them what they would do if they saw a Mussulman and a Christian quarrelling, one of the policemen
replied with the utmost simplicity, that he would take
the Ghiaour to prison, of course. A body of five hundred special constables was enrolled from amongst the
better-disposed Mussulmans, those who had been more
in contact with Europeans, and especially some who
had served during the Crimean war in the pay of England. The general commanding the garrison is an excellent officer, and a brave sensible man, capable of
understanding and of carrying out timely suggestions.
The growing excitement was watched with vigilance;
and, as soon as it was seen that active measures were

not only called for, but also were not to be feared as
productive of a crisis, he sallied forth at the head of the
few troops under his orders, patrolled the town incessantly for three days and nights, posted artillery where
the principal streets crossed, arrested all turbulent characters, and in short so completely convinced the people
that the authorities were not to be trifled with, that
matters soon settled down to their usual state of tranquillity.   He possesses what is notoriously wanting in
Ahmed Pasha of Damascus, personal courage.   The
latter is a scientific officer, having studied at the military colleges of Berlin and Metz, reads much in German
and French on the details of his profession, but he is
naturally a timid man.   I knew him on the Danube in
the beginning of the last war, and every one admitted
that his arrangements for the force under his command
were perfect, but no one ever saw him voluntarily under
fire.   I do not doubt that he was well aware how he
ought to act in the outbreak at Damascus, and that he
would have been quite as successful as others have been
at Aleppo, but he could not bring himself to face the
danger of doing his duty.   His nervousness, not to
use stronger language when talking of an old soldier
and a distinguished general (for the victory of the Turks
over the Russians at Citate, in Wallachia, was entirely
owing to his military skill), has long been known in the
Turkish army.

   All alarm has now been put an end to by the intelligence of the arrival of Fuad Pasha at Beyrout as
the Sultan's plenipotentiary.   He is not only an able

statesman, but also an expert general, and a man of
courage and energy. The first time he was brought
into public notice was during the difficulty between
Turkey and Austria, with Russia as her ally, in the
Hungarian war, when he was sent as ambassador to
St. Petersburgh. This was an arduous mission; for the
Porte had peremptorily refused to give up the Polish
and Hungarian refugees on the equally peremptory
demand of those two great powers, and yet it was
urgently expedient for Turkey that amicable relations
with them should be maintained. The credit of that
noble display of respect for the laws of humanity and
hospitality in saving the lives of many gallant but
unfortunate men, who had thrown themselves on the
honour of the Sultan, is due to our ambassador at the
Porte during that and innumerable other emergencies,
Lord Stratford de Redcliffe, who then added one to the
various titles he has gained, by his lofty English principles of rectitude, to the grateful esteem of his country,
in raising and upholding its name for a chivalrous sense
of what is right and just in foreign lands. The Porte,
after accepting his counsel and support, wished to prevent any disagreeable feeling from being left in the
mind of the Emperor Nicholas by the adoption of Lord
Stratford's views in the matter. This was more than
any one could accomplish; and the proof of the rancour
harboured for years in the imperial breast is the undeniable fact that, if the proximate cause of the Crimean
war was the question of the holy places, its original and
fundamental motive was the more remote refusal of the

Sultan to deliver over to ignominy and death his Polish
guests. Fuad Pasha cannot, therefore, be said to have
been perfectly successful in this mission, but he made
himself known, and deserved to be highly commended,
as he was, for his fidelity to his master, and for his
spirit of independence before foreign arrogance. He
accordingly returned to Constantinople a marked man;
and, when Prince Mentshikoff was sent to pick a quarrel
with Turkey, his first public demonstration was to insult Fuad Pasha, whom he found minister of foreign
affairs, by refusing to treat him even with customary
official courtesy. Fuad Pasha, though entitled to redress, preferred sacrificing his own feelings to aug-
menting the embarrassment of his government, and
resigned his post. He was soon called upon, however,
again to take an active part in public affairs, and was
sent to the Greek frontier, at the time when an incon-
siderate and unhandsome attempt was made by King
Otho to extend his territory at the expense of the Sultan,
in the hope that the latter was engaged in so great a
war that he would not be able to undertake also a little
one. Fuad Pasha found the Turkish and Greek troops
fighting, with some appearance of success on the part
of the latter, owing to grievous blunders committed by
the Turkish commander. Though he had never served
in the army, the Sultan's commissioner at once perceived
where these errors lay, took command of the troops
himself, outmanœuvred the Greeks, and finally defeated
them most signally. The soldiers spontaneously insisted
on his wearing the badge of the army on his fez, which

was confirmed by the Sultan, to whom he had rendered
such good service on this occasion.   Since then he has
been employed as minister of foreign affairs, and on
several important missions in Europe.   I have known
him personally for upwards of ten years, and, if any one
can help Turkey out of her difficulties, I believe Fuad
Pasha to be the man; for to undoubted patriotism and
high-mindedness, he unites indomitable perseverance
and an astonishing power of endurance under fatigue,
both mental and bodily.   A man of such transcendent
natural abilities cannot but be great when he is also a
very hard worker.   Fuad Pasha's first act in Syria has
been to issue a characteristic proclamation, sent here and
to the other towns by express, in which he emphatically
states that, if a single Mussulman should henceforth
dare to injure or insult a Christian, the whole quarter
of the city, in which the said Mussulman lives, will immediately be rased to the ground.

LETTER XVIII.

Execution of Ahmed Pasha—Punishments—Seditious Document
—The International Commission—Military Conscription— Ad-
mission of Christians to Military and Civil Rank—Stagnation of
Trade—Depression of Agriculture—Christian Women in the
Desert—Wars of the Bedaween—A Fight—A Boar-hunt—A
Swedish Camel-driver at Palmyra—A Turkish Governor of the
Desert—A Caravan plundered by an Englishman—A Chase.

Andruse: October 27, 1860.

AHMED PASHA has been executed. He deserved his fate, not as having instigated or even
connived at the crimes which have been committed,
but as a soldier found wanting in the hour of danger.
He died like a man. Until he was brought out to be
shot, he was not aware that he had been condemned.
On seeing troops paraded, he asked the officer sent for
him if his suspicion was founded. The reply being
that it was, he requested to be allowed time to say his
prayers, which was granted. There was great difficulty
in keeping the soldiers steady during his last prayer.
They liked him, I believe. When he stood up, he said
merely that the Sultan might dispose of his life, adding,
'May God not look at his shortcomings!' This expression has been interpreted as implying that the
Sultan sacrificed him, after having wished him to act
as he did. Nothing could be more unfair. The words

are a common Turkish idiom, equivalent merely to our
' God bless him.'   In the same spirit it was asserted,
first, that the government was screening Ahmed Pasha;
next, that they were hurrying on his execution to fore-
stall revelations; and finally, that he was not shot at all,
another man having been put in his place.   The fact
is, that he was formally tried by court-martial, sentenced to death, and shot at once, that the effect of the
example might not be destroyed by unnecessary delay.
Khalid Pasha, who commanded the firing party, was
obliged to exhort the men in strong terms to do their
duty, which they did at last with evident reluctance;
and poor Ahmed Pasha died without a struggle, no
less than twenty-eight balls having hit him.   He thus
suffered himself that violent death which, only a few
months previously, I remarked on his having inflicted
on the Ansairi prisoners, and on the same spot.   Three
other officers were shot with him—the commandants at
Hasbeya and Rasheya, and the colonel who joined the
insurgents with his irregular troops in the Christian
quarter of Damascus.   The latter was the only one
who showed any fear of death.   He was convicted on
the evidence of a French Consular officer with whom
he had formerly been on friendly terms.   This person,
disguised as an Algerine, was with a party of Abd-el-
Kader's people when they met the colonel, who recognised him, and called out to the rioters to put him to
death, as he was a Frenchman; but the latter escaped
to report the fact, and the colonel was executed.   The
commandant at Deir-el-Kamar was also condemned to

death; but he will not be executed till Tahir Pasha's
trial is over, on which he is the principal witness.   A
hundred and seventeen officers and soldiers of the
irregular troops, with the son of the president of the
provincial council, and several civil servants of the
government, have also been shot; while others guilty
of infamy, as well as cruelty, to the number of sixty-
six, among whom were three sons of the greatest
notable of Damascus, were hanged.   Two hundred and
fifty of the insurgents have been sent to hard labour
for life, and three hundred for twenty years.   A very
large sum of money is being levied from the Mussulmans and Druzes to indemnify the survivors of their
victims' families.   These vigorous measures, and especially the number of deaths by hanging, which is an
unusual mode of execution in Turkey, have given to
Fuad Pasha the nickname of the Father of the Rope,
an honourable title under the circumstances.

A seditious document has recently been in circulation
all over Syria.   It purports to be an address from the
Ullema of Damascus to those in the towns of Northern
Syria; and it appears to me so significant that I shall
give a sketch of its tenor.   After commencing, as is
customary, with prolix salutations, it goes on in this
strain:—' You know that the Christians, from the beginning of the reign of Abd-ul-Mejid, have been
quarrelling, and piercing, and destroying the law of
Mahomet, and passing the limits and transgressing the
obligations imposed on them of old from the time of
the Imam Ali-el-Hattab.   And now they struggle

violently with the Mussulmans, bringing a curse on
them in the things which the rules of the just law and
the Koran-el-Shereef forbid, and which hurt them in
their religion, and subvert the duties laid upon them,
all which the Christians should obey. They trans-
gress the regulations by sitting in official places. The
greatest and smallest among them mock the Mussulmans and treat them as equals. They know not that
the Mussulmans are determined to uproot and destroy
their whole race, and for the following legal reasons :
1st, The shedding of their blood, the violating of their
honour, the destroying of their property, the burning
of their churches, the knocking down of their houses,
is lawful, because their capitation tax is remitted.
2nd, Many maxims in the books, Fetwa-el-Hindieh
and Fetwa-el-Baharieh, state strongly that it is not
proper for Mussulmans to allow the strength of the
Christians, and that the weakness of the Christians is
necessary to the Mussulmans by whatever means it be
secured—such as the destruction of their crops and
fruits, and the obstruction of their labour.   3rd, It is
not right to honour the Christians.   May God curse
those who dress them in robes of honour !   4th, The
nations of the infidels are one nation.   In the sect of
the Nakshbendi it is written, that a Christian in an
honourable position must not exist.   It is not proper
that Christians should appear as witnesses against Mussulmans, but it is proper that Ansairi should appear as
witnesses against Christians.   We quote the saying of
God: Be not cowards before the nation of infidels, but

s 2

throw amongst them enmity and hatred unto the day
of judgment! Oh, nation of Islam, awake from your
deep slumber! Come, now, let us exterminate the
worshippers of the cross from the holy cities which
they defile! And let not the name of Christian be
again heard in them! From what we have learnt
from great officials, the powers cannot engage in
war, for they have been weakened by the war of the
Crimea. This then is the time. Let us seize the
opportunity to conquer the Christians, for the day of
their destruction is at hand. If we leave them two
years more, they will become stronger than we are, and
will take our place and destroy our race. For these
reasons we have begun now to show ourselves. We
have made friends with the officials. We have learnt
the disturbances which took place at Stamboul last
year. The greatest part of the men of the government have agreed unanimously to destroy the Sultan
and all the Christians on the face of the earth, for the
reason that the Sultan is a man who turns aside from
the law of Islam; he places images in his palace, and
his own image is placed over his head. He hangs gifts
from Christians round his neck with the sign of the
Christians engraven on them. Things like these defile
the course of Islam, and cause deviations from religion.
Two years ago took place a secret consultation between
the officials and the Ullema and the principal Mussulmans, when they all agreed to destroy the Sultan and
all who adopt his cause; place his brother in his stead,
whose opinions are the same as ours; bring back the

faith of Islam to what it formerly was; weaken the
Christians as they were before; break their pride, and
if possible drive them entirely away from these cities,
for, if wars and battles arise against us, they will be
a stumblingblock to us, and strengthen the Franks.
And now the Christians are exciting the Europeans
and intriguing against Islam, and especially on Mount
Lebanon, where there are two hundred thousand men
rebellious and known to be in every intrigue.   No one
can enter Syria without their help.   How much more
now that they are all in correspondence with the
Franks, in order to help their retaining their hold on
these cities; and, having verified this in every quarter,
we consulted the officials and Ullema, in order to
destroy all the Christians on the Mountain, at Damascus, and at Aleppo, and in the rest of Syria, by whatever means are possible.   And thus we have acted on
the Mountain, and have destroyed them, and dispersed
them in every direction.   And thus also at Damascus
we have destroyed and dispersed them.   And you also,
if anything arise against them, do not help them, but
turn your eyes away from them.   Answer us, in order
that we may continue to instruct you how to act.   And
peace be with you; from your brothers at Damascus.'

When this extraordinary paper first passed from
hand to hand, it was believed to be genuine, and, as
such, it might have done much harm, but soon the
Ullema began to pick holes in it, and finally declared
it spurious.   Then arose the idea that it was a production of the native Christians, for the purpose of

inducing the European powers to take up their cause
more warmly. But the native Christians had never
been known to play so bold a game; and besides,
internal evidence in its tone and purport was incompatible with that theory. Lastly, it has been decided,
and on grounds apparently quite conclusive, that its
composition is that of a European, a good but not a
perfect Arabic scholar, such as are employed by foreign
cabinets after years of study. The style is defective,
and the orthography not always correct. The Imam
Ali is mentioned without the necessary formula of
' Peace be to him!' which is always used when the names
of the Prophet and first four Khalifs are introduced,
whether orally or in writing. El Hattab, moreover,
was not the patronymic of Ali, but of Omar, and such
a blunder could never have been made by any one
capable of writing at all in this country. The word
' kullian ' occurs in the document several times, and its
use is confined to colloquial style. The term ' mukad-
dassi' is applied to the holy cities of Islam, whereas it
is the expression of the Christians in talking of their
holy places; no Mussulman would condescend to use
it, no native Christian would honour a Mussulman
sanctuary so far as to give it that epithet. The word
' kown is employed for 'because' instead of the more
appropriate 'lian.' The name Suria appears for Syria,
which is thoroughly European, the local name being
Arabistan. Not to tire you with verbal criticisms,
which have been multiplied to satiety and complete
conviction, I sum up with two remarks: the manner in

which historical events are recapitulated is concise, methodical, and didactic, three qualities found neither in Mussulman nor in native Christian writings; and, there are various parallel passages to verses of Scripture which would certainly not be known to Mussulmans, and very improbably to native Christians, even supposing them to be in the priesthood. Several suspicious-looking characters have lately appeared in some of the towns of Northern Syria, calling themselves foreign priests, but acting and dressing in exceedingly unclerical fashion. The document was circulated simultaneously in different places, and many copies of it seem to exist.

The institution of an international commission to take into consideration recent incidents and future prospects in Syria, is a measure which meets with universal assent and approbation. The system which had engendered the present state of Mount Lebanon, was the produce of a collective deliberation of the European powers; it is but fair that they should have an opprtunity of verifying the result, and of revising their work at the same time, while it is also not unwise to keep Turkey up to the standard of her duty by the cooperation of foreign commissioners.

A great number of those implicated, but not seriously, in the massacre of Damascus have been drafted into the army. I am not sure that it is quite right thus to lower the tone of military service by making it a penalty; but it will certainly do the recruits a great deal of good to be subjected to discipline, and the army may not suffer by the admission of some such young men. The mili-

tary conscription is soon to be applied also to the
remainder of Syria. The Christians have heard this
with distaste. The recent demand for payment of the
tax in lieu of military service was resisted by them on
the plea that, so long as the Mahometan class was not
required to furnish men, the Christians should not be
called upon to contribute money. But fear seems to
have disposed of that argument, and the tax would now
be willingly paid without the enlistment of Mussulmans,
which is dreaded as a motive for another outbreak. In
some towns the Christians have offered to serve in the
army rather than pay the tax. It appears to me that
the proposal should be acceded to. If it is not made in
earnest, there would be no further opposition to the
assessment; if the Christians really wish to enter the
military service, a great change might be produced in
the political condition of the empire without ferment
or conflict. Were the Sultan effectually to establish
perfect and real equality in this particular, as well as
in others nominally levelled, were religious creeds no
longer to disqualify for military or civil rank, and were
talent, integrity, and meritorious services alone to achieve
promotion, one of two issues must be the result: either
a new impulse would be given to the declining vigour
of the state by the admission of Christian activity and
intelligence into the conduct of public affairs, and by
the healthy emulation it would give rise to on the part
of the Turks; or the superiority of the former in mental
endowments, and in the spirit of enterprise and improvement, would gradually eclipse those of the latter, and

change the dominant race without the occurrence of struggles and violent commotions to disturb the internal tranquillity of the empire and the peace of Europe. That a beneficial influence of Christian energy on public interests would be felt, is proved by the history of Turkey before the Greek revolution, when she was able to uphold her rights against the greatest powers, and when her alliance was sought by those who now impose conditions on her, be they palatable or not. At that time, the exclusive direction of her foreign affairs, as well as the administration of several of her finest provinces, was entrusted to Greeks. Those Greeks may be justly stigmatised for the faults then inherent in their precarious position, when cunning and duplicity were the only shield they could oppose to the sword hanging over their heads. But they made Turkey strong and respected, nevertheless; and they prepared her for a simultaneous progress with other nations, by the institution of schools and colleges for the education of her. Christian subjects all over the land. That class of men, who might almost be called statesmen, is no longer to be found in the Ottoman Empire, having rallied round the nucleus of Greek nationality, but the race is the same, and a class of Christian functionaries, civil and military, might arise if the Porte allowed it as then, with the qualifications and without the defects of their predecessors. If, therefore, a larger share in the administration of the affairs of their country is ever to be conceded to the Sultan's Christian subjects, and one can hardly doubt that such

must eventually be the case, the present appears to be
no unpropitious occasion for making an experiment by
consenting to receive Christian recruits in the army on
equal terms with Mussulman soldiers.

The towns are quiet, but the feeling of security has
not been restored. Some of the wealthy Christian families are leaving Syria to settle definitively in Europe,
apprehending that the catastrophe of Damascus may
any day be renewed. Trade is in abeyance ; the same
motive effectually deterring merchants from embarking
their capital in local speculations. All are, on the
contrary, realising what money they can collect, and
remitting it to their correspondents in Europe, who in
their turn withdraw credits formerly opened for commercial operations in Syria. This state of matters is
not only exceedingly injurious to the general prosperity
of the country, but it also threatens with ruin all those
who were trading on the capital of their consigners, and
this is the usual manner in which the importation of
manufactured goods is carried on. Endless difficulties
arise in the settlement of accounts, lawsuits ensue, and
unproductive ill-feeling takes the place of fruitful
activity in business. The prospects of the upper
classes are thus in the worst possible condition. The
working portion of the population is not more favourably
situated. Cultivators in this country are always to
a certain extent dependent on trade. Small loans are
required by them at seed time, and repaid after the
harvest. The money not being forthcoming, the usual
amount of cultivation is diminished, and next year's

crop will consequently be deficient. The peasants, straitened by the refusal of credit, and less occupied in the fields, fall into violent disputes among themselves for small payments; and trifling and unimportant though they may at first appear, they occasionally result in bloodshed and feuds of whole villages. Several instances of both kinds have occurred of late, which the very defective system of employing irregular troops for the preservation of order in the agricultural districts has been altogether unable to prevent. The corrupt practices, so ingrained in officials that they may almost be called a national institution in Turkey, find an ample scope in these embarrassments of both classes of the population, and ingeniously turn to profitable account every difference arising amongst the high as amongst the low.

It is said that several hundred Christian women and young girls disappeared from Damascus during the massacre. Some are in the harems of the townspeople, and have embraced Mahometanism to conciliate their captors, and obliterate all trace of their miserable fate. Others were carried out of the town by Koords and Arabs who had joined in the pillage. I had heard of a few of these poor creatures being in a camp of the Anezi, and thinking my intercourse with that tribe might perhaps enable me to do something towards rescuing them, I made preparations for the attempt, which were more necessary than usual; for I had been at the Weldi settlement, and found it difficult to pass amongst the tribes now engaged in a general war, originating in the

rivalry between Sheikh Jedaan and his uncle Sheikh
Deham.   They had fought several battles, in which
the former had been victorious, when Deham at last
crossed the Euphrates, and obtained assistance from
the Shammar.   Jedaan then made alliances with the
Sebaa, Mowali, Lehep and other tribes, and pursued
Deham into Mesopotamia.   A great battle lasted several
days, upwards of 12,000 men being engaged.   Jedaan was
totally defeated, and he recrossed the Euphrates in a
wretched plight, having lost all the herds and flocks of
his tribe, and even their tents.   The Bedaween on this
side of the river supplied him with provisions, mares,
and spears; and sent a couple of thousand horsemen
with him to try and recapture his sheep and camels.
In this he partially succeeded, his next attack having a
more favourable issue.   All this warfare, so extensively
carried on to the great detriment of the villages on the
skirts of the desert, was mainly owing to the repre-
hensible conduct of the chief of irregulars, Haji Batran,
who had used a golden key to open his prison door, and
was again at large in the full exercise of his useless and
pernicious functions, inciting tribe against tribe, and
maintaining that state of perturbation which he thought
necessary to his own interests.   The result was a strange
state of affairs.   The Turkish authorities at Urfa took
the part of Deham and the Shammar, and sent all their
troops to protect them against the attack of Jedaan,
while Haji Batran was giving all the influence of the
government at Aleppo to the latter, and supporting
him with the whole force of irregulars.   This could

not, of course, continue under the eye of a man like
Fuad Pasha; and Haji Batran was arrested, and conveyed under escort to Beyrout. When matters stood
thus in the desert, I had gone with F—— to Aisheh,
hoping to get some of the Ferdoon tribe, settled there,
to accompany us to the Weldi camp. They would not
listen to any proposal of the kind, and said all they
could to dissuade us from attempting to pass between
the tribes then daily skirmishing with each other. We
stayed the night with the Ferdoon, undecided what course
to pursue, unwilling to turn back, yet aware of the
difficulty of going on. Next morning a heavy snow-
storm suggested the possibility of getting through un-
noticed. Still none of the Ferdoon would try it.
Knowing the way perfectly, we left Aisheh without an
escort, and having with us only a servant, a groom, and
a lad. For several hours we rode safely under the
thickly-falling snow, unable to see fifty yards around
us, and consequently unseen from any greater distance.
In the afternoon, the weather unfortunately cleared,
and we came in sight of some horsemen towards the
north, belonging to the Shammar Sheikh, Abd-ul-
Kerim, with a few of the worst characters among the
Ghess and other low tribes, which had taken the field
for Deham, in all about sixty. Being only five, we
could not think of simple resistance, but both F——
and I were well mounted, and we could try to avoid
close quarters. The party opened as soon as they saw
us, and we were soon nearly surrounded. Flight in a
straight line was impossible. We had plenty of room,

however, as our enemy seemed to have recognised us,
and evidently feared that we might have firearms. I
told F—— on no account to use his revolver, as we
must be finally overpowered, and by drawing blood we
should only seal our own fate. After ineffectual attempts to force our way through their line, in one of
which I got a spear-thrust through my Arab cloak,
but without wounding me, we kept wheeling and
dodging the attacks made on us within a circle of a
few hundred yards. Our three men having inferior
horses were soon taken, unhorsed, and stripped. Their
cries seem to have been heard by another body of
horsemen, which soon appeared rapidly approaching us
from the south. Encouraged by the hope that they
were friends, we continued galloping about with a
decided advantage in the speed and condition of our
horses; if they were enemies, we could only give ourselves up. F—— was struggling gallantly, striking
out with his fists, like a schoolboy as he is, at four or
five Arabs, who were trying to jostle him. At last
they got him down, and then others tried to close on
me. The shock of several horsemen who ran up against
me at full speed without pointing their lances, brought
my horse to the ground, and rough hands dragged me
from the saddle before he could rise. I contrived to
shake them off, and, giving up my horse, ran towards
the other party of Bedaween who were coming on at
their best pace. The first man who reached me was
Khalifeh-el-Kir, of the Roos tribe of Anezi. He was
a brother, and he shouted to those behind him who I

was. I sent Khalifeh to F——, who was still stoutly
sparring at bay, his horse having been carried off. Not
knowing Khalifeh, he thought him a new assailant, and
struck out at him too. Khalifeh quickly scattered with
his lance the Shammar on foot around F——, unwound
the aghal from his head, threw it over F—— to secure
him, then gave him a horse to ride, taken from one of
his men. The next who came up to me was Ahmed-
Bey-Mowali, who at once charged those near me, and
drove them off with the enormous lance he always uses.
The fear of his very name seemed to disperse the
Shammar. He gave me the mare of his cousin Daher,
who was with him, and a general assault was made on
the enemy. The Anezi and Mowali were only thirty,
but they soon showed their superiority over the
Shammar, who were as two to one. A short *mêlée*
settled the affair, leaving twelve wounded, two of them
severely. One of the latter was on my horse, and he
was set upon ferociously, and knocked off with three
bad spear-wounds and a broken head from the blow of
a mace, which Ahmed Bey carries at his saddle-bow.
In the evening the wounded were carried into the
Weldi camp, where every attention was paid them;
the Shammar and Ghess having galloped off without
bestowing a thought on them. All our horses, cloaks,
and everything we had lost, not excepting the minutest
articles taken from our servants, were carefully brought
to us by Ahmed Bey, who then led the way to
Mehemed-al-Ganim's camp, a short mile further on.
News of the fight had preceded us, and the whole

tribe came ont on foot to meet us; the sheikh with
bare head and feet, and tearing his beard with vexation ; the women brandishing tent-poles, and screaming
imprecations against the Shammar.   It was not until
F—— and I were felt all over by the faithful Weldi,
to convince themselves that we were not wounded,
that they would be quiet, and let us rest after our
lively ride.   All their horsemen mustered next morning
to escort ns on our return, which was diversified by a
very pretty little chase after an enormous wild boar.
F—— turned it after a couple of miles' run, and the
brute charged him.   Excellent horsemanship and the
skilful use of his spear secured to him the victory,
which was cheered by the Arabs forming a vast ring
round the two combatants, when a last home-thrust
laid the huge animal on his side, not to rise again.
Taking the tusks to send home as a trophy, we proceeded on our way, meeting several parties of Bedaween,
who gave so numerous a band a wide berth.   We
slept again at Aisheh, where the Ferdoon marvelled at
our safe return.   Next day, however, we were again
in jeopardy.   Having dismissed our escort, we were
cantering past a large village, when we saw its whole
population sally forth on foot with guns, and commence
a steady fire upon us, which no hailing or signalling
could put a stop to.   Mending our pace, it soon took
us out of range, and the circumstance was explained by
our finding the sheep of the village on our course; we
had been taken for Bedaween intent on driving off a
flock.   Further south, the desert was almost in a worse

state, and it was there that I must look for the Anezi
with whom the Damascene women were said to be.
O—— has also gone through one or two adventures.
He was down near Palmyra, and was determined not to
come back without seeing the ruins. There was so much
fighting, however, that he could not trust to a plain
Arab disguise, and he conceived the bold plan of
becoming a camel-driver. A poor Arab was going to
take a few camels to Palmyra to carry soda; O——
paid him the hire of his camels on condition of the job
being sold to him, with the hire of the driver's ward-
robe included. Thus equipped, he mounted the little
donkey in front, and, giving the Arab call to the camels,
proceeded in his new profession. He met several parties
of horsemen, who disdained to molest one so poor. On
nearing Palmyra, however, he saw a large party emerge
from the ruins, and advance towards him, while behind
them appeared a stronger body, half naked, their long
shirts floating in the wind, and their heads uncovered ;
screaming out their war-song as they rushed at the
other party, which turned to beat them off as they best
could, whenever the pursuers came too near. Three
or four were killed, and about ten wounded. The
appearance of O—— and his camels caused a diversion
in favour of the pursued, for the others came down
upon him like a whirlwind, to rob a caravan as they
thought. When they saw a humbly clad youth on a
little donkey, all alone with a string of unladen camels
in the middle of the worst part of the desert, far from
suspecting that in him they saw a Swedish baron, not

T

inferior in pluck and skill with horse and arms to his
own Gustavus Adolphus and Charles XII., they took
pity on him, and bade him follow them to Palmyra for
protection, as the other party of Arabs had availed
themselves of the incident to get away. Thus O—— saw
the celebrated ruins at a time when few of the bravest
Bedaween venture out unless in great numbers. Considering this state of the desert, it was necessary that
I should take proper precautions before I could expect
to reach the Amarat tribe, which had been near
Damascus during the massacre, and had come this way
to assist the Anezi in their war with the Shammar. I
had ascertained that the Amarat were those with whom
some of the Christian women then carried off to the
desert might still be found. The Turkish authorities,
possessing neither influence to persuade, nor power to
coerce, could do nothing for them.

After the fall of Haji Batran, a governor of the
desert had been appointed. Of all others, the Porte
has selected for this post one of the notables of Aleppo,
formerly a member of the Provincial Council. The
purpose being naturally to promote peace among the
tribes, and to further and protect the efforts made by
some of them to exchange their roving and marauding
habits for those of orderly cultivators, the choice of a
nominee from that class which encourages lawlessness
on the part of the Bedaween in order to mulct them of
bush-money, and preys on the agricultural population
by oppression and extortion in every possible form, was,
to say the least of it, a most eccentric measure. Fuad

Pasha was deceived, and it would take the eyes of
Argus himself to see through all the administrative
delusions of this country when actual presence on the
spot does not reduce them to their real proportions.
Well, this newly appointed governor of the desert lives
in the large village of Tadif, surrounded by a numerous
guard of irregulars, and does not venture beyond its
precincts, while Bedaween in bodies of seven and eight
hundred ravage villages within a few miles of his residence.   A small tribe was coming to join the settled
Arabs the other day after much time spent in persuasion;
suddenly the emissaries of the governor of the desert,
with a party of irregulars, attacked it, and carried off
their eight hundred sheep on the plea that they had
been stolen from another tribe.   No rightful owners
were ever found, but the sheep were not returned, and
the tribe thus plundered, abandoning all idea of settling
and cultivating, went back to Mesopotamia.   When I
reached Tadif, and told the governor my purpose of
seeking out the Amarat, he replied that it was impossible,
that he could not guarantee my safety, and that it was
consequently his duty to prevent my going further.
I heard in the evening that the nearest Anezi tribe was
the Erfuddi, who were encamped at a distance of about
eight hours to the east; and finding an Anezi willing
to take a message to them in the night, I waited his
return, which was not until the next night was far
spent, as no one could move alone in the desert by day.
The poor governor was aroused out of his sleep by the
awful tidings that Tadif was full of Anezi, and he came

to me for advice in great trepidation. To his still
greater horror, he found forty of the dreaded Bedaween
at my door, and my horse being saddled for me. At
first he supposed that I was their prisoner, and that they
were taking me by force to the desert; but I succeeded
in explaining to him that I had sent for them, and was
going with them of my own accord. I left him, still
amazed, but evidently anxious to get rid both of myself
and the Anezi; and we rode out of Tadif at two o'clock
in the morning. Sajer, the sheikh of the Erfuddi, had
sent his son Reja, a lad of eighteen, with some picked
horsemen to accompany me to his camp. Reja is a
perfect type of desert nobility, with delicate features
and splendid eyes, tall but light in figure; wearing
little else than a flowing white garment, mounted on a
beautiful black filly, and gracefully poising his long
spear as he cantered about, his whole appearance was
that of a high-caste Arab. We had not gone many
miles, before loud shouts in front gave the signal for a
furious gallop, of which I was at a loss to comprehend
the motive. I was riding a spirited young colt of the
best desert blood, and he ran off with me before I could
make out what we were after. Our race continued at
tip-top speed, shouts still hieing us on, when I faintly
distinguished a long dark line moving across the plain
before us. Suddenly many flashes emanated from it,
shots were heard, and bullets whistled about our ears.
The shouts waxed louder and louder, our gallop more
and more frantic. My colt became quite unmanageable
with excitement, and his astonishing speed put me in

the first place. The whole dark line fired one more
volley at us, but they had not time to load ere we were
upon them. It was a large caravan. The camel-
drivers begged for mercy, but the Anezi never show
any under such commonplace circumstances. Sundry
hard knocks from the butt-ends of their spears were
the only reply. The head of the leading camel was
quickly turned to our course, and in a very few minutes
we were proceeding eastwards with our prize as if
nothing particular had happened. I began to feel
rather queer at finding myself thus on the less respectable side of the question—a companion, not a victim,
of robbers. Reja was near me, and I heard him ask
what the camels were laden with. It was wheat sent
by Mehemed-al-Ganim to the Aleppo market. I
immediately claimed the privilege of desert brotherhood; Mehemed-al-Ganim was my brother, Sajer
had become my brother; the Erfuddi could not, therefore, keep the caravan. The Weldi camel-drivers
crowded round me, confirming what I had said, and
imploring me to liberate them. Reja, with great
dignity of manner, said his tribe had come from near
Bagdad to fight for the Anezi against the Shammar,
and knew nothing of this part of the country, but that,
if I would give him my oath that Mehemed-al-Ganim
was my brother, the caravan should go free, and the
more readily, for none of us having been hit by the fire
of the Weldi. I pronounced the requisite formula, and
the happy settlers turned back with their fifty camels
and hundred sacks of grain; no dissatisfaction being

evinced by the Anezi at this unexpected result, so
great is their respect for desert law. Shortly after
dawn we reached the Euphrates, and found the Erfuddi
encamped with three other tribes of Anezi; the Ibn
Haddal, the Shumlan, and the Hayaza. I spent that
day with them, trying to get some intelligence of the
Amarat, and getting very little to eat, as these four
tribes had had no provisions for three months but dates
and camel's milk. Yet they gave up the Weldi wheat,
when right was on the other side. Fortunately I like
camel's milk, and kept taking occasional sips of it all
day, which completely banished hunger. I learnt that
the Amarat had been fighting with the Shammar for
three days, and must be somewhere to the south. In
the night I mounted with another party of Anezi, the
Ibn Haddal, and proceeded under their escort, about
twenty strong, in a southerly direction. Somehow, I
felt tired sooner than I should have done ; the air towards morning seemed to me intensely cold, and the
gallop of my colt was surely rougher than usual. As
I kept our party as much as I could at a slow walk, the
day broke before we had reached any other encamp-
ment. The sky was clear, and the sun shone bright
—for the season, very hot, as I thought. A severe
headache, accompanied by aching joints, at last proclaimed an attack of country fever. We had left the
Euphrates far to the north, and I suffered from parching
thirst. I asked one of the Arabs if he knew of any
water near. There was a spring a couple of miles to
our right. Hoping to gain strength by a little rest, I

lay down on a bank, and sent some of the Bedaween
with a leather bottle to fetch me some water. I was
soon fast asleep, but I was suddenly awoke by those
who had remained with me. Their comrades were returning as fast as their mares could carry them. When
they came within hearing, they called out to us to
mount and run, for they were chased. I thought
of nothing but water, and they had brought none.
On coming near the spring, they had seen eighty
Bedaween at it, who immediately pursued them, and
would be here in another quarter of an hour if we
did not mount at once. I wanted to know if they
had water, for, if so, I would wait for them. The
only answer I could get was that they were Shammar, and, if we met, there would be more blood
spilt than water. With my head splitting, and my
back breaking, I bestrode my impatient colt, which
at once bolted with me after the other horses. I let
him run, pressing now my temples, and now the back
of my neck with one hand, while the other held the
useless reins. The Anezi led off into a long hollow,
on entering which we saw our pursuers in full chase.
We held our own without a single straggler, the Ibn
Haddal being one of the best mounted of the Anezi
tribes; and this was our only chance, as the Shammar
behind us were as four to one. On advancing, the
ravine appeared to trend greatly towards the west. An
Arab rode parallel to our course along the higher
ground on each side to keep the Shammar in view;
the one on our right pulled up, planted his spear in the

earth, and with its aid sprang to his feet on the pad,
like a circus rider, to see further.   Quickly he came to
us with the report that the Shammar had left the
hollow, and were cutting across the angle to meet us.
We dashed off to the east, crossed the bank without
being seen, and, pressing our horses awhile in a direction contrary to that taken by our enemy, got clear
away.   In another hour we saw a camp, which the Ibn
Haddal did not know.   I assured them it could not
belong to any other than the Lehep, a friendly tribe;
adding that I would go and rest there, as I felt very
unwell.   They were sorry for me, but their sheikh
would never forgive them for entering a camp they did
not know, and if I persisted in going to it, I must go
alone, as they would return to their own tribe.   I
consented, and we separated.   As I proceeded slowly
to the camp, several horsemen came out to see who I
was; and my conjecture proving correct that they were
of the Lehep tribe, I was received most kindly.   There
seemed to be very few people in the tents, but I asked
no questions, as I had nothing more pressing than to
sleep off my fever.   I told them I had been chased,
however, and lay down on a carpet with another over
me and my saddle for a pillow, after drinking long
draughts of water from the very spring, they said,
which we had been driven from.   When I opened my
eyes it was night.   I felt better and sat up.   A number
of the Lehep were in the tent, and they all crowded
round me to kiss my hands, hoping I would pardon
their having taken me for a Shammar.   During the

chase they had remarked my colt, and had disputed amongst themselves whose it should be when taken; a good one it must be, they said, to have brought me in so long before them. I explained that we had come straight to the camp in leaving the hollow, while they had described a circuit by following it westwards. For supper they gave me rice, which I thought very good after dates and camel's milk, much as I like the latter. I slept well, and next morning I continued my search for the Amarat, taking hourly pills of sulphate of quinine, without a supply of which I have never moved since I have had this tiresome fever. The Lehep escorted me to this place, where another of their camps is pitched, amidst the ruins of the ancient city of Andrene, now called Hanassir. Its wells, still in good order, upwards of a hundred in number, constitute its attraction to the Bedaween, who often place their tents in the open spaces between lines of massive blocks indicating the streets and edifices now levelled with the ground. The citadel occupies a great truncated cone of earth artificially heaped and faced with stone, like many other old forts in Syria. This one is certainly prior to the Saracenic conquest, though traces of that style of architecture are to be found in the fallen buildings on it. The city must have been larger than Chalcis or Hierapolis, but I do not gather that its history was ever remarkable. The tale it tells now is simply that of depopulation in Syria since the Turks have held the country.

I have found the Amarat skulking without tents or

animals around this ancient town. I have visited every
party of them I could hear of. They had just suffered
a great defeat, with the loss of three hundred of their
number, and they were still hunted down by their
enemies, the Shammar. They were dispersed, and
hiding amongst rocks and bushes, not knowing where
their sheikhs were, if alive. I gathered from them that
there had been young women in their camps, whom
they said they had bought as slaves from persons they
did not know, and that they had sold them when they
could no longer feed them. After much cross-question-
ing, I discovered that the purchasers were some of the
Aghel, who passed with desert caravans; and as this is
the tribe which conveys Arab produce from one end of
Syria to the other, and even into Persia, the poor
Christian women are probably now far to the east. A
month had apparently passed since the last of them was
seen, and where to seek them now, was a question none
could answer. I must, therefore, with great disappointment and annoyance, give up all hope of being able to
do anything for them.

LETTER XIX.

Seleucia: July 10, 1861.

WHEN the French troops marched from Beyrout to Deir el Kamar and Zahleh, they were followed by a number of Maronites committing murders on the way. The construction put on the armed intervention of France in the country was thus manifested; its purpose was to take up the quarrel of the Christians, and oppose the Druzes and Turkish authorities, according to the conviction of all parties, not even excluding several most intelligent functionaries of the Porte. At the village of Ain Eyoob, those Maronite camp-followers killed an unoffending Druze, upwards of eighty years of age, and blind. An unfortunate Druze woman happened to pass one day near their bivouac; she was pelted with stones by the Maronites, and, taking to flight, she was stopped by a woman of that Christian community; a struggle took place between them, which brought them both to the ground; the Maronite woman,

having a knife, stabbed the other in the throat, and
when she was dead, the savage cut her enemy's head
off to carry home as a trophy. Without further enu-
meration in detail of the crimes encouraged by the
presence of the French force, I need only say that
there is reliable authority for no less than a hundred
and seventy-six assassinations of Druzes by Maronites
under the eyes of the army of occupation. General de
Beaufort d'Hautpoul is reported to have been utterly
disgusted with the part he has had to play, and with
the effects produced by it in Syria. In many cases
when Maronite murderers fell into the hands of his
soldiers, he is said to have allowed a free use of the
stick to record his opinion of them before sending them
to the local authorities for trial.

The letters of the Maronite bishops, of which au-
thentic copies have been obtained after their circulation
on the mountain, sufficiently demonstrate the existence
of an organised scheme for the extermination of the
Druzes by whatever means might be available; and the
conduct of the Maronites on the arrival of the French
has been consistent with that fixed purpose. Tobias,
the most influential of their prelates, addressed an un-
equivocal charge to the Maronite population of Deir el
Kamar to effect the expulsion and ruin of the Druzes,
while Sophronius, bishop of Tyre and Sidon, wrote to
the Maronites of Hasbeya in a strain which throws so
much light on the origin of the disturbances, and on
the character of the pastor and his flock, that I add
the following translation of his letter: — 'To our

glorious children, exalted and much-honoured, the
sheikhs, nobles, and elders of our nation, the orthodox,
at Hasbeya in the valley. May you ever be honoured!
May the blessings of heaven be upon you! We declare
to you, children, with regard to the events now passing
amongst the Druzes, who are the corruption of the
earth, and the perpetrators of crimes permitted by their
religion, that our well-beloved Christians in the Lord
must awake, and those having the power and being
guarded by the protection of the Virgin must fall upon
the Druzes whom Satan drives to crimes.   There is on
the mountain a gathering of the people of Zahleh,
Deir el Kamar, Kesrawan, Jezzin, and the neighbouring places, and they will all rise like a single hand
against the nation of the Druzes, which is small in
number and weak, and they will destroy it, pour out
its blood, seize its effects and possessions, and drive it
out of the country which belonged to our forefathers,
the orthodox, especially because we have received a
letter from His Holiness our Lord the High Patriarch,
instructing us to give our aid to this gathering of our
people according as they may require it, and this is
why the letter came, in order that each one of you may
be provided with the necessary arms, and that you may
mutually strengthen each other.   Next, give notice to
our Christian children around you, that your enemies
the Druzes may be overpowered.   It is resolved that
on Monday, if it please God, our children shall fight
under the banners of the venerable Emirs, whose zeal
for our whole nation is not unknown to you.   There-

fore be prepared, and, by the blessing of our Sovereign
Mother of God, the country in all directions will be
freed from your enemies, whose hostility to our religion
is known to you. Our blessing be upon you.'

The French troops have done nothing in Syria.
Indeed they had nothing to do, the Turkish forces
having sufficed for all that was to be done. The French
government, however, was unwilling to recall them
after their futile military promenade, and notwithstanding that their presence prolonged the state of animosity
existing between the different classes of the population
and encouraged the commission of crimes to which they
were already addicted. The French troops have,
nevertheless, been withdrawn, and none of the evil
consequences prognosticated on their departure have
occurred, or appear likely to occur. The Mussulmans
regard this cessation of a humiliating foreign occupation with so much satisfaction that little room is left
for rancour towards the Christians, who, on their part,
evince none of that alarm which was foretold as the
necessary result of the embarkation of General de
Beaufort's division.

But it would not have been a French intervention
had it passed without insult to some one, and Fuad
Pasha was insulted accordingly. The French general,
when cooperating with the Turkish troops for the
capture of the outlawed Druzes, officially accused the
Sultan's plenipotentiary of conniving at their escape.
There was littleness in the attack, and there was greatness in the defence. Fuad Pasha, without undignified

resentment, simply pointed out the extreme difficulty of stopping the flight of dispersed bands in their own country, which is mountainous, wooded, and rocky; and explained that, in consideration of that circumstance he had adopted other means by which he had succeeded in arresting fifteen hundred of them simultaneously. Moreover, the commandant of the Turkish force employed on this service was Ismael Pasha, General Kmety, than whom few military men in Europe have earned a better name for the knowledge of his profession, and for straightforward honesty of character. I believe there are not many persons in Syria now that the French troops are gone, who would disparage the merit of the services rendered by Fuad Pasha on the occasion of these disturbances, or impugn the sincerity of his efforts to restore order and administer justice.

Yusuf Bey Karam, whom I visited when at Tripoli, as I wrote to you from there, was appointed Governor of the Christians on Mount Lebanon. He had assembled two thousand armed men at the commencement of the conflict, and was marching to the relief of the Maronites when foreign authorities enjoined him not to advance. Had he not thus been stopped, the massacres might not have been attempted. Fuad Pasha seems to have appreciated his conduct, and in this there was at least impartiality, for Yusuf Bey is an avowed adherent of the French party, and a fanatical Maronite. For a time he rendered useful service, but his inordinate ambition and unbounded confidence in the power of his patrons led him to expect that he

would be invested with supreme authority on the
Mountain, and, when he was disappointed in this, he
retired to his own district, there to raise every obstacle
he could to the fair settlement of all differences existing between the Maronites and the Druzes.

Hoorshid Pasha, Governor-General of Beyrout, has
been sentenced to imprisonment for life ; his culpability
having been proved at his trial to have been confined
to the adoption of weak and ineffectual measures,
which he defended on the not altogether unfounded
plea that the removal of troops from Syria to European
Turkey just before the outbreak had deprived him of
the means of doing better.   Tahir Pasha, the military
commandant, has suffered a similar condemnation for
his blunder, to say the least of it, in leaving Deir el
Kamar when further hostilities were imminent.

Said Bey Jumblat, whom I had met near Sidon,
and whom I afterwards saw frequently at Beyrout,
was sentenced to death; not for having taken an
active part in any massacre, but as being the secret
instigator of the war.   This judgment was loudly
called for by some of the foreign commissioners,
and conscientiously opposed by others.   His health,
however, was such that his doom did not require judicial execution, and he died of consumption, hastened
in its effect by imprisonment and anxiety.   Reports
were spread of suicide, and even of assassination, but
the certificates of European medical men attending him
leave no doubt of the fact that his death was natural.
On the previous day he was visited by Lord Dufferin,

whose universally acknowledged ability in the discharge
of his duties as British commissioner has been accompanied in all such cases, on whichever side of the
question they occurred, by the most humane and benevolent spirit. Said Bey was much gratified by this
considerate attention to a fallen man, of whose innocence
I may add that Lord Dufferin had recorded his full
conviction. That belief is so far borne out by perfectly
conclusive evidence of the Druze chief having saved
the lives of many Christians within the immediate sphere
of his personal influence. On the occasion of his inter-
view with Lord Dufferin, the subject of the assumed
encouragement—or at least connivance—shown by the
Turkish authorities to the massacres perpetrated by the
Druzes, was discussed ; and Said Bey, who knew that
he was on his deathbed, stated that he was not cognisant of any fact corroborating the imputation of com-
plicity on the part of the Turks excepting the otherwise unaccountable departure of Tahir Pasha from
Deir el Kamar at the most critical moment, notwithstanding the earnest entreaty of Jumblat himself and
of others that he should remain there. The dying man's
last request to Lord Dufferin was that in the event of
his recovering, he might be allowed to spend the rest
of his life in England, far from the Turkish government. Strange to say, in his will was found an injunction
that his children should be educated by an English
tutor, and brought up as members of the Church of
England. This has created a great sensation amongst
the Druzes, who, in favour of Said Bey's great sagacity

U

and superior general information, believe that his soul
had once occupied the human tenement of one of their
most distinguished Okkal or initiated. True to their
doctrine of transmigration, they now think that the souls
of his children are those of Christian Apostles, who,
having found out the truth after death, have returned
to convert the British nation to the Druze religion.

Forty-three other Druze chiefs have been condemned
to capital punishment, but have not been put to death,
nor are likely to be, now that the current view has
been fully established that tho Maronites were the
originators of the wish for a trial of strength, and the
aggressors in the consequent hostilities. They will
probably be exiled to distant parts of the empire.

A large sum of money has been claimed as indemnity by those who have suffered loss of property at
Damascus and on Mount Lebanon—nearly a million
sterling. Doubtless most of these claims are exaggerated, and it has been ascertained that in some
instances Christians have tried to make their fortunes
by asserting the loss of what never existed. About a
hundred thousand pounds have already been devoted
to this compensation-fund, and further sums may be
added ; but how much will be actually paid, is another
question. Collection from the Mussulmans of Damascus
and Druzes of Lebanon may perhaps ensure its being
forthcoming. The indemnities awarded to the Christians for their losses in the massacre of 1850 at Aleppo
have not yet been paid, excepting in a few cases of
imperious foreign support.

When the rejoicings of the Mussulmans in general on the embarking of the French troops were beginning to subside, the death of the Sultan occurred, to call forth feelings of a similar nature on the part of the Turks, by whom his brother has been for some time looked upon as a man capable of raising the falling fortunes of their empire. Apprehensions were entertained that the excitement pervading the population, in consequence of the accession of Sultan Abd ul Aziz, might obstruct the settlement of affairs in Syria. The cry of the Mohammedans that Islam is saved, the appearance of an intention to provoke collisions with the Christians, and the rumours spread of the regular army being replaced by a revival of the Janissaries, gave rise to much alarm. Insults in the streets, and refusals to pay for articles bought from Christians in the bazaars, were of daily occurrence. Old prophecies were read aloud in the coffee-houses, manuscript copies of them being hired by the night. Interpretations were given to them, inciting the religious feelings of the listeners to bring about another crisis. Fuad Pasha became an object of vituperation for the executions at Damascus. Hatred of the French broke out in threats and maledictions. Even the more enlightened amongst the Mussulmans seemed to join in the prevalent fermentation. I heard one of them, a young man who had travelled all over Europe, say publicly that France is the worst enemy of Turkey, that he expected to see the realisation of the announcement contained in Monsieur Thouvenel's last note, and that, if French troops should thus again be

landed in Syria, the Moslems would kill the Christians,
burn the towns, and fight till they are exterminated.

Gradually all effervescence subsided, and the affairs
of Syria have now come out of their long-protracted
state of crisis; the results of Fuad Pasha's mission
and the international commission having just been made
public, and the new Governor of Lebanon having
arrived from Constantinople. He is an Armenian
Christian of good antecedents, raised to the highest
civil rank, under the title of Daood Pasha. The administration of the mountain is based on the following
conditions. A Christian governor is to rule over both
Druzes and Maronites, holding his appointment from
three years to three years directly from the Porte. A
representative of each sect, elected by the chief members of the different communities, will be in constant
cooperation with the governor, but without sharing his
authority or responsibility ; in fact they will be merely
his referees. A central council is to be formed of
twelve members, chosen in equal proportions from the
various sects; their functions will be restricted to a
control over the taxation and expenditure, with a de-
liberative examination of all other questions which may
be laid before them by the governor. Besides this
great council, six minor councils will attend to local
interests in the districts of the mountain. Perfect
equality of all classes before the law has been proclaimed. All privileges, feudal and fiscal, are abrogated.
Regular tribunals are open to each nationality on the
nomination of the respective communities, with the con-

firmation of the governor. A mixed police force is to
be raised by voluntary enlistment in the ratio of seven
men to a thousand inhabitants. The services of each
constable will be confined to the community from which
he has been drawn. The governor has, furthermore,
the right to call on the military commandant in Syria
to furnish him with Turkish troops when he may require them. Troops thus detached will be under the
orders of the governor during the time they are serving
on the mountain, which cannot be prolonged without
his consent. A fixed assessment, equal to the average
imposts of past years, will be paid to the Porte as a
virtual, though not a nominal, tribute. This definitive
regulation of the Druze and Maronite interests has
been accepted by the five European Powers which had
instituted the international commission, and the whole
affair is for the present at an end.

We have come to the sea to breathe, after two months
of suffocating summer. Our ride over the rocky wilderness to the east of the plain of Antioch was hot and uninteresting. On the second day we halted on the ancient
Telenissa, or Mount Simeon, at the ruins of a monastery built in the fifth century around the column, now
fallen, on which that crazed enthusiast lived and died
in voluntary chains, leaving his name to the hill. The
scene of the Stylite's aërial penance is forbidding
enough without a pillar or chains, but the utter deso-
lation of the spot formed perhaps its principal charm
to the mind of the savage saint whose distempered fanaticism fell short only of that which lowered the

βοσκοί, or grazing monks of Mesopotamia, to the level
of the herd in their common pasturage. At the height
of sixty feet from the ground, and chained by the
waist, the great Antiochian anchorite passed thirty long
years on a space of three feet square, now praying
erect with his arms stretched out in the figure of a
cross, now bending his meagre skeleton till his brow
rested on the stone so often that twelve hundred and
forty-four successive repetitions of the act were once
counted by the admiring crowd below. He died on
his column, and his remains were conveyed with a procession, headed by the patriarch and six bishops, and
escorted by six thousand soldiers, to Antioch, where
his revered bones were preserved to perform miraculous
cures even to comparatively modern times. Proceeding towards the south, we crossed the circular plain,
clasped in its girdle of rocks, which was formerly the
site of that Imma, where the beautiful Zenobia, more
beautiful than her fair ancestress Cleopatra, rode fear-
lessly from rank to rank in vain encouraging her army
to withstand the overwhelming shock of Aurelian's
Roman legions. We then descended through a long
and narrow ravine to the vast plains of Antioch, which
lie dormant like the rest of the neglected empire to
which they belong. No impulse is given to agricultural production by protecting it from the ravages of
unruly tribes. The Turkomans on this great tract of
fertile country are more troublesome than formidable;
pernicious as an obstacle to prosperity rather than dangerous as enemies of the government. They are ad-

dicted to plundering small caravans laden with the
petty wealth of local traffic from village to village, to
carrying off corn, driving cattle before them when not
adequately guarded, and rifling the slender baggage of
solitary native travellers. The actual damage committed by them is trivial, but the maintaining of a state
of insecurity becomes a serious evil. One year may
pass in *quasi* tranquillity, while the next may see whole
villages abandoned by their inhabitants, who despair of
reaping where they have sown. Then the beys keep
up continual feuds, nominally against the marauders of
the day, really against the possessors of anything worth
taking, however acquired. Thus Ahmed Bey Mursal,
chief of the Rehauli tribe, was last year employed by
the government to protect the roads ; his cousin, Omer
Aga, took the field with a couple of hundred horsemen
to plunder all who passed that way. Ahmed Bey was
forthwith dismissed, and Omer Aga appointed his successor. Ahmed Bey turned robber. Omer Aga became the true man. But not the less do caravans and
travellers suffer. On the western confines of the plains
of Antioch, where the Amanian range shuts them off
from the sea, a large number of Circassians and Tartars, refugees from the south of Russia, have been sent
by the Porte to colonise. They are landing also at
Mersyne, whence they will be distributed over the
plains of Marash, as well as those of this pashalik.
Robbery seems to be their present pursuit, while preparing to form agricultural settlements. It would
surely have been wise to reflect whether or not the

authorities, under whose rule they are intended to establish themselves, are in a position to preserve order before thus adding to the number of a disorderly population. The plains of Antioch, for instance, towards the north where the Russian refugees are located, are in the district of Beylan, the greater part of whose inhabitants rose a few days ago against their Turkish governor, and blockaded him in his residence. Irregular troops arrived from Antioch in time to protect him from further violence. But the insurgents appointed another governor of their own choice, and have kept the Turkish authorities prisoners in spite of the presence of troops. The motive of the outbreak seems to have been flagrant corruption on the part of the governor. However that may be, it is hardly under a similar *régime* that the wild Circassians and Nogai Tartars can be kept quiet.

We did not stop at Antioch, but hurried on to Daphne to lunch under grateful shade beside gushing cascades, once sacred to Apollo. The Persian conqueror, Chosroes, delighted to resort to the groves and fountains of Daphne, though Christianity had then already destroyed its shrines. Nature had done enough without art to make it still the most charming spot in the country. Following the course of the Orontes on its left bank amidst thickets of myrtle, laurel, and arbutus, with the gigantic Casius rising abruptly on our left to a height of five thousand three hundred feet, we crossed the river at a ferry, and left its lovely vale where it burst through a narrow opening into the lower

plain. The lofty cliffs on either side, too precipitous
for a pathway, obliged us to continue our ride amongst
the mulberry gardens to Suadeah, which name is given
to the widely studded cottages of their cultivators.
Several English settlers had built houses, but they are
now all tenantless. There is no harbour; the mouth
of the Orontes, being obstructed by a dangerous bar,
can only give shelter to boats, and the ancient artificial
port, or rather dock, of Seleucia, is entirely filled up.
The ruins of the maritime city of Seleucus Nicator
are extensive, but altogether levelled with the ground.
A fine colossal statue, representing the river Orontes,
lately dug up, and a curious tunnel constructed in the
rock to prevent a winter torrent from flowing into the
basin, with a great many sepulchral caves of considerable interest, are the only remains worth visiting.
After examining these, and bathing in the sea like
Chosroes, whose career of conquest closed here, but
without offering any solemn sacrifice of thanksgiving
to the sun as he did, we cantered along the sandy beach
extending from Mount Rhosus to Mount Casius on our
way to the dilapidated villa of a late British consul,
where we had taken up our quarters. A crowd of
Ansairi near it were engaged, when we arrived, in
something like the act of worship of Chosroes; they
were dancing round a small building in which a fire
was blazing, and they jabbered Arabic all the time
with a richness of gutturals that conveyed the impression of a tracheal epidemic vigorously combated by
universal gargling.

Suadeah has been thought of as a terminus for a
great Indian railway.   Some prefer Alexandretta.
The main consideration for this country is that the
scheme should be soon carried out, be it from one point
or from the other.   To Great Britain it would naturally be advantageous, as bringing her eastern empire
a thousand miles nearer than by any other route, and
it would probably also restore the flow of trade to the
channel in which it rolled its wealth to our shores of
old.   The Syrian desert is the keystone of an arch,
stretching from Europe to Eastern Asia, resting on the
Mediterranean and the Persian Gulf as on two pillars,
and bridging the natural transit and interchange of
commodities between these two quarters of the globe.
Twice have attempts been made to establish their
communication by this way, and, without either having
failed, both schemes have been abandoned.   Five and
twenty years ago, General Chesney successfully navi-
gated the Euphrates by steam, and five years ago Sir
John Macneill gave his high authority as an engineer
in favour of the construction of a railway.   Yet nothing is being done to secure the benefits of such a
line at a time when Monsieur Lesseps is making rapid
strides towards the completion of his Suez canal in the
interest of France.   We shall awake some morning
with the whole Indian trade monopolised by others,
and Napoleon's fleet on its way from Toulon to Bombay
by the Red Sea, while ours may have to go from
Portsmouth round the Cape of Good Hope to defend
our Indian possessions.   Even if the Suez canal should

prove a failure, which I think it will, it may still serve as a pretext for the presence of a French force in Egypt to stop the way to us in the event of a war taking place. Before British power in India rose to its present zenith, we had a rich Oriental trade nearer home. The Levant Company, now a barren tradition, was then a golden reality. The tide of our supremacy has since flowed further towards the east, and by another current, that set in by Vasco de Gama. That stream is now ebbing, and the question of opening new channels has become urgent. British commercial enterprise, like everything else with us, has its fits and fashions. A check in the India, China, or American trade suffices to divert its course. The establishment of a shorter route, a new facility for the importation of raw materials or exportation of manufactured goods, a sudden discovery of a fresh field of speculation, can at any time give an impulse to its coin-compelling flow. Then comes a reaction, and it returns to its previous channel when the diverting cause has ceased to operate. Thus, the introduction of railways may now have the effect of superseding the Cape of Good Hope line, which formerly ruined that on which the improved means of transport may be realised. The chief obstacle to this is the rivalry of Suez. The advantages derived by other states from the previous changes of route can still be annulled; France is open to disappointment in Egypt; Russia may lose her overland trade through Central Asia. A new route may become as beneficial to us as the existing lines are prejudicial.

Whether we regard the subject from a political or from a commercial point of view, and whether we enter into competition with France in the south or with Russia in the north, all present appearances foreshadow an ultimate predominance on the part of Great Britain, both in influence and in trade, if the population of this country were brought into more immediate contact with us by the reopening of the Syrian channel of communication. The question as regards France is as yet prospective, and will depend on the degree of success attending the construction of the Suez canal. But Russia has been our active rival for many years. Her agents have systematically represented her in these parts as an overwhelming central power fated to predominate over the destinies of the world. In this they are consistent with the political tendency of their nation towards despotism after the manner of Asia, and they find an echo in the political tendency of the population of Syria, which is essentially Asiatic. It brings them to the feet of the greatest despotism in the world, be it, or rather especially if it be, the very incarnation of oppression. Ivan the Terrible or Nicholas appears to them as legitimate a sovereign as Gengis Khan or Timour the Tartar. They do not penetrate the spirit and essence of a government, but are captivated by its form alone, if it be in harmony with their own inherent sympathy for visible power. The massive strength of Russia is thus homogeneous with the nations of the east. She has hitherto been without a rival in this respect. But the rise of trading

energies is now giving her a rival in Great Britain, in
whose favour they militate.   The original elements,
which enriched bygone generations of dense populations, still exist in this country ; in proportion as trade
brings them into play, Syria is drawn towards England.
Each cargo of cotton shipped is a blow to Russia.
From the gradual development of resources to adoption as a channel for the trade of distant lands the pro-
gression is natural and easy.   Geographically situated
between Europe and the far east, especially since steam
has made seas and continents the means of union rather
than the cause of estrangement between widely-sepa-
rated nations, the rich and level expanse of Syria and
Mesopotamia must, one would think, soon act as a link
for the binding together of the hitherto broken chain,
and for the assimilation of divergent interests in some
of the most important parts of the world: Such a
union would be the greatest fact of modern history.
Russia has been yet alone in her influence over this
vast field of action.   Our name is hardly known beyond
the boundaries of the states' conterminous with our
Indian empire, and it is respected only as that of a
great maritime power without a hold on the interior.
France and the other European countries may be said
to be utterly ignored, as far as present political influence is concerned, at any distance from the eastern
shore of the Mediterranean.   Russia, on the other hand,
stretched her fame years ago beyond the Uralian and
Altai mountains.   She formed establishments and
raised fortresses, as stated in the work of Haxthausen,

n the northern regions of the obsolete Mogul empire. She boasts, through her poet Pushkin, of her sway extending from the Cremlin to the wall of China. Fifteen millions of Russian subjects press on two sides of Central Asia; they are made to learn the official Slavonian language, to attach them to Russia, while they are allowed to retain their vernacular Tartar, Mogul, and Manchoo dialects, which bind the non-annexed populations to them. They are called Christians, though practising Mohammedanism and Shamanism. Their customs, wants, and tendencies differ in no way from those of the neighbouring hordes whom they have taught to look up to them as a civilised people, and to envy the protection of the white czar, as they call the emperor of all the Russias. And this has been effected by a state which had neither political nor commercial existence a century and a half ago, when our Levant Company possessed a fleet of three hundred large boats of their own on the Euphrates for the transport of their merchandise. We were not wise when we conceded to the factory of British merchants at St. Petersburgh the exclusive privilege of trading with Central Asia. Both the Levant Company and East India Company had applied for it in vain. The route by the Caspian Sea and Astrakhan soon gained an advantage over the more southern line, a due of eight per cent. being the only charge. When, exhausted by constant warfare, Persia and Turkey had lost the power of protecting the Caucasian states, Russia, moved by feelings of compassionate humanity as recorded in the manifesto of

Alexander I., marched a couple of regiments through
the Dariel pass, and occupied Georgia. To keep the
various adjacent tribes from internecine feuds, the Persian provinces of Erivan, Talcih, and Nakhchevan, and
the independent territory of Imeritia, Mingrelia,
Abassia, and Gooriel, were taken possession of; and
the north-eastern coast of the Black Sea became subject to Russia. All the country from the Euxine to
the Caspian was thus annexed. The latter sea is now
a Russian lake, connected with the centre of power by
the great navigable river Volga. Seventeen steamers
ply on the Caspian. Caravans convey goods from its
southern and eastern shores, landed in three days from
Astrakhan, to Khiva in twenty-five, Bokhara in thirty,
and Samarcand, the ancient Tartar capital, in thirty-
five; to Meshed and Herat, the principal marts towards
the south-east, in fifteen and twenty-five days. The
exports of Russia by her Asiatic frontier exceed the
value of ten millions of roubles per annum, and her
imports fifteen millions. Even Prussia sends her broad-
cloth by this route to China to the annual amount of a
quarter of a million sterling. Were a channel of trade
encouraged through Syria, Mesopotamia, and Persia, all
these results, so unfavourable to our interests, would fall
to the ground, for it would be a cheaper line; and our
trade would take the field on an equal footing with that
of other countries. To the Turkish provinces, through
which it would pass, it is a question of the greatest
interest, for no other contingency could better or more
rapidly enable their former prosperity to revive.

LETTER XX.

Circassians—Massacre of Musulmans by Christians—Rebellion
of Armenians of Zeitoon—Their positions stormed by Circassians
—Priests murdered—Zeitoon attacked—Monk killed—Treachery
of Turkomans—Defeat of Government Irregulars—Cannon taken
—Musulman Conspiracy to massacre the Christians of Marash—
Reinforcements procured from Aleppo—Tranquillity restored—
Negociations with Zeitoon—Blockade commenced—Submission of
the Armenians—Robberies—Murder of a Missionary—Crime in
Turkey—Misgovernment—State of Turkey—Reforms—Coloniza-
tion—The Hatt Humayoon—Results?

Marash: August 25, 1862.

THE principal change I find here since my last visit
is a change of persons. There seems to be little
or none in the state of the country. Drunkenness was
apparently not the sole vice of Hoorshid Pasha, who
was then governor of Marash. He has recently been
removed from his post for venality. His successor,
Aziz Pasha, is a young man bringing an excellent reputation with him from previous posts. He has had to
commence his functions here by the dangerous task of
redressing the wrongs inflicted by his predecessor, who
accordingly left the place, after justice had been done
between him and those aggrieved by him, with threats
of vengeance on Aziz Pasha. An opportunity was not
long waited for. Hoorshid Pasha, like most others
similarly circumstanced, soon found means of obtaining
favour at Constantinople, and he has returned to this

part of the country in the higher rank of Governor of
Adana.   His influence at Marash, exercised from so
near a point, has been most injurious to Aziz Pasha, as I
shall explain presently.

I find also a great change in the physiognomy and
costume of the inhabitants. I left here only Turkomans
and Armenians ; and now the majority of those one sees
in the streets are Circassians.   These hungry refugees
treat Turkey as a conquered country, swaggering about,
all bristling with arms, and abusing every person
daring to make the least objection to their insolence and
lawlessness.   They sell their children freely, both male
and female.   One Turk has bought eight for about
three hundred pounds.   They are even accused of
kidnapping children of the country to dispose of as
slaves.   A caravan of natives rescued, it is said, a boy
of four years of age, whom a Circassian was carrying
in a large saddle-bag, and who happened to cry as they
met on the road.   The capture and sale of prisoners
from hostile tribes was the origin of this nefarious
traffic.   The market for slaves was in Turkey, where
the menial offices were performed chiefly by foreigners,
and where polygamy offered a provision for well-
favoured Caucasian damsels.   The supply having
become unequal to the demand, the Circassians began
to send their own flesh and blood to the market.   It is
truly a strange spectacle to behold a people, always
ready to fight valiantly for its liberty, and yet basely
selling that of its offspring.   It is idle to gloss over the
barbarism of the practice, as some writers have done,

x

by alleging that paternal solicitude finds in it the best
mode of securing a comfortable establishment for handsome daughters, and a means of opening a high career
for clever sons, or that patriotism sacrifices even the
ties of family to provide for the purchase of ammunition to defend an invaded country.   The plain prose of
such poetic flights is that the Circassians regard their
children as property of the same nature as their mountain goats, and dispose of them accordingly.   The mild
character of slavery under the Turks, the kindness of
the Mussulman husband, tainted with contempt though
it be, in domestic life, prove that Turkish cruelty in
families was a fable, or has been mitigated; but the Circassian father is not the less unnatural on that account.
The Circassians, on the contrary, have in this respect
continued in the barbarous state they were in when
Jason led Greeks thither in search of the mythic golden
fleece; which, by the way, meant probably the mode
of collecting gold in the beds of rivers, still practised,
by sinking sheepskins to catch the precious particles
washed down by the stream.   That the Phœnicians
also entertained commercial relations of a similar character, and perhaps at an equally remote epoch with
that of the Argonauts, is evident from the foundation
of their colony of Pronectus, and from the mention of
them by Ezekiel under the names of Tubal and Me-
shech as traders in the persons of men.   It was probably a custom all over the thinly-peopled globe in
very ancient times, and it is remarkable that the progress of enlightenment should have failed to do away

with it only in the region first inhabited after the flood.
The Circassians deserve, however, all credit from us
for their protracted opposition to the advance of Russia,
which is indirectly advantageous to England. Shut
out from the south by eight hundred miles of sea,
Russia had but two lines of conquest to follow. That
round the western shore of the Euxine has been con-
tested by a long series of wars, and is closed for the
present by the Treaty of Paris; the other, turning the
eastern flank of the barrier, and leading through Armenia, Koordistan, and Turkish Arabia, to the Persian
Gulf, has been opened by the Crimean war. The Circassian struggle to retain independence is an obstacle
in her way, for Russia, though possessing Georgia,
would not leave an armed foe in her rear, as Turkey
did with Montenegro in Europe and the Armenians of
Taurus in Asia, to her frequent great discomfiture.
Napoleon III. well understood the importance to Great
Britain of this eastern outlet for Russian conquest,
which might seriously endanger our relations and com-
munications with the far east. He was our sincere
ally in the Crimean war until the siege of Kars involved an English interest alone, when he placed every
possible impediment in the way of its relief, and allowed
Mouravieff to take and destroy the only fortress on the
Armenian frontier of Turkey. This was a victory
over England, which Russia, taking advantage of our
having a Queen's Commissioner and his small staff of
British officers with the Turkish army, represented as
a defeat of British forces, but which was more serious

to us than a mere military disaster, because it removed
one of the bulwarks of the east against Russia, and
Turkey will not probably ever construct another. The
first line of defence is still unbroken in the gallant resistance of the Circassians. It may appear ungracious
on the part of an Englishman to say anything against
them. But I cannot see in them the least merit as a
nation beyond that of great personal bravery. They
have played a prominent part here during the last few
weeks, in which they have fully maintained that national reputation.

A dispute arose between two Mussulman villages in
this neighbourhood, by name Ketma and Beshen, regarding the boundaries of a field. The claimants of
Beshen asked the chief of Alabash, an adjoining Armenian village, to act as umpire between them and
their adversaries in the suit. The inhabitants of Ketma
refused to accept his judgment when he repaired thither for that purpose with some of his people. An
altercation ensued, then a scuffle, in which the son of
the chief of Alabash, four other Armenians, and two
Moslems, were killed. During the following night,
the Armenians went to the village of Ketma in a large
body. Of sixteen men, whom they found, only three
left their houses alive. Even these lost their lives
afterwards by drowning in the river Jihoon, which they
attempted to swim when pursued. The Armenians in
the village, supposing the three men had escaped, declared that three children should answer for each of
them. Nine children were accordingly put to death.

The women of Ketma sought protection and justice at Marash, one of them showing a deep gash in her shoulder, inflicted by an Armenian in the act of cutting off the head of an infant in her arms, while her three other children lay murdered around her. The villagers of Alabash were called upon to give up the perpetrators of these atrocities. On their refusal, an irregular force, numbering nine hundred and forty men, was sent to capture them. The Armenians then took up arms, and marched towards Marash, about eight hundred strong. Three days were given them to reconsider their rebellious refusal to surrender. It was repeated at the expiration of the term. They were then attacked. During the three days, the Armenians had dug trenches and raised breastworks to defend themselves. The resistance on their part was obstinate. Some Circassians, amongst the irregular troops raised for the expedition, carried the first earthwork with the greatest gallantry. They were all wounded in the assault except their Bey, who rushed on alone to attack the second trench about fifty paces higher. He was shot down before reaching it. Others came up, and the Armenians were finally driven from all their defences, leaving thirty-eight killed. The irregulars lost ten men. A guard was immediately placed over the women and children in the village. The houses were plundered. Amongst those who escaped were the murderers of Ketma; they took refuge at the principal Armenian town of the district, Zeitoon. The irregular force was then augmented to the effective strength of three thousand one hundred,

310 RAMBLES IN SYRIA. [LETTER XX.

six hundred of whom were Circassians, and the remainder Turkomans of the neighbouring plains, and
townspeople of Marash. The expedition marched
against Zeitoon under the command of Aziz Pasha.
On the way through a mountain pass leading thither,
the Armenian villagers of Mukhal attempted to stop
its onward progress. After a short action the village
was taken, sacked, and burnt; and its inhabitants retired to Zeitoon. The convent of Perghich was also
on the road; some Circassians forced its gates, and
butchered the superior, two deacons, and an old woman
servant, whose bodies they stripped, mutilated, and
piled on the roadside with the carcase of a dog placed
on them, in a manner too abominable to bear description in detail. The total loss of life had amounted
hitherto to about a hundred and twenty on the side of
the Christians, and between seventy and eighty on that
of the Mussulmans. Of the latter many were conveyed to Marash wounded; the Armenian inhabitants
of the town finding safety in keeping within doors,
while the convoys were passing through the streets,
so great was the rage and excitement of the Moslem
population at sight of wounds inflicted on the true
believers by Christians. When the expedition reached
the vicinity of Zeitoon, the town was summoned to
surrender, and to give up the murderers. Negotiations
were commenced with every prospect of a favourable
issue, the only condition proposed by the Armenians
being that the Circassians should not be permitted to
enter their town. A corps of irregulars, about eight

hundred in number, forming part of the expedition,
suddenly advanced upon Zeitoon without orders from
Aziz Pasha. It was commanded by a certain Ahmed
Pasha, a native of Marash, who had raised it from
amongst the lower orders of his Mussulman fellow-
townsmen.   He is the intimate friend of the ex-
governor, Hoorshid Pasha. Seeing themselves attacked,
the Armenians of Zeitoon sallied forth in a well-armed
body to give battle, for they enjoy a high character for
martial qualities.   The irregulars were at once withdrawn by Ahmed Pasha, but the Circassians, who had
come forward to support them, engaged the Christians,
and a sharp and bloody contest was sustained between
them for about an hour.   The Armenians were driven
into their town with great slaughter.   The Circassians
followed them, fighting in the streets, and plundering
the houses in spite of a most courageous defence by
their inmates of both sexes.   A large convent stands
on the hill above the point attacked.   The monks barricaded its doors and windows, and fired from the roof
on the Circassians.   A field-piece was brought up.
One monk came out, to parley as was supposed, and
prevent the cannon being pointed at the convent.   He
was immediately cut down by a Circassian, who called
him an accursed Russian.   The building was set fire
to.   Aziz Pasha, who was near, succeeded in saving
it; and rendered thereby meritorious service to his
government, which might have been seriously embarrassed by the consequences of the destruction of a
Christian monastery full of friars and priests when

foreign cabinets are known to be watching for such an
opportunity. Indeed Monsieur Thouvenel's note on
the withdrawal of the French army of occupation says
so most unequivocally. The Circassians, while fighting
with the Armenians, frequently reinforced in front,
found themselves in the most unexpected manner vigorously assailed on the flank by a body of nine hundred Turkomans of the Tajerli and Kiligli tribes, who
were with the irregular troops. These Turkomans
were led on by Suleyman Aga, who had given us hospitality in his camp on our previous visit to Marash,
and who had afterwards become a devoted adherent of
Hoorshid Pasha, and had been amnestied as a rebel by
the Porte on the recommendation of that governor.
He is said to have hurried off to Adana to receive instructions from his patron when he was called upon by
Aziz Pasha to take command of the Turkomans with
the expedition. This treacherous onslaught by those
regarded as comrades threw the Circassians into confusion. The Armenians rallied. They captured the
whole party in charge of the field-piece, and took the
gun into Zeitoon in triumph. All the irregulars commenced retreating in the greatest disorder. The Circassians were the last to run, but they too joined the
rout, leaving sixty-two of their men dead on the field.
The Armenians, who buried those killed on both sides,
declare that they were more than four hundred. Towards
evening the remains of the irregular force poured into
Marash, wild with disappointment and rage. Aziz
Pasha reached the town about midnight. Exposure

to the sun, fatigue, anxiety, and shame at his defeat, brought on typhus fever, which has kept him prostrate in mind and body ever since.

The greatest excitement arose in the town when the circumstances became known. Nothing less than a general massacre of all its Christian inhabitants would satisfy the indignant Moslems. Outbursts of grief and resentment, over dead and wounded, threatened at every moment to give the signal. The head of an Armenian, brought by a Mussulman from Zeitoon at his saddle-bow, was carried about the town, and money was paid to him by the Mussulmans to whom he showed it, as a pledge that they would rise and fight. Boys afterwards kicked it through the streets, and it was finally thrown into the river. Thirty of the chief Moslems assembled in a mosque with closed doors to organise their revenge. The different quarters of the town inhabited by Christians were distributed amongst them for murder and rapine, that each might have his due share for his followers. But regular troops had, meanwhile, been procured from Aleppo, and, on the morning after the repulse at Zeitoon, a battalion of rifles, two squadrons of dragoons, and two field-pieces, marched into the town. Patrols and pickets were immediately established in the streets. An intimation was sent to the thirty Moslem conspirators, with a paper containing all their names that they might see they were known, to the effect that, if they ventured to stir out of their houses, they would all and each of them be at once marched off to Constantinople under an escort of regulars. The Armenian Bishop of Marash was then sent to Zeitoon with a warning that the bridge of the Jihoon and the three mountain passes leading to that town would be occupied by riflemen, if the murderers of Ketma were not given up within three days. All the grain of the Armenians, being still on the threshing-floors when the irregulars passed the villages, some of which were abandoned by their inhabitants, had been burnt, and Zeitoon could thus be starved into submission. It was announced, however, that the women and children would be allowed to remove to the Armenian villages whose population had returned to their homes, and that Zeitoon would be supplied with corn by the authorities as soon as it should show obedience to them. On the fourth day, no answer having been received, fifty irregulars were sent to the bridge, to precede the regulars about to blockade the place on all sides. The bishop was sent back when it was thus seen that the threat had been made in earnest. He brought proofs that all the murderers of Ketma had been killed in the fight before and in the town of Zeitoon, excepting one who was lying so badly wounded that he could not be moved. A full submission to the government was made at the same time. The captured field-piece was returned. A Turkish governor was then sent to Zeitoon, and was well received there. A sum of thirty-five thousand piastres was paid by the Armenians as arrears, and further instalments were promised. A mixed commission was formed to verify the losses of unoffending persons with a view to compensation. The

question of the treatment of the Circassians still remains
to be settled. I hoped that those who had been guilty
of atrocities, especially such as were committed at the
convent of Perghich, might be severely punished, but
it appears that the services they have rendered to the
government will be regarded at Constantinople as a
set-off. The whole irregular force has, meanwhile,
been paid and disbanded. This was necessary and
urgent, although disorders might ensue, for their insolence and lawlessness exposed the population to greater
dangers when they were in the service of the government than after their dismissal. Robberies still occur
daily, however. No Christian dares to offer his wares
for sale in the bazaars of Marash, or take out his mules
to bring grapes from his vineyard, for the Circassians
at once seize them, and, when objection is made, draw
their long knives, demanding the blood of their bey,
killed by the hated Russians, as they persist in calling
the Armenians. Indeed, the whole country is in a
worse state than ever. The Turkomans, having betrayed their trust in the fight, and fearing the consequences of their act, make themselves more formidable
than usual as robbers in hope of bringing the authorities
to treat with them. When hard pressed, they go to
the woody and rocky recesses of the Ghiaoor Dagh,
whither no pursuit can overtake them, and whence
they descend to make fresh depredations. Even at
Alexandretta merchants' stores and warehouses are
invaded, and goods carried off with impunity. One of
them, well acquainted with the Turkoman chiefs,

having suffered a loss in this way, knew so well where
to look for his missing bales that he wrote to them at
once; and found them next morning before his door
uninjured.   A very shocking murder took place a short
time ago on the road from Adana by the Ghiaoor Dagh
to Alexandretta.   The Rev. Mr. Coffing, a much-
respected American missionary, accompanied by a servant, two muleteers, and one irregular soldier, was
suddenly fired at from behind some brushwood.   Mr.
Coffing was mortally wounded, as also his servant, and
one muleteer severely, the other slightly.   The soldier
galloped off at once unhurt.   Three horses bearing
their baggage were taken.   Mr. Coffing contrived to go
on for some time, but was at last from loss of blood
unable to proceed further.   He lay down on the sandy
beach.   The muleteer, who had suffered least, went as
far as Alexandretta to give the alarm.   Mr. Coffing
was conveyed thither, and died next morning.   His
servant was brought in on the following day, and lived
only to tell the particulars of the attack, which Mr.
Coffing was past explaining when he was found.   The
muleteers both recovered, the soldier was not forthcoming, and the horses were sold by some Turkomans
in one of the villages.

Crime in Turkey differs essentially from crime in
Europe.   Here we have no gangs of housebreakers, no
shoplifters, or pickpockets.   The vigilance of the police
is not eluded; it is defied.   No stigma attaches to acts
of violence.   In Europe towns are infested by malefactors, while the country is comparatively free from

them. In Turkey it is rare to hear of murders or
robberies in towns, and this absence of what would be
called elsewhere ordinary crime is very remarkable,
but the population of the country is a prey to lawlessness. Police is not what is most wanted in Turkey; it
is government. The want of government creates here
lawless classes, not individual criminals. Lord Macaulay
says that no ordinary misgovernment will do as much
to make a nation wretched as the constant effort of
every man to better himself will do to make a nation
prosperous. The constant effort of most Turks to
better themselves belongs to one of two descriptions;
plunder and bribed connivance. High and low, official
and unofficial, rich and poor, all follow the tortuous
groove of peculation, corruption, and extortion, on the
one hand, or are addicted, on the other, to armed
depredations. I allude, of course, only to the provinces
of Turkey, as I have already more than once specified
in remarking on the state of the country. Were the
astonishing perseverance and ingenuity employed in
the pursuit of illicit gain, and the great courage and
skill displayed in acts of violence, turned into the wide
and legitimate channel referred to by our distinguished
historian, they would, by a parity of reasoning, make
the nation very prosperous. But, to effect anything of
the kind, a new social order must be inaugurated,
which would admit of both classes earning their livelihood honestly, and some moral distinction must be
established between what is right and what is wrong
that crime should be stigmatised. For the usual

isolated disturbances, remedial measures, more or less
prompt and efficacious, may be expected from the
Turks, but, when a people is thus perverted, as well as
misgoverned, all practical improvement to be looked for
from the Porte can, I fear, be of little avail. The evil
is deep-seated in a country where labour is not allowed
to be productive, and plunder in all its varieties is
encouraged by sharing its profits. Lord Macaulay's
ordinary misgovernment theory has no application
here. This is a stupendous misgovernment, and the
nation is very wretched.

The state of Turkey can only be judged fairly in
connection with her history since the commencement
of the present century, and by the light of all the
collateral evidence which that history is able to furnish.
Many writers have treated the problem as being, what
we should think of a single unfavourable occurrence,
and what deductions should be drawn from it. Certainly, if this is all that has to be answered, Mussulmans
are simply monsters, and the sooner they are exterminated from the face of the earth the better it will be.
But the first point which history and common sense
concur to call in question is, that the existing evils
arise from an overweening sense of strength. I believe,
on the contrary, that they originate in a source diame-
trically opposed to this, a galling sense of weakness, in
presence of a rising Christian supremacy, and a designing foreign exasperation. I have no sympathy now,
however, with the apologetic literature of the philo-
Turkish school. The former class of publications found

favour in the eyes of our grandfathers; the latter became more or· less popular some twenty years ago.
Both are obsolete. Theories are out of fashion. This
is the age of facts, and one must grapple with them,
and find out what they are made of. I have stated
my idea on the subject, and I have narrated many circumstances and incidents which have come under my
notice since I have been in this country; it remains
for others to judge whether or not my idea is borne
out by them.

There have been collisions between religious sects,
hostile tribes, and factious parties. These I regard as
symptoms of the decline of a dominant race, bursting
forth in occasional recrudescences in proportion as the
rise of another social order becomes felt, and allowing
conflicting interests to fight out their own battles.
Such contingencies were more rare before the struggle
commenced between absolute predominance and the
assertion of equal rights. They prove, therefore, that
a change is taking root in favour of the Christians, and
not merely that the Christians are oppressed by the
Turks. Yet, these same Christians appeal to Europe on
each recurrence, whining out their fears, festered into
grotesque and monstrous forms of fanaticism, of which
they mysteriously reveal portentous specimens. An-
tiquated foreign enthusiasts, loving to parade forgotten
lore, and indulging the play of fancy at the expense of
rigid truth, rave in the very madness of philanthropy,
grown cruel to Moslems in assumed mercy to Christians. People, who know nothing of Turkey as she

really is, having only taken the bird's-eye view of the
traveller, or studied the aspect of her capital, go home
to echo the strain till all Christendom is ripe for
another crusade. Then, certain continental cabinets
consider it their duty to interfere. Encouragement on
one side, exasperation on the other, do their work sooner
or later, and another outburst arises from the embers of
the last one. Thus it goes on, and will go on, till the
game shall have been played out, and foreign policy
shall have attained its object. Acrimonious language
publicly held with regard to Turkey also envenoms the
relations between the two communities, and between
one of them and other states, for it is always translated
into local newspapers, to the wild exultation of Christians, and the bitter resentment of Turks. So much,
indeed, has this been the case, that every disturbance,
be it even a result of agitation from abroad, becomes
an engine for the production of another, while it un-
happily arrays, at the same time, some of the leading
minds of Europe against even what is least unsound in
Turkey, and least imputable to the Turks. In the
strength of the assertions, people overlook their want
of verisimilitude. My belief is altogether of a general
character, and unaffected by particulars adduced to
give colour to narrations and foregone conclusions.
What happens in Turkey might happen, I feel convinced, were the whole population of one religious
faith. It is composed of two distinct antagonistic elements, the reciprocal asperities of whose relative position are not smoothed down by the double attrition of

any intermediate class.   The Mussulmans are a land-
holding aristocracy ; the Christians are peasants and
tradesmen.   In most other countries, a third element
occupies a species of neutral ground, deriving an easy
independence from both agriculture and commerce, and
serving as a shield to the labouring classes against a
spirit of encroachment on the part of the nobles, while
it is ready to uphold the rights of the latter against
popular lawlessness.   This is wanting in Turkey.   The
tilling, trading, and industrial portion of the population, not being bound to the dominant race by the ties
of mutual interest, as employed and employer, knows
no feeling in unison with that of the Turk, who arrays
against it, not only the overwhelming lawful power of
a despotic system of government, but also the still
more debasing and the less legitimate form of oppression, founded on personal position gained by bribery,
with the consequent necessity of draining the produce
of labour and industry to supply the means of corruption.   This has no reference, it will be perceived, to
religious distinctions, and it exists as much in districts
inhabited by Moslems alone as in those having a mixed
population.   In such a state of society patriotism cannot live.   The noble seeks only the patronage of a
greater noble.   The boor strives solely for the tranquil
enjoyment of his due share in the fruits of the earth.
The trader, or artisan, toils for the realisation of the
fair profits of hisshop or loom.   Tax-gatherers are the
dreaded enemies of all except the noble, in whose service
they are.   No class has thus a care beyond its own

Y

immediate wants. The first thirsts for money to purchase favour, and desires favour to amass money. The
second and third hoard a pittance to meet the exactions of
the local administration. It is self-evident that reforms
are called for; equally so, that they must come from without. The Mussulman grandee, if consulted by the Sultan, would assent to the premises, and then propose, as a
remedy, that he should himself be made Governor-General of his native province, or Grand Vizier, concluding
with the insinuation that he would in that case feel
honoured by permission to supply the imperial kitchen
with butter and cheese gratis for a year. The Christian
labourer or tradesman would first wonder what his Imperial Majesty could want from him so important that the
demand should be preceded by holding out such unrealisable hopes, and, when convinced that only his own advantage was sought, he would accept the benefits offered
on the one indispensable condition, that he should be
taken into foreign consular protection, in order that his
life might be saved in the massacre which the improvement of the state of the Christians would infallibly give
rise to, or, if it should not be saved, that his family,
through that protection, should receive an indemnity
ten times greater than the fortune they might have
lost. Reforms must be introduced in Turkey by foreign
pressure; not nominally, as heretofore, but really introduced; not merely to affect the political position of
the Ottoman empire, in relation to other states, as
heretofore, but to supply a remedy so loudly called for
by the evils within it. Turkey is received into the

concert of Europe, as it is styled; this does not modify
the domination of the Turks, which must be admitted
to be the first desideratum; it only enables them to
contract loans, so far as I can see, and other loans
to pay the interest of the previous ones. The integrity
of the Empire is guaranteed; this, again, does nothing
to arrest the internal decline; it only makes the Turks
look about them to see which of their provinces is to be
taken from them next; after Transylvania and Hun-
gary had been wrested from them by Austria; the
Crimea, Bessarabia, and the Kuban, by Russia; Ser-
via made independent; Wallachia and Moldavia nearly
so; Greece, a separate state, after the destruction of
the Turkish fleet at Navarino, by England, France, and
Russia; Algeria taken by France; and Egypt made
an heir-loom in the family of Mahomed Ali, by England,
Russia, Austria, and Prussia. The Turks think us
strange people. But, as they accept a guarantee for
their frontiers, they submit also to the changes imposed
on them in their system of government. They admit
them in principle, but defeat them in detail. In this
latter operation, they have proved themselves more
skilful than their advisers. Still we go on advising,
I believe.

Reforms are brought about in Europe without danger
or difficulty, because their necessity or expediency is
felt by the people, and the government grants them
accordingly. Here the people do not wish for reforms,
the Moslems knowing they have everything to lose by
them, the Christians fearing lest they lose more than

they gain. Reforms must therefore be applied without
any preparation of the public mind. It is still doubted
by many that Sultan Abd ul Aziz really desires reforms;
but, supposing him to be seriously and sincerely disposed to introduce them, the question of the means he
can employ is full of difficulty. The Koran forbids his
following the example of Peter the Great, and bringing
able men from Christian countries, while the few
Europeans in the Turkish service are rendered powerless by being obliged to assimilate themselves to the
Turks, or lose their posts by refusing to do so. Had
it been otherwise, Turkey might have been saved
by the same iron hand which raised France from the
ruins of her revolution, for Buonaparte had determined
on entering the Sultan's army after the siege of Toulon,
and only wanted a little encouragement to carry out
his purpose. There is little to be hoped for from the
plan of sending clever young Turks to be educated in
Europe, and to serve an apprenticeship in the different
departments of administration there, for, if we may
judge by many of those Turks who have adopted
European ideas, the sacrifice made of what is respectable
in the old Turkish character is greater than the gain of
a mongrel civilisation. Islam once betrayed, as the
good Mussulman says, nothing remains to be moulded
into the perfect form of an upright public servant.
The Turk is emasculated when his Mahometan principles are taken from him. Yet the formation of a
body of honest officials is a measure which, if possible,
would go far to place Turkey in a hopeful position.

The open plunder practised is strikingly inconsistent with the indubitable honesty of a numerous class of the Turks in their private and commercial relations. Whether it be a lingering remnant of a past state of society, in which rapacious Satraps left no defence but roguery, and no other feeling towards them than hostility, or the more immediate result of a deep abhorrence of all innovations on the ancient Mussulman law, is uncertain, as indications of both origins are discernible. Mussulmans often seek foreign protection during litigation before Turkish authorities, implying thereby a rooted distrust of them; and Mahometan merchants are unwilling even to give receipts for the payment of duty on their goods, or of new imposts, because they are not sanctioned by the Koran, evincing a disapproval of them, from which there is an easy transition to defrauding the state. The benefit derived, moreover, from applying a curb to venality and corruption can at best be only partial and temporary, unless it be accompanied by the development of the vast resources of the country. The two questions act and react on each other. Money circulates, whether honestly or not, without increasing the national wealth and prosperity, when it is not employed in a productive form. It flows from the threshing-floor of the industrious cultivator to the coffers of the grinding tax-gatherer, who passes it on in bribes, through a graduated hierarchy of needy spendthrifts, till it supplies the superfluous profusion of the imperial household. Supposing its progress to be confined to the purest possible channels, still the country

would remain impoverished if the mines of riches it
possesses are left closed by neglect and by the want of
adjustment in their essential conditions. Thus, Syria
might send incredible amounts to the Sultan's treasury,
were cultivation extended over the boundless fertile
plains on its eastern frontier, were the Nomadic tribes
encouraged to settle in the many deserted towns and
villages with which they are studded, and were the
rivers and smaller streams diverted into canals, after
the manner of the ancient Babylonians, for the irrigation
of crops and plantations suited to the soil and climate.
To effect this, the only thing wanted is security. The
elements of prosperity are abundant, but they cannot
be made productive as long as the Arabs, Koords, and
Turkomans are allowed to commit depredations at will.
In the present state of the Turkish Empire it may
seem utopian to contemplate such a career of improvement, but the means would be forthcoming if the
energy to use them could be found. It would require
some annual outlay to enable the better-disposed tribes
to complete a cordon of military colonies on the skirts
of the desert, and to maintain a sufficient force for their
protection against the more unruly tribes. This might
be supplied by recasting the establishment of irregular
troops, now kept up at a great expense and with little
advantage, and by small savings in other less important
branches of the provincial administration. The different details of the organisation of this country are so
dove-tailed into one another, that in tracing them one
is led from effect to cause until the higher sources of

evil are exposed; economy is the keystone of the
administrative arch; and, when one sees the magnates
of the nation squandering in official pomp and private
luxury the hard-earned gains of the productive classes,
the impulse is irresistible to remind the Turks of that
simplicity of habits, both public and personal, which
formed the characteristic trait of their brilliant rise as a
nation, and which can alone save them from their present advancing decay. Instead of seeking to realise
the means of establishing tranquillity in the desert, the
Turks make discord amongst the tribes inhabiting it a
source of corruption. This policy is as short-sighted
as it is demoralising, for the hardy sons of the Syrian
plains, had the Turks secured their allegiance by acts
of justice and humanity, might have become an element
of internal consolidation and a bulwark against aggression from abroad, rather than one of the many existing
causes of the weakness and decline of the Ottoman
Empire. The country can never remain long quiet, I
feel convinced, until the evil of Bedaween disorders be
taken seriously into consideration. Remedial measures
are obvious, and by no means difficult of realisation,
but the importance of the subject is not duly appreciated in the proper quarter. It is not the desert alone
that suffers, as I have shown in previous letters. The
whole territory of Syria is crushed by the weight of
misgovernment. Its extent and fertility sufficed for
the support of ten millions of inhabitants, as recorded
by both Strabo and Josephus; now there are barely a
million and a half. Perfect salubrity of climate, and a

patient, frugal, and laborious race of cultivators, with
an active and intelligent trading community, leave
little wanting in Syria, for a rapid increase of population, and a degree of welfare now unknown, but the
security of life and property, and the construction of
roads for the cheap transport of produce to the coast.
It is true that the agricultural and industrial classes
are arrayed under hostile creeds, both under the domination of an oppressive aristocracy.   We hear of
Christians oppressed by Moslems, but there are two
other categories of which little is said, though their
existence is equally undeniable; I mean the oppression
of Mussulmans by Mussulmans, and that of Christians
by Christians.   All this, together with the intolerable
evil of foreign protection of classes and interference in
religious differences, renders the prospects of Syria
more clouded than those of other portions of the
Turkish Empire.   Greece, for instance, was one of its
provinces thirty-five years ago; that she enjoys some,
if not all, the benefits of political development, is
evident in the fact that her population, without having
augmented, draws twenty times the amount of manufactured goods from England that it consumed when
the Sandjaks of Morea and Roumelia existed; but
Greece possesses a perfect unity of faith and nationality,
while Syria, on the contrary, is a prey to religious
factions and national enmities, impeding all progress,
and furnishing a pretext for the subversion of tranquillity by foreign states.   On the whole, however, the
results of the experiment made by George Canning

with that portion of the Turkish Empire do not encourage Europe to try another.   Volney narrowly
escaped the Bastille for advising France to join Russia
against Turkey, when Joseph of Austria had shaken
the equilibrium of power by his alliance with Catherine
the Second, and to form a Christian empire, as a geo-
graphical necessity, with the command of the Bosphorus.
Leibnitz proposed to Louis the Fourteenth the conquest of Egypt, which he felicitously styled the
Holland of the East, to form a Christian empire with
Syria, and open the route of trade from India.   In
spite of the authority of two such distinguished philosophers, the facts of the present day point to another
solution of the fate of Turkey.   The political education
of the Sultan's Christian subjects has made so little
progress since those days that a violent change would
still find them greatly in arrear of all opinions regarding
them as prepared for self-government.   Nor do I see
that their political education stands much chance of
being speedily perfected, if time and opportunities are
not allowed and improved for the maturing of the seeds
sown by the edict of Gulkhaneh.

A long residence in the Turkish provinces must produce the conviction that nothing can be worse for their
Christian inhabitants than the measures adopted by influential cabinets on the occurrence of sudden disasters.
Momentary necessity moulds their will to try strong
remedies.   Success, however sagaciously pursued, remains unrealised; and the most skilful combinations
leave effects widely different from their logical conse-

quences in a country where the diversities and intricacies
of social interests are proverbial. Thus, an intestine
feud on Mount Lebanon and violent outrages at Damascus produced an armed intervention. France sent
troops. The Christian population is divided and subdivided into religious denominations inveterately hating
each other. The French have an exclusive and un-
masked sympathy for the Roman Catholics. The
priesthood of that persuasion, and of its satellite Maronite Church, maintains an organised persecution of
the Greek, Armenian, Jacobite, and Protestant churches,
as well as of the Druze community. These latter were
exposed to all the overbearing arrogance of those especially protected by the French, which went so far as
the perpetration of many murders and acts of barbarous vindictiveness. The Mussulmans, too, were
exasperated against the Christians in general by the
character of the protection exercised in favour of a
portion of them, and were irritated still more by the
insolence of those who were so protected. Disunion
in the country was thus more firmly established. Instead of helping the Christian population to qualify
itself for future beneficial changes, intervention in that
case rendered them less fit than ever to hold a more
advantageous position; and I am of opinion that it
will generally have that effect if adopted on other such
emergencies. It appears to me that the best chance
for Turkey is to make desirable changes grow, as it
were naturally, out of the course of internal events, by
a steady but not violent pressure from without, inducing

the progressive admission of the Christians to a share
in the government of their country, and afterwards
founding on that social improvement a new political
position, more advantageous to the empire itself and
less incongruous with the state of feeling in Europe.
I should like to see this country gradually transformed,
not suddenly emancipated. The more vigorous energies
of the Christian would no longer be without a scope,
and drive him to the feet of foreign influences.   The
pride of the Mussulman would be appeased by material
gain, and the cessation of interference from abroad.
The only European influence I should wish for on the
spot is that of *settlers*, which, I think, would act as a
safeguard against a continuance of unapplied reforms.
In Asiatic Turkey three-fourths of the population are
Mahometan; in European Turkey, two-fifths.   The
government of the whole is an absolute despotism, formerly tempered, as Chateaubriand said, by regicide on
the part of the Turks, but still also by what is much
more to the purpose, by those municipal institutions of
the Lower Empire which survived its fall.   Each community has its individual liberty, though all are collectively ruled by an arbitrary system.   With the relative
proportions above-mentioned in the numerical strength
of the two great distinctive creeds, and notwithstanding
the proclaimed will of the sovereign in behalf of
equality, the privileges of the Christians, municipal or
political, present and future, may at any time be im-
perilled by popular resistance to the realisation of
decrees, be it openly violent or latently inert.   Then

would the infusion of foreign blood and the influx of
foreign gold act as a powerful diversion in favour of a
peaceful settlement of differences.   There would be a
difficulty with regard to jurisdiction, for it never could
be expected that land should be held by persons not
amenable to the laws of the country ; but the capitula-
tions, sanctioning foreign protection, must soon undergo
some modification, whether there be colonisation or not.
The wide circulation of British coin during the Crimean
war went far to teach the inhabitants of the interior a
salutary lesson, which the admission of foreign enterprise and capital would complete.   That image of a
stranger queen, of fabulous wealth, imprinted on apparently uncountable pieces of money, finding their way
to every obscure hamlet or Nomadic camp, where a
bushel of barley, a baggage-mule, or an ox for slaughter, was to be found, while it struck them with astonishment, awakened a keen appetite for gain in
hundreds and thousands who had theretofore been content to doze away existence beneath a blazing eastern
sun, in the cheap enjoyment of the simple necessaries
of life.   The apathetic Mussulman conciliated the more
active Christian, whose gold-loving instincts responded
promptly to the chink of pounds sterling, whose very
reverence for co-religionist Russia oozed from his heart
in proportion as his pockets filled with British gold, or
whose Papistic fraternity itself became estranged from
France by that potent metal.   Immemorial foes became
partners in contracts, great or small, for ship-loads of
corn as for the solitary bullock and beast of burden,

owned by the lazy Turk and sent to the allied camp by
the energetic Greek or Maronite. All eyes naturally
turned to the quarter whence benefits accrued, and
sought to learn its will. The flow of wealth from peaceful agriculture and trade would set in the same way,
and its consequences be the same as those produced by
warfaring requirements. Stale old enmities would be
buried under heaps of jointly accumulated bales of
cotton and wool, and stores of grain produced by united
capital and labour. The natural resources of the country are unbounded with respect to tillage and pasture.
Millions of deep alluvial and thickly-wooded acres pant
for the plough and the axe. The land is broad and
rich; industry would go in and possess it. Vast tracts
of fertile soil lie waste; for the rude and desultory cultivation of the Turkish provinces is hardly deserving
of the name of husbandry. Desolating wars and se-
cular bad government have reduced them to such a
pitch of abasement, that their meagre population barely
elicits from the profuse and varied bounties of nature a
scanty subsistence. Internal security and a ready remunerative sale would of course extend and improve
cultivation. Consumption of manufactured goods exchanged for raw materials would augment. Vigour
would be imparted to a country, languishing but containing the elements of power, created but dormant
century after century, and waiting only for profitable
employment. Suitable marts demand only the exercise
of activity to produce a copious influx of wealth. That
activity would be called into existence were the classes

of the population of Turkey not only nominally, but
really equal before the law, and were the implantation
of foreign enterprise encouraged. By putting a check
upon the abuse of power through its equal distribution
between Mussulmans and Christians, by effecting a
more equitable arrangement of the respective and relative rights of conflicting sects, and by opening the
country to foreign colonists, along with an absolute
prohibition of foreign protection and local interference,
these ends might be attained in so far as legislative
means can avail. Interests now antagonistic would
thus be bound together. The labourer or artisan, no
longer forced to work for another, might then work for
that other while working for himself. A middle class
would spring up from such a regulation of social rights
in proportion as prosperity might enable the cultivator
and tradesman to extend their operations, and according
as necessity might oblige the great proprietor of land
and looms to become himself industrious. Trade would
then be indigenous, and wealth would cease to be
monopolised by local magnates and foreign speculators,
while money, instead of filling the coffers of a favoured
few, leaving the provinces to purchase influence, or
being sent abroad by strangers, would circulate at
home, begetting affluence, producing what is now imported, and remaining in the country as the stock of
future generations. The missing links in the social
chain once supplied, the equilibrium essential to productive harmony established, the different wheels of
the machine so adjusted as to work well alone. and the

population brought to the normal state of well-regulated
society, prosperity would become possible, and good
government certain. The hour of redemption from
starving pride on the one hand, and from debasing servitude on the other, sounded for millions of human
beings at the close of the Crimean war. The lapse of
a certain interval between the shock of a great conflict,
and the realisation of its stipulated and proclaimed
results, naturally took place. The shaken supremacy
of the dominant race oscillated for a time, and Europe
looked on in expectation of the final practical abolition
of all class privileges. Matters have settled down,
however, on their former basis. The decree, comprising
the germs of such important social and political changes,
has remained a dead letter, in so far as regards all
practical results. The warning conveyed to the tottering throne of Turkey has hitherto been disregarded.
Unaided and unwatched, one can have but little confidence in the administrative abilities and political
morality of any man or set of men in Turkey. With
the exception of Fuad Pasha, Ahmed Wefik Effendi,
and a select few, too few to achieve the rapid trans-
formation of so vast and so corrupt an Empire, the
best-intentioned sultan has not instruments at his disposal for such an undertaking. Hence arises the
grievous evil of foreign local interference in the details
of government, to which it may not be unfair to attribute in a great measure the failure of Turkey to keep
her promises. She is not left time nor temper to do it
under the constant teasing of embassies about trifles.

Every one knows that our own ambassador has never
followed that course, and that Sir Henry Bulwer has,
on the contrary, contributed very efficaciously towards
the realisation of every good purpose of the Porte,
while his not having always succeeded either in effecting progress or preventing evil is not to be wondered
at in presence of other influences, less disinterested
and beneficent, but equally entitled by position to claim
the Sultan's careful consideration. I cannot doubt,
however, that by a moderate and justifiable insistence
on the adoption of obvious principles and practice,
emanating directly from a friendly power, so as to
escape the Scylla and Charybdis besetting the local
approaches to the Porte, Turkey might be placed and
kept in a train of improvement advantageous to herself
and satisfactory to Europe. It must, certainly, be a
work of time; for I imagine that a people cannot at
once be raised, as was expected, from the actual state
of the Sultan's subjects by international stipulations
and imperial enactments, however beneficial and comprehensive they may appear, without passing through
a period of transition. That period has commenced;
whether or not it will ever arrive at a favourable issue,
is still an unsolved problem, involving the peace of
Europe.

www.ingramcontent.com/pod-product-compliance
Lightning Source LLC
Chambersburg PA
CBHW021118270326
41929CB00009B/932